CREATING A NATION WITH CLOTH

ASAO Studies in Pacific Anthropology

General Editor: Rupert Stasch, Department of Anthropology,
University of California, San Diego

The Association for Social Anthropology in Oceania (ASAO) is an international organization dedicated to studies of Pacific cultures, societies, and histories. This series publishes monographs and thematic collections on topics of global and comparative significance, grounded in anthropological fieldwork in Pacific locations.

Volume 1
The Anthropology of Empathy: Experiencing the Lives of Others in Pacific Societies
Edited by Douglas W. Hollan and C. Jason Throop

Volume 2
Christian Politics in Oceania
Edited by Matt Tomlinson and Debra McDougall

Volume 3
Big Men and Big Shots: Reciprocity, Disaster, and Conflicts about "Custom" in New Britain
Keir Martin

Volume 4
Creating a Nation with Cloth: Women, Wealth, and Tradition in the Tongan Diaspora
Ping-Ann Addo

Creating a Nation with Cloth

*Women, Wealth, and Tradition
in the Tongan Diaspora*

Ping-Ann Addo

berghahn
NEW YORK · OXFORD
www.berghahnbooks.com

First published in 2013 by

Berghahn Books

www.berghahnbooks.com

©2013 Ping-Ann Addo

Library of Congress Cataloging-in-Publication Data

Addo, Ping-Ann.
   Creating a nation with cloth : women, wealth, and tradition in the Tongan diaspora /
Ping-Ann Addo. -- 1st ed.
      p. cm. — (ASAO studies in Pacific anthropology ; v.4)
   ISBN 978-0-85745-895-7 (hardback : alk. paper) — ISBN 978-0-85745-896-4 (ebook)
   1. Women—Tonga—Social conditions. 2. Women—Tonga—Economic conditions.
3. Textile fabrics—Tonga. 4. Tonga—Social life and customs. I. Title.
   HQ1868.A44 2013
   305.4099612—dc23

                                                                          2012032448

British Library Cataloguing in Publication Data

A catalogue record for this book is available from the British Library

Printed in the United States on acid-free paper.

ISBN: 978-0-85745-895-7 hardback
ISBN: 978-0-85745-896-4 institutional ebook

For my parents, Christopher, and Leomana

Contents

Illustrations 🌼

Figures

Tables

Maps

Acknowledgments 🎭

A book documents many journeys, some of them happy, some of them challenging, but all of them dynamic and full of opportunities for introspection, planning, and gratitude. I am greatly indebted to innumerable people in several places, all of whom I endeavor to mention here. Any failure to recognize the assistance or guidance of someone is entirely my own.

I began the research for this project as a graduate student at Yale University, whose faculty and staff I thank for creating a dynamic environment for my intellectual growth. My Ph.D. advisor in the Department of Anthropology, Eric Worby, became a rigorous mentor, but also a treasured friend, as I learned from him in courses such as "The Anthropology of the Object" and chatted with him over cups of tea in his office or at his family's dining table. Other faculty members to whom I am deeply indebted include David Graeber, Kamari Clarke, and Ilana Gershon. David's "Anthropological Theories of Value" course taught me to read the classics of socio-cultural anthropology with a new and more purposeful eye. The many formal and informal conversations we had about the study of exchange and grassroots activism made me think and hope and laugh in new and life-altering ways. Kamari's steady encouragement of my work and my ambitions to teach and mentor, from the days when I served as her "teaching fellow" for two undergraduate courses, continues to this day. Ilana, whose research at the time was perhaps closest to mine substantively, challenged me not just to think, but to write in original terms. Because of Ilana, I will continue to try to "avoid bad puns." I will never forget members of my student cohort and other student friends at the university, among them: Yasmina Katsulis, Dodie McDow, Alison Norris, Christine Pettet, Stephanie Rupp, Yuka Suzuki, and Gilbert Mireles. Mieka Ritsema and Helena Hansen, Alethia Jones, Jennifer Tilton, and Judith Casselberry especially deserve special mention here. We wrote, read, ate, and laughed together so many times over the years during and since graduate school. Having shared times like this, I know we will be friends—sisters!—for life. Mieka, especially, has been a helpful editor, steadfast fellow thinker, and a treasured friend on this intellectual journey. Other friends whose minds brushed the pages of this book as I was writing it include Simone Ferdinand, Kim Alleyne, and Mahmoud abd el Wahid.

For research funding (2000–2002), I am grateful to the Wenner Gren Foundation and the Yale Center for International and Area Studies. My startup funding from the University of Massachusetts Boston, where I have worked since 2005, has helped me continue my research during shorter trips to "the field" in 2007 and 2009. My colleagues in the Department of Anthropology have provided welcoming ground on which to carve out an intellectual and emotional space that continues to feel like home. Indeed it is my UMass Boston colleagues who model for me ways to teach, write, mentor, and live my life as much for "the people" as I do for my own fulfillment and career. I must make special mention of Elora Chowdhury, Amy Den Ouden, Marisol Negrón, Rosalyn Negrón, Patricia Nielson, Denise Patmon, Aminah Pilgrim, Pratima Prasad, Steve Silliman, Peter Kiang, Tim Sieber, Rajini Srikanth, and Karen Suyemoto, Lynnell Thomas, and Shirley Tang. Our friend and colleague Jalal Alamgir was taken from all of us too soon, but I will never forget how he reached out to me, soon after receiving his own positive tenure decision, to inquire about my book project and other work. My students ground me daily with their intellectual curiosity and idealism—things that brought me to and, in some ways, keep me in academia. If their worlds are made better by half the measure of which they better mine, then I am gratified. To former research assistants Sanea Magalhaes, Amanda Bock, and Katie Joe Markman: thank you.

Numerous Tongan people welcomed me into their villages, churches, and communities as I did my research in Nukuʻalofa, Tonga, and in Auckland, New Zealand. Those to whom I owe the deepest ʻofa are Henry Kilifitoni and Longo Quensell, and their extended family in Tonga, New Zealand, and Australia; their daughter Nita, my Tongan "twin" and her family; Pasemata (Holani) Taunisila, with whom I stayed on my first trip to Tonga and who is now resident in Australia; Nunia Huni and her extended family, my village family in Tonga; and Filipe and Seini Nau, who rented me a small house in on their family compound in Nukuʻalofa where I could peacefully type up my notes and quietly receive visitors of my own. I also thank Tuna Fielakepa, Latu Lavulo, Filisi Savieti Beswick, and their *kāinga*, Vāleti Taupeafe and the women of Langa Fonua ʻo Fefine Tonga ʻi Aotearoa, and, especially, Kesaia Pulu and her extended family in Auckland for sharing their homes, life stories, and perspectives on Tongan culture with me.

Meeting and getting closer to numerous colleagues immersed in the study of Pacific culture and society has been invaluable to me. Tevita Kaʻili, Hūfanga ʻOkusitino Māhina, Melenaite Taumoefolau, Heather Young Leslie, Phyllis Herda, Helen Lee, and especially Niko Besnier have been staunch sources of support and guidance in so many aspects of my journey in the anthropology of Tonga. Rochelle and Dionne Fonoti, along with Faʻanofo Lisaclaire Uperesa and Nuhisifa Seve Williams, have been sisters in the struggle; Stacey Kamehiro has enlightened my understanding of Pacific artistic sensibilities; and Jane Horan has been an intellectual companion and immense support on my trips to Auckland. Adrienne Kaeppler, Loketi Latu Niua, and the late Besi Wood-Ellem have always been most gracious in discussing their views on Tongan society and culture with me. Ty Kawika Tengan deserves special mention as perhaps my oldest friend in Pacific Studies. As undergraduate anthropology majors at Dartmouth College, it never occurred to us that we would end up sharing not just a discipline, but area studies as well. For repeatedly demonstrating that Pacific Anthropology is as much about listening with one's heart as with one's ears, I want to thank Ty, along with Tevita, Hūfanga, Lisa, and Rochelle. *Mālō 'aupito, mahalo nui, and faafetai tele* to you all.

In completing and revising the manuscript that became this book, I am indebted to friends and colleagues I met through the Association for Social Anthropology in Oceania have provided a decade of intellectual engagement. Jocelyn Armstrong, Laurence Carucci, and Michael Rynkiewich provided helpful suggestions about publishing my manuscript. Rupert Stasch has been an immensely supportive series editor, Ann DeVita, Elizabeth Berg, Melissa Spinelli, and Marion Berghahn at Berghahn Books, have all been extremely encouraging and professional. I am very grateful to Helen Lee and Margaret Jolly, who reviewed the manuscript, for their detailed and constructive criticism and for recognizing my book's potential. I recognize Claudia Castañeda for her invaluable services as a line editor.

For unwavering personal support throughout this research, my mother, Lily Nyuk Mui Chin-Addo, is unparalleled. She endured months and years without seeing me when I was in graduate school, in the field, or working jobs that kept me far away. With her strong faith, she has been always been my rock and, most recently, provided childcare as I completed the revisions to this book. My in-laws, David and Esther Fung provided just the right amount of "How's the book coming, Pingi?" over the last few years. My husband, Christopher, also provided editing help and moral support at all stages of preparing this manuscript. He and our daughter, Leomana, continue to be constant sources of joy, optimism, and love; they make all aspects of life just beautiful.

My father, Dr. Herbert Christian Addo, passed away before I ever thought I would live and work in the Pacific. He and my mother supported tirelessly my passion for arts and handmade objects of beauty, and they put all their love and resources into enabling me to make a career out of the study of these things. Their own personal histories as diasporic people who carved out an abiding sense of "home" in a tiny twin-island nation—Trinidad and Tobago—prepared me for this research in unforeseen ways. It is to them, and to Christopher and Leomana, that I dedicate this book.

Introduction 🍀

Nation, Cloth, and Diaspora
Locating Langa Fonua

In November 2000, I walked into the foyer of an old church in Grey Lynn, a suburb of New Zealand's largest city, Auckland. Up until two decades ago, this run-down, yet beautiful building had been used for worship by the Loto Tonga Methodist Church congregation of Tongans, who emigrated from their small island archipelago homeland, some 1200 miles away. It was now used as an ancillary space by the church, which had relocated to a newer building further back on the property. Two rooms near the front of the church were occupied by rectangular tables on top of which were spread a range of hand-crafted items made from the treated leaves of the pandanus, or screw pine plant (*Pandanus utilis*). These objects included placemats and baskets, as well as some decorative items made from *ngatu*, the conventional form of barkcloth made by Tongans today. This space spoke of commerce and pride in the artistic products of the constitutional monarchy of Tonga. There were small hand-written price tags on the many handicraft items that had been woven and painted with patterns and hues characteristic of Tongan barkcloth. Nearby, several elderly Tongan women were seated on chairs and pandanus mats on the floor. Their relaxed positions, warm smiles, and the hushed tones of their chatting spoke of leisure and communion. They initially greeted me with a simple "hello," but immediately struck up a conversation when I responded with the Tongan greeting *malo 'e lelei*. In their replies, they asked me, "'*Oku ke ha'u mei fonua fē?*" (Where do you come from?). In their question, they used the word *fonua*, the term for land, nation, country, and place that I would hear innumerable times during my research. Their use of the term indicated that they wanted to locate me in the transnational social fields through which I, a non-Tongan student of Tongan culture, would have learned to greet them in their native tongue. They were pleasantly surprised that I had sought them out because of their production and marketing of Tongan material arts in New Zealand.

I had sought these women out because, like other elderly commoner women I had met in Tonga, they perform as agents of a modernity that involves people from small states engaging in global travel and circulation of valuables, and thereby incorporate more conventional sites of modernity—the cities of industrial capitalist nations—into their local world. Even the name of the group I met in Auckland incorporated New Zealand into a form of Tongan tradition that remains the purview of women: the production and exchange of traditional textiles valuables. The women revealed that their group was called the Langa Fonua 'ae Fefine Tonga 'i Aotearoa, a title that, in part, resonated for me as a borrowing of the name of an important women's organization that I had encountered in Tonga earlier that year. Established in 1954 by the kingdom's third and only female monarch, Sālote Tupou III, the Langa Fonua 'ae Fefine Tonga was a national organization whose aims included standardizing women's knowledge of textile making, while providing local commercial outlets for women with particularly neat or innovative work to sell textiles, baskets, and other crafts. The element "'i Aotearoa" in the Auckland group's name marked the group as ensconced, in its own way, in New Zealand—"Aotearoa" is the name for New Zealand in Maori, the language of its native people. The textiles, known as *koloa faka-Tonga,* or simply as *koloa,* constitute a category of valuable objects made and presented ceremonially only by women, and associated with women's generative powers. These giftable valuables primarily include textiles such as barkcloths and fine mats, but also include scented coconut oil and decorated baskets that Tongan women have long made (Gailey 1987). The Langa Fonua women in Auckland, like women throughout Tonga, used the same technologies and materials to make objects for non-Tongans who were interested in consuming a particular image of Tonga.

One of the women selling *koloa* in the old church told me of her group's related mission: "to lift up our Tongan culture in New Zealand and to make it possible for people to share in our gifts, our *tapa* [barkcloth] and our fine mats." Women not only make, but customarily gift textiles from their families to other families as an integral part of the observance of life-cycle ceremonies—birthdays, weddings, christenings, funerals—or to commemorate an event of civic or institutional importance, such as a church or high school's anniversary. As long as Tongans have been emigrating, they have been carrying such textiles with them and gifting them for similar purposes in diaspora. Flows of textiles accompany, retrace, and remap people's own movements between Tonga, New Zealand, Australia, Hawai'i, the continental United States, and most recently Japan. The women I met in the old church in Auckland also used *koloa* to achieve other important aims: to distinguish themselves and their ethnic community as producers of unique crafts that, when sold, afforded them some measure of financial independence in this new country.

Exchanges of unique cultural products can serve as means to construct and represent the modern "nation" as a collectivity of people who share values, aspirations, and culture—as when a US president presents Elvis Presley memorabilia to the South Korean head of state, or the president of South Africa presents a chess set with pieces in the shape of Zulu warriors to the Queen of England. When political leaders of modern nation-states exchange gifts, acting as representatives of their nations' citizens, they make statements about the values that they and their fellow citizens share as well as about the meaning of being a sovereign nation. Ordinary people visiting their overseas relatives and friends may also present their hosts with a unique craft object from their homeland, for example an ornamental wooden fork and spoon set from the Philippines, carved soapstone animal ornaments from Kenya, or a knickknack patterned with the stars and stripes from the United States. So too Tongan families have been leaving their homeland for the diaspora for the last half-century and have been carrying with them *koloa*—primarily textile *koloa*—that they gift to relatives in diaspora.

This book explores how commoner women in diaspora re-create the Tongan homeland in diaspora through the various ways they work on, with, and through *koloa* in their daily and ceremonial lives. The particular agents on whom I focus for this study are elderly Tongan women of commoner status who connect the distances between themselves and others through their production and exchange of textile *koloa*, the supreme valuables in Tongan society. The women are agents of a particular kind of modernity characterized, in part, by their regular launching of these gifts into circulation outside of their territorially grounded homeland. Here, I attend to how they use these practices to intertwine tradition and modernity, and kinship and capitalism, in processes of global nation building. This ethnography thus puts human faces on globalization and diaspora studies and takes seriously the role of women in nation building.

Other questions this book explores include: When Tongans exchange these objects at events such as celebrations to mark life passages of kin group members, what statements do they make about Tongan identity? And, when they exchange objects over multiple generations and include kin from far-flung places, what particular cultural histories do they reference and what forms of value do they materialize? More specifically, this book asks: what role does the traditional view of *fonua* play and how does it change, for the women of Auckland and their communities, as they continue to make and exchange *koloa* in diaspora? In answering these questions, I draw upon the notion that these textiles function as texts through which ideas about gender, family, competition, and solidarity are realized and reworked in ways that incorporate traditional and modern notions of what it means to be part of the Tongan nation in the twenty-first century. Specifically through ceremonial gift exchange, the women and their communities resituate the *fonua* in urban New Zealand. To understand how they do so, we must first examine the way *fonua* was understood and enacted in Tonga before the time of European contact.

Fonua as Gift Exchange

Fonua is variously translated as land, placenta, and homeland (Churchward 1959)—as in the place of one's birth, ancestry, nationality, or allegiance. Before European arrival in Tonga, *fonua* was an ontological principle that was materialized in everything around a Tongan person. The relationship between individuals, land, and ecology traditionally began when a Tongan child was born, and its placenta—also called *fonua*—was buried near his or her family home. In pre-contact Tonga, *fonua* indexed the use of the land to fulfill responsibilities to kin and to chiefs, through subsistence and respect. As part of their *fatongia* or "duty," commoners grew surplus crops on tracts of land on estates that were governed by chiefs. Men grew crops, the most important of which were long yams and *kava*. They also reared pigs that, together with these crops, constituted men's wealth or *ngāue*. Tongan commoners regularly exchanged gifts of these foods that they cultivated and, more importantly, offered these products of the land as tribute to their chiefs: men presented *ngāue* and women presented *koloa*. Chiefly families consumed some of these products and presented the rest to one another as gifts to shore up alliances and to celebrate life crisis events such as births, marriage, and deaths. In ceremonies called *'inasi*, chiefs also presented such valuables as first fruits to the Tu'i Tonga, the supreme ruler of the Tongan territory, who in turn propitiated the gods on behalf of all his subjects for continued sustenance from the *fonua*.

Inherent in the meanings of *fonua* are relationships that ground people in space at different stages of their lives: at birth, *fonua* is placenta; during life, *fonua* is constituted in exchange relationships; and at death, *fonua* is the label used for one's grave. In this ancient reckoning, *fonua* is a concept that indicates that people and place are mutually constitutive, thus Francis's definition of *fonua* as the "conjuncture of people and place" (Francis 2007: 346). Tongan families cultivated crops on the land (place) for food and ceremonial exchange. Eating was itself considered a privilege derived from *tauhi fonua* (caring for the land) and gifting food was an obligation. For early modern Tonga, the most basic exchanges that defined a place as *fonua* were those between chiefs, who were the only human beings of any consequential personhood; at this time commoners were not even considered to have souls (Martin 1991 [1817]). While they were obligated to engage in processes of exchange, this did not grant them the status of persons.

After commoners were granted "emancipation" and allowed access to plots of land on chiefly estates through the 1875 constitution of the Kingdom of Tonga, they followed chiefly practices of exchanging food and *koloa* between their kin groups who lived on these lands. Moreover, the modern nation-state continued to be a place of sustenance whose relationship to people was maintained through exchange. Hierarchy remained intrinsic to *fonua*, as commoners continued to gift to chiefs who were themselves ranked within the institution of the nobility. Commoners also gifted valuables to their churches and celebrated the links between church, nation, nobility, and their own families through the proffering of valuables.

The practice has continued until today, with modern valuables more accessible to commoners, and imported foods available in local shops. As in ancient times, the objects gain or are afforded value in and through the process of *exchange*. Whether at the state level, between families, or between individuals, recognition of others' humanity—and in particular recognition of those higher in rank than oneself—is demonstrated through a particular kind of social and economic input: the gift. That the practice of establishing *fonua* through the gift has continued, even through the profound changes that Tongans experienced with "emancipation," and then later with diasporization, suggests the endurance of a society based on the bonds manifested by giving, receiving, and reciprocating gifts (Mauss 1990 [1925]). To Tongans, the gift is a "total social fact" (ibid.), a concept that encompasses processes, pervades societal institutions, and can be used by analysts to explain the meaning of social life for a given people (Sykes 2005:12).

Adrienne Kaeppler has stated that, by producing their respective categories of ceremonial wealth, Tongan women and men "regenerate and reproduce society" (2007:146), extrapolating to gift exchange the agency of symbolically producing new generations of inhabitants or citizens. Women and men also *reinvigorate* society—through cultural reproduction, physical sustenance, and genealogical memory—using, and in this case gifting, their wealth. My own analysis of *koloa* as a means of re-creating society in diaspora examines how Tongans can and do use them in a variety of ways to construct versions of Tongan society that draw on both Tongan cultural history and memory and on the local conditions of the diasporic hostland. This is a practice that can happen almost anywhere, and certainly anywhere that Tongans choose to exchange gifts.

Just as nation building can take place in many physical locations, so too *fonua* is more than just land, and material resources such as food and textiles have always been more than mere commodities that carry exchange value. They are also more than simply consumables that provide use value, to Tongans. They are material expressions of connections and obligations between a Tongan individual and groups from whom that individual derives her identity as a Tongan—ethnic community, church, kin group—and the gifting of objects reiterates connections and creates bridges between people, regardless of location. Knowing that Tongans in faraway places are doing likewise allows people in one place to experience a sense of simultaneity of action that is essential to the sense of nationhood (Anderson 1983). Thus, ceremonial gifting helps people feel grounded—physically and culturally—in places that matter, or come to matter, because they engage in meaningful activity there.

Gifting makes materially manifest Tongan values—that is, the very meanings of being Tongan and the things that are worth striving for as a member of a Tongan community. This shared sense of worth is reflected in the value that people assign to the things they gift, which is further reflected in two other considerations: what the giver considers the recipient to be legitimately entitled to and what the giver sees herself to be entitled to when her turn to be a recipient comes around. Anthropologist David Graeber states: "values are the criteria by which people judge which desires they consider legitimate and which they do not" (2001:3). In communities of Tongans, the desire to create and exchange *koloa* is entirely legitimate because it occurs in the context of "collectivist giving"—a term Yunxiang Yan uses to denote gift exchange on behalf of family, lineage, or community (Yan 2005:246). The value of gifting *koloa* thus remains deeply rooted in reciprocity. So, when a woman prepares a gift, the material contribution, good will, and reputations of many people are encapsulated in and affected by her gift. Yet the value of the gift object—meaning or esteem she will gain from presenting it—exists as mere potential until that thing is exchanged (gifted) such that everyone involved experiences a culturally readable effect in their relationship(s) with the other (ibid.).

Thus, the value of Tongan *koloa,* even in modern situations where it has little everyday utilitarian significance, lies in its capacity to be gifted and, when gifted, its capacity to bind together givers and recipients in a reified sense of their already shared values and emotions. *Koloa* are largely valued for this *capacity* or potential to connect, therefore I use the term *value potential* to indicate the as-yet-unrealized opportunity for someone to experience the shared sense of worth evoked by an object or its exchange. In addressing women's *koloa* production and exchange in the Tongan diaspora, I am interested in tracing the globalized value potential of objects and of people's actions and interactions with objects. Of course, not all *koloa* end up being gifted: some are kept and others are sold, both instances posing challenges to prevalent notions of what people traditionally and ideally do with *koloa.* For some contemporary Tongans, moral norms of transacting *koloa* in diaspora are different from norms in the homeland; one may eschew gifting in diaspora while being sure to engage in gift exchange when one is in the homeland. I thus also explore contexts in which co-ethnics negotiate which cultural values they share, which values they profess not to share, and what role their geographic location plays in navigating between such values.

Anthropological research on the Pacific region has long been a key part of the academic literature on value, and scholars working in this region have produced many ethnographically based analyses of material culture and exchange (Forshee 2001; Herda 1999; Hereniko 1995; Hoskins 1998; Kaeppler 1995, 1999b; MacKenzie 1991; Schoeffel 1999; Thomas 1991), with a particular focus on systems of giving (Akin and Robbins 1989; Kuehling 2005; Malinowski 1922; Munn 1992; Strathern 1990). These studies examine the myriad contexts in which the exchange of material things is a crucial social fact for different peoples in the region. Besides overtly addressing material culture, much of this literature links objects to how people map space or make a "place" of connections to one another through these things; and how they use objects to assert their identities within particular spaces. Here I add my own examination of material culture's role in expanding the limits of "local" worlds into contexts that analysts refer to as "the global." In focusing on *koloa* gift exchange in diaspora I do not simply regard objects as inanimate things that accompany social processes. I am interested in objects as embodiments of meaningful processes in society—processes of production, and status reification and negotiation; of value creation; of nation building; and of modernity. In keeping with the intellectual tradition of understanding the peoples of the Pacific region through analyzing the gift and, therefore understanding "how people relate to things and, through things, how they relate to each other" (Yan 2005:249) my study examines how one such people see their "local" world as being made through globalized transaction with objects.

Pacific nation building is derived largely from indigenous practices and ways of constructing the world. Enacted by indigenous people—those who descend from the original inhabitants of a place—Pacific nations are not confined to the bounded territories of landmasses, as the ocean and the underworld are also part of the space inhabited by Pacific peoples (Hau'ofa 1993). Following on from this characterization, modern Pacific nations are also not confined to the boundaries of single nation-states, but encompass networks of overseas communities of co-ethnics who are also constructed as parts of the *fonua,* or nation as it is lived. It is not only recent migration that "diasporizes" Tonga, extending it beyond the borders of the nation, but a complex web of exchanges between homeland- and diaspora-based Tongans and between Tongans in various locations in diaspora.

Diaspora: Modernization by Commoners

A nation can be defined as "an imaginative construct that constitutes persons as legitimate subjects of, and in, a territorial state" (Foster 1997:4). For Tongans, this description can be applied to *fonua* as an ancestral land as well as a modern(izing) nation, keeping in mind the particular meanings of *fonua* and the Tongan *nation* mentioned above. Tonga's development into a modern state began under the influence of the ideas of one particular chief who united the territories of Tonga under his rule in 1875, converted to Christianity, made his subjects do likewise, and constructed a religious state with a Westminster-type government system. This chief united the island groups of Vava'u, Ha'api, Tongatapu, and the Niua islands under his rule, becoming Tonga's first monarch, Taufa'ahau Tupou I. Committed to modernizing Tonga, its economy, and its culture, his Constitution approved commoners' working to accumulate their own wealth in the form of *koloa* and *ngāue;* he also encouraged the production of some form of *ngāue* as commodities for paying taxes to the church. Under his great-grandson, the monarch Taufaʻahua Tupou II, the kingdom established a Treaty of Friendship and Protection with Great Britain as a British protectorate, a status it held from 1900 to 1970. Tonga is the only Pacific country that was never formally colonized by a European power and perhaps one of the few island nations to have avoided overt imperialist control, but it was still subject to histories of power and dispossession through introduction of Christianity, the capitalist market, and laws forbidding, among other native practices, the production and exchange of traditional valuables, including *koloa* (Gailey 1987). During the operation of the Law on Tapa (1885–90), barkcloth production declined, but the textiles did not lose significance. Since then, Tongan women have been steadily producing *koloa*.

Sālote Tupou III, Tupou II's daughter who had been educated in Auckland and who ascended the throne in 1918, was highly concerned with harnessing commoner skills and loyalty to aid Tonga's burgeoning modernity in the early 1900s. It was she who established Langa Fonua, the women's group mentioned earlier. Queen Sālote—who, like other chiefs, had long been beneficiaries of overseas education and Western-style material fineries—was convinced that Tongan modernity would be advanced through people of commoner rank also benefiting from increased participation in modern amenities such as healthcare, sanitation, and education.

After Sālote's death in 1965 she was succeeded by her elder son Taufaʻahau Tupou IV, who began to encourage out-migration among the members of the commoner rank in 1970, based on his notion that a civil service populated by people with tertiary levels of education was crucial to Tonga's modernity (Campbell 1992; Marcus 1993). As Queen Sālote had espoused before him, a modern, educated commoner population—not just an educated chiefly and clergy population—was essential to the development of the kingdom's human capital and, thus, its modernity (Lātūkefu 1974). This would be achieved by providing government scholarships to high-performing students of commoner backgrounds who would study in the tertiary institutions of the Western nations closest to the Pacific—Australia and New Zealand.[1] Tonga's churches, and in particular the Catholic Church of Tonga, were supportive of such plans (Campbell 1992:217).[2]

When Tongans moved to these places—and later when they would move, with the help of the Mormon church, to Hawaiʻi and Salt Lake City—they established the familiar village associations, women's craft groups, churches, and other "traditional" institutions designed to nurture themselves culturally by recreating homeland practices and values, and by creating and maintaining links to family, co-villagers, and fellow congregation members back in Tonga. Over time, these institutions became sites in which Tongans in diaspora could perform their cultural identity and transform their new sites into a form of *fonua.* As in the homeland, exchanging cash, *koloa,* and *ngāue* were symbolic expressions of loyalty, love, and mutual help, but in diaspora they grew also to be ways of supplementing the resources necessary to meet the high cost of renting halls, buying feast foods, and reciprocating other cash gifts. Diasporans continued to send money as their contributions to exchanges taking place in the homeland, including the hefty contributions that Christian churches were demanding from congregants. Exchange linked diasporans, or emigrants, with Tongans in the kingdom as traditional gifts of *koloa* and *ngāue* valuables, modern food, and cash necessary to critical life-cycle rituals flowed between family members in Tonga and in the diaspora. In addition, as the Tongan population in diaspora increased, more exchanges began to take place in diaspora itself, augmenting remittances (money and valuables sent back to the homeland) as ways in which Tongans could demonstrate their allegiance to the notion of *fonua* as kin-based gifting. By engaging in these different forms of exchange, Tongan diasporans were able to maintain strong links across globally-dispersed communities: between their new homes and Tonga, and with others living in diaspora. This latter aspect—what Helen Lee (2009) refers to as interdiasporic transnationalism—is a relatively understudied aspect of diaspora and one to which my ethnographic effort in this study pays considerable attention.

The Tongan *fonua* has now been effectively globalized by Tongan emigration from the kingdom, resettlement in other lands, and exchange of material valuables. Used as either commodities or as gifts, it is through enhancing and exchanging these valuables that Tongans materially and symbolically re-create their ancestral land (*fonua*) of Tonga in urban diasporic spaces. In so doing, diasporic Tongans effectively augment the distance, or space, over which the *fonua* is able to stretch. With the maturation of Tongan communities in diaspora and their interdependence with the Kingdom of Tonga, it is as though every location in diaspora is imagined as another island, extending the reach of the 171 islands that comprise the Tongan homeland (Young Leslie 2004). Indeed, I would go so far as to say that this traditional *fonua* model of society owes its evolution to the diasporization of Tonga—the creation and growth of diasporic communities that remain materially and symbolically connected to one another and to communities in the homeland—just as the traditional *fonua* model makes this diasporization particularly Tongan.

Langa Fonua: The Nation and the Women of Tonga

Queen Sālote Tupou III realized her commitment to commoners through a variety of modernity projects. A hospital, ship dock, and paved roads were built during her reign, to enable Tonga's burgeoning modernity (Wood-Ellem 1999), but she also held the strong belief that commoner women would be crucial in the development of Tonga's human capital. This was to be achieved through strengthening the skills women used to look after their families. Elizabeth Wood-Ellem reports that Queen Sālote was especially interested in spreading the idea among her people that maternal health and child health were integrally related. She requested that Elizabeth Bott, a British anthropologist, conduct a study on "mother-and-child health" over a six-month period in 1958 (Wood-Ellem 1999), following notions about the interconnected nature of mother and child health that had been popularized by the British government in the earlier part of the twentieth-century. This idea rendered women both agents and pawns in nation-building projects through their production of children—and explicitly healthy children—who would survive epidemics, live to adulthood, and fight wars, if that was what the nation needed (Davin 1997).

Sālote saw an emphasis on family and tradition not only as a way to strengthen the nation, but also as a building block for the new forms of subjectivity demanded by modernity. In proclaiming that Tongans should be guided by their kinship-focused traditions and cultural obligations as they joined the community of modern nations, she also foresaw that Tongans would increasingly come into sustained contact with non-Tongans. She was essentially reminding Tongans that they should adhere to traditional Tongan values, treating all people as they would their own kin when interacting with them (ibid.). These principles were similar to those that guide the idea that democracy, citizenship, social security, and national self-determination are to be considered the "vertexes of the world order" (Wimmer and Glick Schiller 2002)—concepts meant to guide people who are citizens of modern, democratic nation-states in treating one another as individuals with particular human rights. Langa Fonua, the organization, was thus a modern reinvention of the traditional notion of nation, and an especially Tongan one, in that specific traditions would guide citizens in their relations with people of other modern states.

One example of the increased emphasis on commoner women's participation in the modern nation-state was Sālote's addition of a law prescribing Tongans to wear hand-plaited waist wrappings (*ta'ovala*) over their clothes as formal attire required when they were to enter a church or any government building (Wood-Ellem 1999). As the makers of *koloa*, commoner women were charged with ensuring that all members of their families had this attire available and wore it as was appropriate to venue and occasion. These media of dress were central to creating new public and self-oriented notions of respectability and liberal personhood (see also Hau'ofa 1993; Stoler and Cooper 1997). In this and other ways, duty to God and duty to *fonua* (nation) were reinforced by the same visual and bodily means, and traditional *fonua* was modernized as part of the monarch's vision of the nation. Commoner women were finally being asked to put their unique mark on the nation—and the modern nation, at that.

The emerging nation's lowest-ranking citizens consequently had a sense of themselves as contributing to Tonga's unique form of indigenous modernity. The concept of indigenous modernity or the "indigenization of modernity" (Jolly 1992; Sahlins 1999; Young Leslie 2004) denotes an ongoing history of indigenous people actively co-mingling the seemingly incongruous categories of modern and indigenous but on their own terms. The indigenization of modernity, especially as elaborated in research on Pacific cultures by Margaret Jolly and Nicholas Thomas (1992), Roger Keesing (1989), Jocelyn Linnekin (1990b), and Nicholas Thomas (1991), among others, celebrates "tradition" as intrinsically creative and innovative, and rejects outright the opposition of pre-contact and introduced aspects of culture reified by the confining and objectifying binary of traditional versus modern. Thus, innovation does not occur through the wholesale adoption of forms and processes from the West, but through indigenous peoples adapting, melding, and regrounding forms and practices from other peoples within the indigenes' long-standing concerns. By the same token, and as I have argued elsewhere (Addo 2007; Young Leslie and Addo 2007), this book investigates how contemporary Tongans have "Tonganized" modernity. The indigenization of modernity literature developed, in part, in response to an older debate about "culture." The "invention of tradition" was theorized by Eric Hobsbawm in his now classic volume edited with Terence Ranger (1983). In Hobsbawm's formulation, traditions are seen as strategic innovations in service of perpetuating long-standing practices. A better parallel to the more dynamic "indigenous modernity" debate can be drawn with Roy Wagner's treatise on the "invention of culture," in which the author focuses on what is really at stake in co-mingling cultural forms from different sources—that is, people—when he states "It is people, and the experiences and meanings associated with them, that they do not want to lose, rather than ideas and things" (1981[1975]:26). Wagner's stance resonates with mine in this book.

Before Sālote's era, Tongan women had rarely been cast as being at the forefront of the nation in any way, even though they produced the objects that were symbols of the nation at both the state and familial levels. For example, women were not granted the right to vote until 1960—near the end of Sālote's reign—while men had been voting since soon after constitution (Wood-Ellem 1999). As is the case with indigenous women from other Pacific territories, Tongan women have been thought of as participating in the nation primarily through producing persons who are cultured to work for the nation; their role has long been cast, in official discourse, as merely rooted in their gender and kin-based roles as mothers, sisters, daughters, and daughters-in-law, and this discourse still pertains today (Young Leslie 2004). But are Tongan women so completely bound to these roles in actuality?

I suggest that while these roles have roots in traditional kinship roles for women, many women remain far from mired in them. These Tongan women take the security and comfort of having such roles to resort to if they desire, but they have long pushed the boundaries of *how* they carry out the roles of mothers, sisters, and daughters; more often than not they do so *by* engaging with modernity and diaspora, interacting with both co-ethnics and non-Tongans, and stepping outside of traditional roles and beyond Tonga as a location. What I argue in this book is that object exchange is also an invaluable lens onto such gendered processes of globalization—the increased interconnection between sites that results in more intense and intentional engagement between people in far-away places. These processes include the transnational distribution of identity production, as exemplified in the growth of the Tongan nation by the resettlement of Tongans in other nation-states. These globalized forms of landscape constituted by interactions, emotions, and exchanges within and between groups of actors with a common identity are what Arjun Appadurai (1996:33) refers to as "ethnoscapes." The continued interconnection between communities thus formed is intrinsic to a uniquely Tongan form of modern nationalism that women spearhead by doing "tradition."

Women and Nationalism

In the literature on modern nationalisms, women's roles in nation building are usually analyzed in relation to their activism around statehood and their biological abilities to physically reproduce citizens, and thus the nation. These roles may be especially crucial in the midst or wake of conflicts that highlight nationalist narratives and that include war, post-war rebuilding, and other contexts in which civil society, peace, and the thriving of children and families are adversely affected (see Enloe 1997; McClintock 1997, amongst others).[3] However, as many Pacific woman writers and other theorists on the Pacific remind us, the role of women in nation building usually goes beyond these singular, dramatic moments whose primary agents are typically identified as men, moments when women fulfill roles assigned to them by men and are therefore symbols of nationalism rather than agents of indigenous nation building (Jolly 1997 and 2005, Bolton 2003; see also volume edited by Lukere and Jolly 2002). These authors might be described as rejecting the idea that nationalisms have "typically sprung from masculinized memory, masculinized humiliation and masculinized hope" (Enloe 1997:89), a view that excludes and marginalizes women and denies them any direct relation to national agency (McClintock 1997:90). Similarly, Grace Mera Molisa from Vanuatu refuses the term *kastom* (a transliteration of the English word "custom," used in some areas of Melanesia to designate male-imagined indigenous practices that form a core basis for communal or national identity in the region) because it is often applied to honor the practices of men, merely pays lip service to women or is "conveniently recalled to intimidate women" (Molisa 1983:24), and thus reifies patriarchal relationships (see also Bolton 2003:58–60 and Jolly 2005). Native Pacific women activists, such as Molisa and Haunani-Kay Trask, reject the idea that women's roles in nationalism should be primarily relegated to performances that commemorate the nation in touristic ways (Trask 1996; see also Alexeyeff 2008 and Sissons 1999) or in ways that marginalize women's welfare, especially as pertains to their roles as daughters and mothers (Molisa 1983:47; and see Bolton 2003:60). They seek an indigenous nationalism in which women's issues are decided upon, not by indigenous men or foreign feminists, but by indigenous women in all their diversity of roles and ambitions.

Where nationalism is bound up with transnational populations, both male and female diasporans face the issue of who works toward the homeland's growth or toward global nation building.[4] This notion that women's activities comprise *work* is crucial to a more just analysis of nationalism as gendered and power-laden. Patricia Hill Collins has critiqued the prevailing idea of women as culture bearers—literally based on their child-bearing role—and refers instead to women as culture workers, because they actively work at jobs, at relationships, at finding resources, at socializing and providing for families, and at maintaining many of the processes and symbols whereby their peoples define their uniqueness in the world (Collins 2006). Consciously cultivating and publicly espousing the unique culture of the nation becomes one means to expand the nation's global presence, but it is also a way to produce citizens who are proud of and love their nation. In Tongan communities, women are indeed culture bearers, as they are charged with rearing their children with Tongan values and the concomitant "rules"—rules about how to live in the Tongan way (Young Leslie 2004). But, as I will show in this book, some women also emphasize vocations such as entrepreneurs and textile innovators as crucial to how they perform their love of the nation.

For Tongans today, global flows are crucial in their families' survival because of the material and symbolic need to share resources. Global paths and markets are essential to how women in numerous societies meet their subsistence, kin-based, and other social responsibilities, including those that contribute to nation building (Forte 2001; Meintjes 2001). They can also be fundamental to a community's production of identity, as "the constant and various flows of such goods and activities have embedded within them relationships between people" (Glick Schiller et al. 1992:11; see also Yan 1996). These intertwined projects of creating cultural value and promoting cultural values find some of their greatest meaning as nationalist projects. By "nationalist project" I mean (following Yuval-Davis 1997) social and political contexts in which people interact with the intention of sharing moments of emotional expression that are both derived from, and contribute to, a sense of shared identity. Sometimes these are in dynamic relationship with material processes of resource sharing, and often the emotions shared are compounded with common memories of, or experiences in a homeland. As a system of communication and embodied value, *koloa* can, and regularly does, embody these emotions and encode these memories, thus becoming a tool for performing nationalism.

Langa Fonua and Diaspora

My study addresses the particular set of conditions, whereby the *fonua*— "homeland" and "nation"—has been transformed by people engaging in the connected processes of movement and dwelling as they develop communities outside of their original homeland. The expanded, globalized, encompassing *fonua* on which I focus here emanates from ongoing exchange processes in which Tongan women—wherever they are located geographically—through their activities contribute to their communities' augmentation (*langa*) of the *fonua*. The textiles they produce, gift, and counter gift maintain relationships of affect, inter-dependence, and reciprocity between people, culture, and their environment (Māhina 1999; Tuʻitahi 2007), thereby producing the nation. In the context of urban New Zealand, Tongan diasporans engage in familiar activities while effectively replacing the ecology of Tonga's natural world and its local villages with city infrastructure, grocery stores, planned parks, and modern transport systems.

The modern Tongan concept of *langa fonua* is used in Tongan government discourse as a catchall for women's activities that not only build up a family, but also build up a nation (*fonua*). A diasporic woman said to me that *langa fonua* is "doing something with your own hands to help your family." She added that moving to the diaspora was a decision that her family made to help themselves, especially when it came to meeting the rising cost of donating money to their kin-based obligations (*fatongia*). Many other Tongans I spoke to during my fieldwork in Auckland responded similarly, suggesting that diasporization is a highly desired and perfectly logical process with which to continue the practices that are basic to *fonua* because it enables the continued pursuit of material sustenance through kin-based exchange. As Kwok Bun Chan suggests for Chinese diasporans, diasporic families are the result of rational decisions to maintain traditional notions of family as a key form of sociality and as "a resourceful and resolute way of preserving it" (1997:195). *Langa fonua* is the Tongan concept that I use to frame my analysis of contemporary strategies of transnational migration and exchange. My study examines how women, in particular, continue to project and reformulate an ancient concept, *fonua*, into new times, places, and activities.

Most notably, the symbolic exchange of cash and *koloa* as gifts remains crucial in the ceremonies associated with the forging of new connections between Tongan people, and is one of the material aspects of diaspora that I explore here. Material gifts possess the potential to increase allegiance and to affect relationships. This book argues that Tongan modernity has entailed commoner Tongans adapting their traditional idea of nation (*fonua*) into "modern" terms, in response to the opportunities afforded by globalization. In the process, I argue, commoners have engaged with globalization on their own terms and thereby enable a particular conception of *fonua* as a process of *langa fonua* (nation building) that they practice diasporically.

According to Sione Tu'itahi, a Tongan theorist and health worker based in Auckland, *langa fonua* refers to "the intricate web of connected, on-going social relationship between the entire physical and social environment and humanity" (2007). To be committed to *langa fonua* is to actively acknowledge that one's existence is dependent on appropriate and fulfilling reciprocal relations between oneself, other people, and the land(s) that sustain(s) all concerned. When people restore or maintain a balance in relationships of dependency and reciprocity between themselves and others, as well as between themselves and the land that is Tonga, they ensure sustenance for people and place. Thus *langa fonua* has never simply about a particular, territorially bounded nation-state; and while it has been tied to place, but it is not set within the boundaries of physical space. Diasporic Tongans therefore can perform *langa fonua* by attending to daily and ceremonial responsibilities in diaspora, which becomes the "place" where nationalism is performed. Moreover, performing *langa fonua* facilitates a sense of belonging to, and an active engagement with, an imagined *global* community of co-ethnics who, ideally, neither forget their cultural rootedness in Tonga nor are content with being anonymous, "faceless" immigrant "others" in the states where they now dwell.[5] Acting according to Tongan values and principles gives immigrant Tongans a way of engaging with people on their own terms, while also taking into account the local ecology and the forms of valuables it offers. In urban New Zealand, ecology encompasses the effects of human populations' varied and often technologically intensified use of land and environment, and work is largely performed for wages that are then used to purchase things to gift rather than directly producing objects. In such contexts *langa fonua* is a *conceptual* place for Tongans to stand as they engage in cultural production while interfacing with a new environment, often using foreign cultural forms.

Diasporic Tongans also frequently apply the general label of "*langa fonua* group" (combining Tongan and English words in a single expression) to designate a specific group whose members engage in activities to share or learn particular skills that help them re-create a sense of being in the homeland. *Langa fonua* groups typically comprise elderly people and sometimes a few middle-aged members, although elders are always involved and are in leadership positions because their age gives them cultural authority. Whether they meet to create a new textile product, teach traditional songs and dances to Tongan youth, or knit blankets and pillow cases in one another's company, members of *langa fonua* groups in Auckland perform aspects of their culture that others recognize as value, this recognition adding to the group's members' their sense of personal worth. The women I met at the old Methodist church in Auckland are one such group. Interacting across generations and across distances, they engage in a crucial form of *langa fonua* and embody a globally-cultivated homeland through its material arts.

History and Demographics: Homeland, Diaspora, and Migration

The Tongan diaspora currently comprises over 110,000 self-identified ethnic Tongans, a number that has exceeded that of the population in Tonga for many years. This is a tantalizing statistic for modern demographers and development specialists perhaps because such an apparent imbalance in population distribution challenges the idea that the citizens of a nation live *inside* that nation's territorial boundaries, while also reifying a colonial notion of the economic and sometimes political non-viability of these small homelands. These small countries, inhabited mainly by people of color, and with somewhat traditional economies, are equally of interest to people invested in the idea of the West's bigness given that they are usually former colonies of European nations—"small islands removed from large landmasses of Europe" (White in Hau'ofa 2008:xv). Yet native Tongan anthropologist 'Epeli Hau'ofa rejects this Eurocentric framing of the Pacific nations for, in his words, "the idea of smallness is relative" (1993:6). Because Pacific Islanders crisscross and master oceans both historically and contemporarily, connecting on the ground through resettlement and exchange, their worlds are "anything but tiny" (ibid.). Hau'ofa challenges developmentalist language insisting that Pacific nations have long been considered to be "small, remote, and dependent" territories by Western analysts (ibid.). He argues that the islands, connected rather than separated by the ocean, are far from insular; indeed, they are the vanguard in the very connectedness and transnationalism—of people, capital, ideas, information—that globalization theorists espouse today. He tacitly rejects notions of the nation that rely on assumptions that Lisa Malkki (1997) critiques as "the metaphysics of sedentarism."

Tonga has substantial diasporic communities resident around the globe, yet there are specific political economic and policy-based reasons for different-sized

Tongan populations living in particular host nations today. What Hauʻofa (1993) seems to identify as Tongans' cultural propensity toward travel and transnationalism is only a part of the reason that the Tongan diaspora has developed, and become multiply rooted, in its particular way. Host-nation immigration policies, globalization by particular churches, and national and personal desires for economic growth have all played a part in how Tongans have become routed to, and rooted in, their diasporic spaces.

During the 1960s and 70s, increasing numbers of Tongans emigrated from Tonga to New Zealand. In 1970, New Zealand introduced several urban work schemes aimed at attracting temporary workers from Pacific Island nations, and by 1971 there were 1273 Tongans in New Zealand, according to the census (Taumoefolau N.d.). By 1974, the Tongan population in New Zealand reached 3965, a tenfold increase in size since 1955 (ibid.). In 1976, New Zealand granted an immigration amnesty to Tongans already resident there, regardless of their legal status. Around the same time, a change in immigration laws in the United States enabled Tongans to apply for work visas, which were issued preferentially to families who would be reunited with a member already resident in the US (Levin and Ahlburg 1993). Emigration to all three of these nations has continued and today, large and vibrant diasporic communities exist in the major cities of Australia, the western United States, and Hawaiʻi. There are also growing Tongan diasporic communities in Britain, Canada, and Japan (ʻEsau 2007).

Australia has long been a destination for education, as well as for theological training since the 1920s. Tonga's King Taufaʻahau Tupou IV earned his bachelor of arts and LLB at Sydney University in the late 1930s, as have several members of Tongan noble families since then. Tonga's formal relationship with Australia was very tenuous before World War II, save for the influence of the Australian Methodist Church on Tongan Methodism between the 1860s and the 1920s. In the 1970s, Australia gave many scholarships for Tongans to study in Australia, and some of the commoner families with the longest residency in Sydney, Melbourne, and Canberra descend from migrants who traveled to Australia for this purpose. While in the 1970s, the emigration of commoner Tongans to Australia began to rise significantly, it has never reached the pace and volume of emigration to New Zealand and the United States.[6] The White Australia Policy that restricted immigration by people of non-European descent until 1966 to 1973 (Lee 2003) was a significant factor in Tongans' difficulty in obtaining visas for entry. For example, according to Lee (2003), it seriously affected the number of Tongans already in Australia who were able to sponsor family members to immigrate on "parent-visas" (ibid.).

In the United States, the 1965 Immigration Act abolished the rules that restricted immigration to specific quotas from most countries. Thus, any Tongans who had already immigrated to the US—for example those who had settled in La'ie, Hawai'i, with the help of the Mormon church in the interwar and post–World War II years—were able to bring members of their family to this part of the United States (Ka'ili 2008). Secondly, a visa category called the Fifth Preference favored the reunion of siblings whose families had a member already resident in the US. Between 1980 and 1990, the Tongan population in the US saw an almost threefold increase (from 6200 to 17,600).[7]

New Zealand boasts the highest total Tongan overseas population, with over 40,000 self-identified ethnic Tongans living there (Lee 2004). *Koloa* plays no small role in mainstream New Zealanders' recognition of Tongans as worthy immigrants. It is a commodity New Zealanders can buy from Tonga women sellers at almost every craft fair. Barkcloth graces the walls of public institutions such as libraries and commercial spaces such as cafes, and many contemporary artists of Tongan and non-Tongan descent use *koloa* as inspiration or as materials in their artwork. In addition, groups of Tongan women may receive funding from the New Zealand government to promote and teach their textile skills to others in their communities. These varied uses of *koloa* are examples of the ways in which Tongan nationalism is manifested in small but growing pockets of New Zealand's urban landscape.

Globalized *Fonua* as Multiterritorial Nation

Joanne Wallis has used the term "deterritorialized nation-state" to describe the phenomenon in which "people can live anywhere in the world yet retain ties to their nation-state of origin" (2008:409). Writing specifically about contemporary Tongan constructions of identity and nationalism, Wallis argues that while the state may remain the geographically bounded territory of Tonga, the "nation-state" may be seen as "all Tongans, including those who live overseas" (ibid.). I agree with this idea whole-heartedly. However, Wallis also characterizes homeland and diaspora as constituting a "deterritorialized nation," which suggests that such a nationalist construction is devoid of physical connections to established places on the ground. On the contrary, I would argue that diasporans engage in sociopolitical constructions that create *multiterritorial nations*.

My notion of multiterritoriality captures lives that are simultaneously characterized by movement and dwelling—routedness and rootedness, in the words of James Clifford (1997)—in both physical and conceptual terms. The multiterritorial Tongan nation takes into account the fact that communities are often far-flung and physically distant from one another, but are also physically linked by land and sea and conceptually connected to and by the people who comprise them. Hau'ofa's specific (1993) treatise on the importance of the ocean reminds us that Pacific Islanders' ancient worlds were much larger than

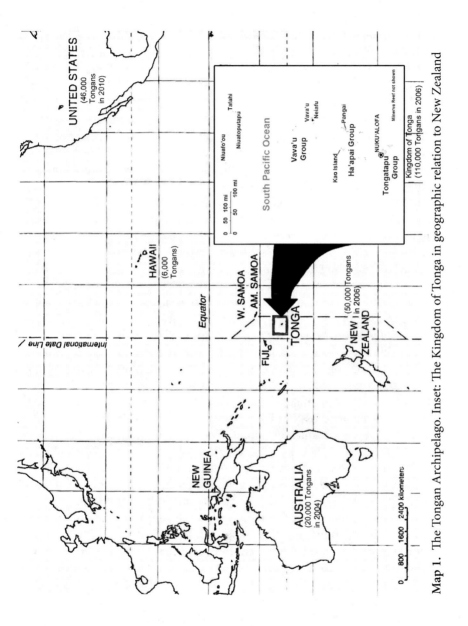

Map 1. The Tongan Archipelago. Inset: The Kingdom of Tonga in geographic relation to New Zealand

their islands because they traveled the ocean to connect with others. Likewise, today, the watery spaces between the Tongan homeland and sites in its diaspora mediate persons' sentiments of nationalism, where nationalism can be defined as allegiance to a place and a people or as the sentiments that exist because of a person's shared heritage, language, and self-definition with a specific group of people. Thus a multiterritorial nation is also one whose constituents engage in long-distance nationalism, a set of identity claims whereby people in dispersed locations connect themselves and their communities and express belonging to a specific ancestral homeland (Anderson 1998; Glick Schiller et al. 1992).

However their connection is not only to that homeland. My ethnography reveals that there is often a kind of simultaneity of concern, orientation, and interaction between people in different parts of a multiterritorial nation, meaning that people are keeping multiple places central in their nationalist consciousness and commitment. Navigating specific geographies and territories has become crucial in the economic strategy of numerous households across the globe today. Hence, the nation emerges as a multiterritorial concept—evoking communities, to whom concepts of place such as *fonua* matter immensely, interacting together in numerous places—rather than one that is merely "deterritorialized," as Wallis has suggested (2008). Specifically, in the multiterritorial Tongan nation, people interact within and between ethnic communities in different nation-states through exchanging valuables as gifts. Sometimes those communities are rooted in Tonga, and sometimes they are rooted in diaspora; interactions between diasporic communities are as common as interactions between Tonga and a given place in the diaspora.

As this study suggests, the movements of valuables across the distances separating far-flung kin and communities may constitute micro-level flows of remittances, goods, and individuals that seem insignificant in the shadow of global capital and trade (Appadurai 1996; Levitt 2001; Shankman 1993; Werbner 1990). Yet cross-border exchanges between kith and kin are far from trivial: they are maintained by a multiplicity of modern mechanisms that enable the global social relations that are some of the crucial building blocks of modern transnational communities-cum-nations. The phone calls made, gifts sent, money wired, debts repaid, capital invested, commodities transported, and kin who travel connect modern diasporans to their points of origin and to one another, and are far from insignificant. Examples of the importance of these links in different "globalized" communities range from the transnational political role of US-resident Haitians in the electoral politics of Haiti (Fouron and Glick Schiller 2002; Laguerre 2006) to Zionist American Jews' fundraising in the US for schools and youth programs in Israel (Fouron and Glick Schiller 2002). Such transnationalism is the link, the central process through which non-commercial globalization operates; and, in this context, globalization is nothing without people's particular links to one another within a system (Tsing 2005).

These interconnections—both lived and imagined—can be the basis of an alternative modern form of nation, even when they are based on practices, such as gift exchange, that actors themselves tout as "tradition." Whereas nation-state theory focuses on the nation defined as a group of people who live in a particular place—a limited territory over which they have sovereignty (Smith 2001)—and who are connected through print media and an active imagining of themselves as a "community" (Anderson 1983), diaspora theory focuses on the agency of diasporans in determining the daily practice and sometimes even the political path of the homeland. Contemporary diaspora theory does not assume, furthermore, that diaspora is subordinate to homeland, or the "bastard child of the nation …, [an] impoverished imitation of the originary culture" (Gopinath 1995; see also Braziel and Mannur 2003, Hall 1990, and Safran 1991). On the contrary, diaspora theorists insist that diasporas and homelands are mutually dependent and mutually constituting even when, in many cases, homelands are dependent on diasporas for economic sustenance, primarily through emigrants' sending of remittances to kin in the homeland (Lee 2009a and b).

Second- and third-generation members of diasporic communities often have a very strong cultural affinity and allegiance to the nation-state(s) in which they have grown up, but they are not devoid of relationship to their homeland. Instead, their concepts of the homeland are filtered through a consciousness shaped by the countries in which they were born (Levitt 2009), and they often blur the boundaries between the center of the "nation" and its periphery, or diaspora. For these later generations of Tongans, the ability to look simultaneously to Tonga and to diaspora, in turn facilitates their meaningful interaction across space in ways that might be described, not as Tonga-centric, but as what I call *multicentric,* even as it potentially generates differences between the generations.

This book, in focusing on the role played by *koloa* and its globalized production and circulation, tells a crucial part of the story of how Tongan people have created their own modernity. The significance of *koloa* in this story lies in its being a category of objects that has become a focal point for concerns that all Tongans have, in some place, at some time, and for some specific reasons, about moving between tradition and modernity (Besnier 2011). Thus, *koloa* is also a site of debates and negotiations between Tongans themselves about what their multiterritorial nation should be.

Objects categorized by commoners as *koloa* fulfill multiple functions as gifts, commodities, and ceremonial dress, as well as encode complex sentiments about the nation. If the production of *koloa* is an activity that is primarily the province of older people, is it still relevant for younger generations within the Tongan diaspora? Many young people—members of the second generation of Tongans in New Zealand—see the cloths as old fashioned or simply irrelevant to their own lives, as Lee (2003) has also noted for Tongan youth in the wider diaspora and as Peggy Levitt (2009) has found for Indian youth in the United States. I am interested in the complexity of the sentiments that are encoded by *koloa* for second-generation Tongans in diaspora, people who were born in the diaspora to parents who immigrated there. These sentiments are an important determinant in how people who have not lived much, if any, of their lives in the homeland negotiate belonging in their ancestral *fonua*. In later parts of this book, I briefly examine the role of *koloa* in the lives of second-generation and 1.5 generation kin group members (those who emigrated to diaspora as youth) to consider the potential longevity of these objects as repositories of value in the future. Studies like mine that emphasize the experiences of the first, or immigrant generation, or of the interactions between multiple generations, still make an important contribution to the anthropological literature on 1.5 and second generation immigrant populations.

The Significance of This Study

Giving and reciprocating material things gives people the power to create bonds that *they* constitute and consider essential to society. In other words, gift exchange becomes a way of producing a culturally valued and connected self. Of this process, Karen Sykes (2005:113) writes: "by calling gift exchange a knowledge practice, anthropologists understood that people understood both ceremonial exchange and little acts of give and take to be social acts that expressed conscious and non-conscious belief, and made social relationships at the same time as it recreated social structure." Such a habitus—a set of habitual, non-conscious "dispositions" that people acquire socially and that constitute their way of being in the world (Bourdieu 1977)—is central to how Tongans interrelate affectively and economically. Insofar as the gift is Tongans' means of recognition of another's belonging in a community—indeed, of their humanity—I would argue for their having a habitus of the gift. For this study, which shifts from a particular "culture" or "nation" to the multiterritorial space, the gift becomes a conceptual map both for the movement people make physically and symbolically when they engage with globalization and a lens through which to focus my analysis on the people who, I argue, are at the center of community and nation building in diaspora—elderly Tongan women of commoner status. My characterization of the Tongan nation as a multiterritorial construction of place highlights the integral role played by the Tongan gift as it articulates with three distinct yet related approaches to diaspora. The first sees diaspora as intertwined with, and often maintained by the needs and dictates of kinship. Helping kin in the homeland and seeking new opportunities for themselves and their families are often the reason that emigrants settle down in new countries, becoming diasporans. The desire or obligation to maintain ongoing connections to kin, claims to land, and to a homeland that anchors one's heritage are the driving forces behind diasporans' movement, and consequent dwelling (Chan 1997; Gershon 2007).

Pacific Islanders have been moving across the globe for centuries to explore, marry, conquer new territory, settle disputes, trade, gift, and forge alliances. Since the turn of the twentieth century there has been much more travel to developed nations, in part because of the need people feel to seek capital that their own nations' economies cannot regularly afford them—as David Harvey has said, where there is a shortage of capital one will find movement of people, or labor, to places where there is an "over-accumulation of capital" (2001). This is precisely the case with the increase in the number of Tongans in New Zealand since the 1950s. One might say that wherever one finds an under-accumulation of kin along with an overabundance of capital, transnational movement will result. People often become diasporans, not for individual self-gain, but as a form of family strategy for surviving rising costs of living in a homeland, fleeing war and political strife there, or to reunite with kin who live outside the homeland.

A second notable quality of the concept of diaspora lies in its force, as Clifford describes it, as a "traveling term" (1997). By this I take Clifford to mean that diaspora is an experience to which movement between places is, and has always been, central. Not only does diaspora evoke movement of people, between places, over time, and with multiple political-economic, social, and religious implications, but the meaning and mechanisms of diaspora change as the concept moves and is applied to case studies in different times and places. Thus, the kinds of conditions and experiences that give meaning to the concept of Jewish diaspora are very different from those that give meaning to African diaspora and contemporary Pacific diaspora. Here I examine the particularity of Tonga diaspora, and contribute to the anthropological literature on how people use objects to map space—or trace their movements, activities, and modes of dwelling. I ask: how, under what conditions, and with what consequences do people use objects or valuables in their overseas ethnic communities? Anthropologist Christopher Tilley has called for more research on the role of material culture in transnational social relations and, in this study, I also examine what he calls the "objectifications of transnational and diasporic communities" (2006:70). By this I take Tilley to mean the processes and assumptions whereby objects or material forms are embedded in people's lives as members of groups, institutions, and societies (ibid.:60). My study contributes an exploration of diaspora by illuminating the centrality of traditional valuables in contemporary Tongan institutions of transnational kinship, religion, and gendered exchange, all of which rely heavily on movement and dwelling between homeland and diaspora.

The third area of my study characterizes diaspora, not just as a state of being or as the maintenance of connections to an ancestral homeland, but also as an economically and socially purposeful mechanism whereby people accumulate resources needed to meet modern costs of living and to develop their own social value—or reputation. In Tonga, many gifts are the products of the land or can be made by hand from cultivated resources. *Ngāue* and *koloa* are two such (gendered) categories of gifts. In diaspora, however, Tongan ceremonial gifts require givers to have access to money, or in other words to economic capital. I find capital a useful notion with which to analyze the Tongan gift in diaspora because intrinsic to the concept of capital, as Marx and Bourdieu have used it, is the idea that people are able to accumulate capital and that they can further invest it in an existing system so that it "reproduces itself" (Marx 1990 [1867]). Furthermore, referring to the kind of value that people derive from exchanging *valuables* as capital highlights the assumption of such value being transactable, or exchangeable by people for value that will grow from being exchanged in future social interactions. Finally, in the notion of capital, there exists a sense of the instrumentality or calculation with which people transact the forms of value that they accumulate (Bourdieu 1986). This instrumentality is highlighted in one convention of Tongan exchange: Tongans do not generally gift important valuables such as *koloa* indiscriminately, but gift when they are obligated to because of the relative social rank of, and history of debts between their family and others' kin groups. This "rule" about exchange is built on the notion that value can be accumulated and transacted through the gift.

What Tongans value most in their interactions with other Tongans are their reputations as people who recognize obligations to give and reciprocate gifts and, thus, as people who have and express *'ofa* (love, compassion) most appropriately. These reputations are most decidedly augmented by their further engaging in gift exchange. When people gift, they typically receive reciprocations in the form of valuables—*koloa*, food, cash, etc. These constitute material capital and can be further gifted in service to enhancing reputations; Bourdieu (1986) would refer to the reputations themselves as embodying "social capital," the respect and honor an individual receives when others recognize that he or she has presented a gift. The concomitant positive effects that such recognition accrues to a person's reputation can be used to her advantage in social transactions. But among Tongans, engaging in gift exchange affords individuals a chance to accrue cultural capital, or a rise in their status due to others' recognition of their mastery of cultural knowledge. Such mastery is evidenced by things like their competence in matters that regenerate the values of the community, such as organizing and staging a ceremonial occasion wherein kin group members can engage in "collectivist giving." In this way, a person's value or reputation can be augmented by further investment in enabling the reputations of others.

Thus, individual and family reputations, which in themselves constitute value, also become capital that can be invested in a social system and made to grow. Transactions of gifts between kin groups are the very things that lead to the growth and accumulation of such capital. This is how gifts embody value—they represent Tongan people's best efforts at maintaining or augmenting their kin group's reputations. Because reputations bridge the time between generations and because kin groups abide through time and, increasingly, over space, there is longevity built into diaspora, in part, facilitated by gift exchange. Gifts also provide a way for people to accumulate various forms of capital needed to navigate the costs of living as Tongans in a new society.

Accumulating cultural capital thus relies on the conscientious attention to resources that is part of the work people do to maintain or augment their sustenance and their ties to kin in other parts of the ethnoscape (Chan 1997). There is a global twist to such a basis for Tongan reputations, however: ceremonial exchanges can sometimes occur so close together temporally, yet so far apart physically, that a family has to plan carefully how it will finance its daily expenses and its ceremonial obligations in order to ensure economic survival in diaspora from one week to the next (Ka'ili 2008). Tongans who can give in ways that other consider to be generous at ceremonial events, and with no detriment to their family's finances, are generally highly admired. However, there is always a risk that others will think their large gifts are an attempt to appropriate the prerogative of chiefs—that is, that others will label them *"fie 'eiki."* Presenting an appropriate and affordable gift involves a person evaluating her own current social status, the status of recipients, what wealth she has on hand or can acquire quickly, and future occasions when she will, again, be obligated to gift. As I explore in later chapters, sometimes individuals or families make strategic decisions to reduce the size of everyday expenditures of both modern and traditional wealth or to extend the timing of a reciprocation while making ready, exchanging, and reciprocating a gift.

Lisa Malkki (1997) and other anthropologists who study culture and place argue that linking national identity to one geographic territory fails to capture the complexity of the multigenerational interactions around which sentiments and material commitments that produce the nation actually develop (Clifford 1997; Gupta 1997).[8] Transnational people's ties to a nation develop alongside connections to and interests in citizens of other countries, beyond even what has been considered the "globalized" or "diasporic" nation. People living such transnational lives—like so many others in the world—often want these lives to be materially satisfactory, socially fulfilling, and modern ones. They want to travel, consume, communicate, work, relax, invest, and be trendsetters. They also often want to engage with other modern people using global tools—such as mass-produced commodities, fashion, technology, and cash wealth—while remaining true to the cultural principles and practices that afford them a sense of their own uniqueness in the world. They hold dear their own senses of tradition and the objects that symbolize their belonging in particular groups and places, however contingent and negotiated the definitions of tradition and the forms of the objects may be. In examining contemporary Tongan culture, this book is as much about those aspects of life that people count as "tradition" as it is about people's interface with modernity, but its lens is the revaluation and redeployment of tradition in ways that cannot be named either tradition or modernity. It considers the time, place, and social conditions, as well as gendered and generational aspects of a shift that is about globalization manifesting as the particular diasporization of a contemporary Pacific Island people.

Getting Here: This Study and This Volume

In designing the fieldwork on which this book is based, I followed a multisited ethnographic process (Marcus 1998) to research Tongan material culture in the homeland and diaspora. In June 2000, I began conducting fieldwork on *koloa* and their forms and functions in Nukuʻalofa, the capital of Tonga. Located on Tongatapu, the Kingdom of Tonga's main island, this city is home to about one-third of the kingdom's population. My time there was my foundation for the more expansive study I would undertake on diasporic communities of Tongans who lived in New Zealand. I was intent on learning all that I could about the aesthetics of *koloa*: from the cultivation of plants to the beating and softening of the bark for producing barkcloth; from the processing of pandanus leaves for plaiting fine mats to the weaving of these mats; and from the meanings of decorative patterns to the combinations of *koloa* that were suitable for being gifted. I also gained indispensable knowledge about the unique role played by the communities of the diaspora in island-based Tongans' sense of their own presence in the world. People in the diaspora provided cash remittances and familiar communities in which to live when traveling or studying abroad. The diaspora has also been responsible for increasing the export of *koloa*. Numerous people in Tonga had told me, many doing so with no small sense of pride, that "there is more *koloa* in New Zealand than in Tonga ... those Tongans overseas, they take all the *koloa* and their *katoanga* [ceremonial occasions at which *koloa* are publicly gifted] are bigger than the ones we have here."

Interested in how this perceived imbalance in Tongan and diasporic exchanges affected the status and self-perception of women in diasporic communities, I interviewed more women in New Zealand, noting the paths they told me their *koloa* had taken to get to them in diaspora. In following the routes whereby people in Tonga "export" *koloa* to kin in diaspora, I traveled to New Zealand in 2000 where I lived for four months during that same first fieldwork period. Like a Tongan migrant, I had been initially socialized into Tongan culture in the homeland and then began a transition to New Zealand. I returned to Auckland to do ethnographic research for another seven months, from January to July 2002. I initially lived for a short period of time with Fatai, a young Methodist woman struggling to raise three children on a single salary in this "new" country. In her home, I learned how *koloa* can be strategically included, and sometimes excluded, from the economics of daily life and ceremonial obligations. Later, I shared the home of Kakala, an elderly Methodist woman who was the keeper of *koloa* for her entire extended kin group in Auckland, and whose life—a life steeped in involvement with *koloa*—I write about in chapters 3 and 4.

My movements back and forth from Tonga to New Zealand afforded me a range of experiences of Tongan family life; in each country I accepted invitations to live for several months with two different kin groups. These family experiences also impressed upon me the diversity of ways in which Tongans live according to principles of *langa fonua,* not least because of the differing church donation practices expected by their Christian denominations. In the Kingdom of Tonga, the Free Wesleyan Church has the largest following of adherents, with 37 percent of the population of Tonga.[9] The majority of Tongans who live in diaspora continue their affiliation, if not devotion, to one or another Christian congregation. There is some denominational switching evident when Tongans move abroad, but people primarily remain loyal to the denominations they grew up in or, in the case of women, married into.

In Nuku'alofa, I lived near another mainline Methodist family with whom I became very close. When one of the daughters of this family, who lived in Auckland, died unexpectedly, I accompanied the family to Auckland for her funeral. Participating in their process of mourning reinforced my conviction that, even though I was concerned with documenting the movement and aesthetics of *koloa,* what I was ultimately studying was the movement of, and bonds between people. Thus, in applying the methodology of "follow the thing" (Marcus 1998:93), I came to an embodied understanding of the efficacy of another methodology: "follow the people" (ibid.:92). Most of the time, however, I practiced "follow the story" along trajectories embellished with objects, value(s) and people. In recording life histories from my informants, I learned how they and others launched particular (pieces of) *koloa* on trajectories of connection between relatives located in different parts of the ethnoscape and how, sometimes, these objects reappeared in stories that they told one another, and me, about Tongans in different parts of the globe. Other details of my research methods emerge through this ethnography and weave a parallel story of how I, as a researcher, came to understand "my people" by being *there*—that is, *anywhere* they choose to be, or needed, to be—with them. As Jana Braziel and Anita Mannur (2003:7) have stated, "diasporas force us to rethink the rubrics of nation and nationalism, while refiguring the relations of citizens and nation-states." My methodology of being in different parts of the multiterritorial nation, negotiating tradition and modernity along with my informants proved

invaluable in understanding how they—especially commoner women of a senior generation—generated the nation while living it.

Chapter Summary

As one might unfold *koloa* one has received as a gift, I have organized this book
to unfold the entangled issues addressed so far in this introduction: the history
and value of particular varieties of *koloa,* women's life histories as revealed in
their involvement in *koloa* production—both in the diaspora and in the homeland—, the roles that the *koloa* system plays when Tongans gift money and
other forms of modern wealth, and how *koloa* operates as a value-laden notion
in the lives of multiple generations of Tongans in diaspora today. In chapter 1,
I argue that the notion of global commodities and valuables should include
traditional forms that contribute to kin-based connections as they embody
memory, desire, and even contention over modernity. The chapter analyzes
Tongans' debates surrounding the authenticity of *ngatu pepa,* a textile that encodes both rupture and continuity because it was "invented" in diaspora and
is composed of non-Tongan, synthetic material. I explore commoner women's
prerogatives to authenticate new material cultural forms that they introduce
into the *koloa* system. My analysis thus illuminates the role of the diaspora as a
site of women's "authentic(ized) innovation" and nation building through the
deployment of "traditional" objects in new forms. By producing things and
relationships Tongan women respond to and create new conditions of production in diasporic locations.

Chapter 2 analyzes the role of women's associations in the process of indigenizing foreign forms, thus preserving tradition through innovation. I argue
that diasporic women's cooperative work groups extend and augment the ancestral homeland as a place of Tongan culture through specific (womanly) processes of negotiating older practices in new homelands and with new social and
economic affiliations. I ask: what roles do women assign their objects in nation
building through their work in these groups? And how, and to what effect, do
the women reinterpret host-country notions of development and modernity
through their own cultural lenses when they seek public funding in diaspora
to support their production of *koloa*? I argue that the women Tonganize or
indigenize these modern resources, retranslating them back into gifts.

Chapter 3 traces the life stories of three elderly women to capture the tension between women's traditional roles in kin groups and community and their
modern ways of performing *langa fonua.* This chapter asks what is at stake for
women who engage in the work of kinship, culture work, and nation building,
while also balancing household finances, sourcing and caring for *koloa,* and
gifting it ceremonially? The life narratives tell how the women harness help

and resources from people in different parts of the multiterritorial Tongan nation in order to fulfill these kin-based duties and to re-create their society in diaspora. Aspects of these life narratives also seem to challenge women's kin-based duties.

Chapter 4 asks why entanglements in relations of debt are such an integral part of what it means to be a Tongan woman, and especially a Tongan mother. The chapter further illuminates the entanglements of money with the gifting of cloth in complex ceremonial gifts comprising cash, cloth, *koloa,* and consumer goods. It analyzes case studies of a commoner wedding and a first birthday celebration in Auckland from the point of view of the mothers of the celebrants, analyzing their recollections to trace the movement of valuables between various nodes in the multiterritorial nation. I also analyze how recognizing and reciprocating *'ofa* (a gloss for the emotion "love") ensures that families avoid *mā* (shame, another emotion), and how *'ofa* constitutes a cultural project, motivating contributions from younger-generation members who normally eschew ceremonial gifting.

Chapter 5 documents why the form of a Tongan gift is highly subject to negotiation in ceremonies that take place outside of the homeland. The chapter focuses on a funeral—the type of ceremonial occasion in which being perceived as respectful of tradition evinces its highest stakes for participants. By analyzing the effects of the grieving family's refusal to accept *koloa* as gifts, I underscore how, by both its material presence and its consequential absence, *koloa* can deeply affect diasporans' efforts to perform *langa fonua.*

Tensions arising in the use of both *koloa* and money as ritual gifts symbolize the continuity, as well as the rupture, between Tongan tradition and a distinctly Tongan modernity. Yet, money plays a crucial role in how Tongan diasporic communities perform their allegiance to Tonga and compete for places of recognition among their co-ethnics in the multiple sites of diaspora. Chapter 6 examines two fundraising events, discusses the role of 1.5 and second generation Tongan youth in performing their families' allegiance to church and homeland, and demonstrates how the privileged place of the "center" of the ethnoscape must be continually negotiated and publicly performed with the proffering of valuables.

The conclusion recapitulates some of the major themes of the book, and suggests the need for further study of how second generation members of Tongan-New Zealand communities live out the complexity of their identity as Tongans who are rooted—both physically and in terms of heritage—outside of the homeland. This chapter recognizes that, in Pacific worldviews—as in the habitus of transnational people more generally—moving and dwelling are in dialectical relationship to one another (Appadurai 1996; Clifford 1997; Francis 2007 and 2009; Gilroy 1993; Hau'ofa 1993). Studying exchange in Pacific diaspora brings this to the fore because, insofar as ceremonial exchange connects people who are separated because of movement, it takes place because people dwell in particular places; that is, exchange is always situated *somewhere.* Commoner women invest in the creative possibilities in this tension between movement and dwelling and, through exchange of *koloa,* they lead Tonga's modernity as a multiterritorial nation.

Notes

1. In 1970, the authority of the Australian High Commissioner to Fiji was extended to include Tonga (Grainger 1998). Chiefly Tongans had been emigrating to cities like Sydney and Canberra for at least two decades prior to this, seeking education and clerical training. The London Missionary Society, based in Australia, coordinated the establishment of the Tongan monarchy and international markets for Tongan products and provided Tonga's first prime minister, the Methodist Reverend Shirley Baker.

2. Since the mid–nineteenth century, Tonga has been a Christian country; Catholics today account for only 11 percent of the Tongan population, but many highly influential Tongans belong to this denomination. Following denominational splits during the reigns of the first Tongan monarch, Taufa'ahau Tupou I, and of Sālote Tupou III, nobles have belonged to any of the three largest denominations: the Free Wesleyan Church of Tonga, the Church of Tonga, and the Roman Catholic Church.

3. Modern Tonga has largely been free of war, so much so that several days of unrest in the capital, Nuku'alofa, that started on sixteenth of November 2006 sustained the attention of much of the international press. Dubbed "16-11," the burning of significant commercial establishments throughout much of the town was allegedly instigated by unrest among supporters of the long-standing pro-democracy movement who had been awaiting a parliamentary response to their demands that more elected parliamentary officials be put on future public ballots. Protesters sought to counteract the cronyism that has characterized the history of Tongan parliamentary practices due, in part, to the monarch's constitutional power to appoint the majority of officials (Māhina 2010; Young Leslie 2007).

4. The quality of homeland-diaspora ties determine whether participants in the nation consider remittances put into the service of growth of the homeland also contribute to global nation building. See Lindley (2009) for an analysis of remittances from a diaspora perspective, including an analysis of how forced, rather than voluntary migration affects remitting practices.

5. In a recent survey-based analysis of attitudes held by people within what the authors call the "Tongan Transnational System," Mike Evans, Paul Harms, and Colin Reid (2009:121) state that their respondents identified several core manifestations that distinguish them, as Tongans, from others in the world. The survey suggested that Tongans "will always return to Tonga, value their families' interests over their personal interests, and share generously." The respondents are essentially stating that these are the core defining characteristics that one will find among Tongan people who live according to *anga faka-Tonga* (the Tongan way) and they constitute a measure of their uniqueness in the world.

6. In 1980, an Australian High Commission was established in Nuku'alofa (Grainger 1998), and in the late 1980s, Australia began to take a leadership role in developing the

Tonga Defence Force. It continues to pride itself on being extremely attentive to Tonga in matters of economic aid and disaster relief (see Australia Government 2009).

7. By 1995, there were 25,000 ethnic Tongans—both first- and second-generation immigrants—registered as living in the US (Small 1997). In 2000, half a decade later, the US census reported that there were 36,982 people who claimed Tongan ancestry (either entirely or partially) living in the United States (US Census Bureau 2005; also accessible online at: http://www.census.gov/prod/2005pubs/censr-26.pdf). Similar figures are reported by the US Census Bureau, 2001, "The Native Hawaiian and other Pacific Islander Population: 2000," which is accessible online at: http://www.census.gov/prod/2001pubs/c2kbr01-14.pdf. By 2004, the total had risen to 39,052 (US Census Bureau 2007:2).

8. For example, the nation of Israel, by definition, comprises all ethnic Jews; however, not all Jews are citizens of the nation of Israel (Braziel and Mannur 2003).

9. Other religious leanings include the Church of Jesus Christ of Latter-day Saints (Mormons) with 17 percent, the Free Church of Tonga with 16 percent, and the Roman Catholic Church with 11 percent. Seventh-day Adventists, Assemblies of God, and Anglicans, make up about 14 percent of the population (Tonga Department of Statistics, 2006). A much smaller percentage comprises people of Baha'i, Hindu, and Muslim faiths.

❀❀ 1

Migration, Tradition, and Barkcloth
Authentic Innovations in Textile Gifts

Through exchange, members of Pacific transnational communities forge and maintain the intersecting webs of obligation, desire, and value transfer that connect them to kin and co-ethnics in other homes, villages, and countries. Their exchange practices involve both high-status traditional valuables and modern cash wealth. In the case of textiles that are particularly prominent in exchange practices of Tongan diasporans, the objects' value stems partly from the fact that Tongans have historically invested them with power and shared meanings.

Textiles are symbolically "open" to a range of categorizations and associations that depend, in part, on the qualities of the textiles in question. Some people have taken their softness and apparent fragility as metaphors for the deeply enveloping, but entirely fleeting nature of emotion (Weiner 1989; see also Rethman 1999 and Rovine 1990). But in many societies, textiles do not signify the same impermanence, because people make textiles—or "cloths" as Weiner terms them—to last; they intentionally keep, repair, and renew them (Weiner 1989; Young Leslie and Addo 2007). So too the construction of textiles from interlaced or otherwise fused fibers gives them a degree of durability that supports a different set of metaphors. For example, in Pacific cultures, the plaited construction of cloths is a metaphor for how society is composed of human beings intertwining, and even reaching over and past one another as they negotiate their place in society. In the Tongan case, the proverb *'oku hangē ki he lālanga 'a e kakai*, or "human kind is like a mat being woven" (Young Leslie 1999; 2007) provides a useful example of this metaphoric use, where the interlaced fibers of Polynesian fine mats (*lālanga*) are symbolic of the interlacing of human beings to form society.[1] This interlacing is accomplished through marriage, childbearing, and the assembling of communities to observe life-crisis events.

Not only are the materiality and technology of *koloa* made to manifest social ideals or values of societal strength and solidarity, Tongan women *make* their cloth to be durable and enduring. These qualities of textiles are directly attributable to women's action on raw materials. While not directly indexed by the proverb above, barkcloth shares with other interlaced textiles a social technology wherein women work collectively to join its basic materials with their hands. When women overlay strips of beaten and felted paper mulberry tree (*Broussonetia papyrifera*) bark, then paste them together with vegetable starches and rub dye into the surface, the barkcloth that results is assumed to embody a certain physical and cultural durability. Women also regularly repair tears and holes in fine mats and barkcloths, a practice that reinforces the long-standing notion that cloths, as objects of value, should be preserved.

In Pacific societies more generally, the material *and* cultural durability of cloth is socially assured because objects made using textile techniques—plaiting, weaving, pressing, pounding, and pasting—belong to a category of things that are considered unique and valuable.[2] Andrew Arno (2005) describes a similar relationship between durability and value when he suggests that *tabua*, whale teeth prized in Fijian society and usually individually mounted on braided sennit (coconut shell) fibers, bear the status of gifts of the "supreme material valuable" in Tongan culture. Like *tabua* for Fijians, no other material goods are equal to *koloa*, neither can they permanently replace them in exchange (ibid.). Similarly, Rod Ewins (2009) argues that, for people from Vatulele Island in Fiji, *masi* barkcloths are "signs in history": these objects that are often ancient and preserved for decades, if not centuries, encapsulate a sense of both material and temporal value. Meredith Filihia (2001) adds that Tongan women hammer the *mana* of Pulotu—the home of the goddess Hukuleʻo and other ancestors and ancient deities—into their barkcloth, such that they literally embed the symbol of womanly *mana*, spiritual potency, in the barkcloth.

In this chapter, I show that, even without hammering bark to create barkcloth or plaiting pandanus fibers to create *lālanga*, Tongan women are able to imbue their *mana* as well as their *ʻofa* ("love") into a different type of cloth. I introduce *ngatu pepa*, or *ngatu* made from "paper" and describe its production techniques. "Paper" is what Tongans call vylene, a synthetic fabric from which women can now produce barkcloth and which eliminates the need to use paper mulberry bark. I analyze *ngatu pepa* making techniques as a diasporic innovation in traditional barkcloth production that has been taking place in the homeland for centuries: *ngatu pepa* becomes a type of cloth that they can potentially gift and that enables them to perform *langa fonua* in diaspora. I explore the aspects of *ngatu pepa* aesthetics, production, and use that enable it to serve the purposes of tradition. My analysis suggests that Tonga is not the sole site of authentic Tongan cultural production; indeed, both homeland and diaspora can be contexts in which women exchange valuables in newly "traditional" ways. Producing *koloa* in diaspora makes a break with former total dependence on Tonga as a source for traditionally styled *koloa*. Moreover, producing *koloa* for commercial purposes—as some *langa fonua* groups do in New Zealand—also eschews the notion of women's assumedly (subservient) roles and analysts' assumptions that *koloa* are primarily connected to

Table 1. Handmade women's exchange valuables mentioned in this book: Types, Uses, and Sizes

Name(s)	Use	Material base	Color	Layers	Length in native textile units (*langanga*)[1] or approximate equivalent in feet
Barkcloth					
ngatu ngatu	gift, dance costume, ceremonial floor covering	*hiapo* (paper mulberry bark)	brown	2	*launima* (50 langanga)= 65 feet *lauteau* (100 *langanga*) = 130 feet
ngatu pepa	gift, dance costume, ceremonial floor covering	vylene	brown	2	Can be 50 *langanga* (65 feet) *but* usually 10 *langanga* (13 feet)
ngatu hafekasi	gift, dance costume, ceremonial floor covering	*hiapo* and vylene	brown	2	Can be 50 *langanga* (65 feet) but usually 10 *langanga* (13 feet)
ngatu kāliko	gift, ceremonial floor covering	white or off-white calico	brown	2	usually 10 *langanga* (13 feet)
fuatanga (rare; made from different joining technique than *ngatu*)	gift, ceremonial floor covering	*hiapo*	brown	2	10-50 *langanga* (13–65 feet)
Lālanga, woven *koloa*					
fala paongo	gift, floor covering	pandanus (*louʻakau*)	brown	2	optional; usu. room-sized
fala paongo fakakulasi	gift, floor covering		brown	2	optional; usu. room-sized
kie tonga	gift, waist mat		pearly white	1	3'x5'–4'x6'
taʻovala (eg: taʻovala lokeha)	waist mat		various	2	5'x2'–7'x2'
kie fau	waist mat		blond	2	3'x5'–4'x6'
taʻovala liponi	waist mat	ribbon, plastic lacing, video tape strips	Various; incl. brown, black, rust, green, purple, rose	1 or 2	5'x2'–7'x2'

Kato (baskets)					
kato teu	gift	basket, covered with cloth	various; shiny, sequins	n/a	1–1.5 feet in diameter
kato alu	gift	shallow basket; alu fibers	brown or black	n/a	1–2 feet in diameter
Lolo niu (coconut oil)					
	gift, skin care, hair care	expressed flesh of dried coconuts; scented	clear yellow to green	n/a	presented in tall bottles; store-bought toiletries are often substituted
Koloa si'i (little koloa")[2]					
monomono (patch-work quilt)	gift, bedding	fabric sewn with machines	various		8x8 feet
kafu niti (knitted/cro-cheted blankets)	gift, bedding	colored yarn	various		8x8 feet
kafu sipi (synthetic 'fleece' blankets)	gift, bedding	store-bought 'fleece' blanket	various		8x8 feet
kafu satini "satin bedding"	gift, bedding	shiny bedspread w matching pillows	various		8x8 feet

Source: adapted from Young Leslie 2007 (p. 118)

Notes

1. A barkcloth is typically width of the worktable used to construct it, a minimum of twelve feet. The length of a barkcloth is measured in native units called *langanga*. One *langanga* is about eighteen inches long, although there are some that are larger (see Arbeit 1994:14). Today, one can find *ngatu* with shorter *langanga*, fourteen inches being the minimum I have seen. A woman measures *a langanga* by "walking" her outstretched fingers over the surface of a cloth, adding twice the distance between her middle finger and thumb to the distance between thumb and forefinger or middle finger and forefinger. Thus, these native units can vary by a few inches between different women. In any given piece of *ngatu*, the *langanga* will be roughly equal, however, since the size of the measures sections conforms to the size of the wooden worktable on which women assemble the cloth.

2. See Herda 1999:164; this category includes store-bought bedding such as "fleece blankets" and satin bedding sets.

domesticity (Young Leslie 1999), fertility (Veys 2009), sacred potency (James 1988; Rogers 1977), and rank (Kaeppler 1999b). As I argue here, the resulting shifting value of barkcloth forms indicates there is a continuum of textile materialities that comprise the category of *koloa*. Moreover, in a process Homer Barnett would label "recombination" (1953), textile forms change continually, with elements added and subtracted according to how women choose to accomplish particular tasks.

The commodification of *ngatu* for purchase by outsiders is evident in Tonga's marketplaces, such as the central Talamahu market and the local commercial outlet of the organization that Queen Sālote started in the mid-1950s, the Langa Fonua 'ae Fefine Tonga. Tourist brochures identify these places as good locations for obtaining barkcloth, plaited baskets and mats, fans, handbags, and other things categorized as *ngāue fakame'a'a*, or "handicrafts." These barkcloth-based items are not *koloa*, but they are sought out by Tongans traveling to overseas locations and by diasporic Tongans returning to their host countries, who are often proud to buy and publicly make use of such objects. They thus play a role in reinforcing overseas Tongans' devotion to and performance of *langa fonua*. The work of women's hands thus continues to be linked to women's *mana* and to *koloa* and its meanings.

Technologies and Histories of Tongan Barkcloth and Plaited Fine Mats

Most commoner Tongans I have spoken to do not always know, nor are they very concerned about, when their ancestors first began to be make *koloa*. They also have rarely thought about whether the knowledge and plants needed to produce these textiles were brought with their ancestors on their migration eastward from the New Guinea region to settle the Tongan islands.[3] What is known is that *koloa*'s origins are sacred and associated with the time of *āpō*— the time of darkness and the time before human beings, when only deities existed. This is the time of Tongan origins, and associating *koloa* with this time period helps to establish the sacred origin of *koloa*. As Maurice Godelier (1999) states, sacred objects have their origins at the beginning of time. Thinking of *koloa* as things with a primordial or pre-temporal past—as things that have "always existed"—associates them with Pulotu, the dwelling place of the goddess Hikule'o and the place where chiefs go after death (Filihia 2003). Indeed, *koloa* were once made only by chiefly women (Martin 1991[1817]; Kaeppler 1978a, 1999b). Kerry James writes that, in pre-Christian Tonga, "high ranking women were specially valued, not so much as producers of goods, *koloa*, but as reproducers of the sacred quality they were believed to embody and which they transfer to their children" (1988:34).

In pre-contact Tonga, *koloa* was included in first fruits offerings that *tuʻa* (commoner) people made to *ʻeiki* (chiefly) people, including the divine paramount, the Tuʻi Tonga (Bott 1982; Martin 1991[1817]). Similar exchanges continue in Tonga today, and within each ranked grouping—*tuʻa* and *ʻeiki*—such exchanges also reinforce a particular set of ideas about people's obligations to contribute to the physical maintenance of *fonua*, or place and the people who are nurtured by it. Enshrined in the 1875 Constitution is the notion that all Tongans have the additional duty to maintain *fonua* by honoring the Christian God.

Tongan women consider their textile wealth to be durable and they purposefully keep it so that it stands the test of time and regenerates people culturally (Kaeppler 1999b:7). Like *koloa*, *ngāue*—agricultural wealth items produced by men—are valuables that originate from the *kelekele* (land).[4] *Ngāue*, which also includes pigs, comprises perishable objects that can potentially be quickly consumed, such that items of *ngāue* regenerate people physically (ibid.). Historically, men also produced elaborately carved wooden weapons, head rests, and *kava* bowls that were exchanged between members of chiefly families. While *kava* bowls, which Adrienne Kaeppler refers to as "the centrepieces of Tongan ritual" (1997), are essential in chiefly ceremonies, it is the consumption of the drink made from the *kava* root—also a product of the *kelekele*—that renews people physically, rather than the implements used for mixing and distributing the drink. Today, unlike *koloa* that women continue to make throughout Tonga and in some places in the diaspora, carved wooden objects have limited use in daily life for Tongans. With the exception of *kava* bowls that men use and wooden beaters that men make for women to use in their barkcloth making, carved utilitarian wooden objects are rarely employed outside of the realm of tourist objects except as gifts between high-ranking people. In contrast, *koloa* is historically connected with the development of Tonga's earliest global commodity economy and continues to be relevant in the later burgeoning of transnational migration as an enduring feature of commoners' gift relations.

Even after missionaries had converted Tongan leaders to Christianity, starting around 1826, some elites—including Taufaʻahau who eventually became Tupou I, the first Tongan monarch—continued to make offerings to the gods that included *koloa* and yams (St. Cartmail 1997; Kaeppler 1999a). Foreign missionaries and would-be colonists sought to suppress local practices related to ancient religion. Between 1826 and 1875, chiefs who followed Tupou I embraced Christianity and led their commoner followers to new religious beliefs and modernistic practices (Gailey 1987). Dress was a key tool in these "civilizing" practices. Conventional expressions of rank had disallowed commoners from wearing anything other than roughly plaited mats and plain unpainted *tapa*. After the adoption of the Tongan Constitution in 1875, commoners were given constitutional rights to make *koloa* for their own consumption, including for dress. However, when Shirley Baker, Tonga's first Prime Minister, saw that increasing the demand for imported, loom-woven cloth would yield both profit for allied European firms and support for the mission's civilizing causes, he ensured that wearing barkcloth was banned among commoner and chiefly Tongans between 1885 and 1890 (ibid.; Rutherford 1996).

Fine mat plaiting probably continued throughout this period because missionaries—as they did in many parts of the Pacific (Eves 1999)—must have regarded as useful the plaited (floor) 'mats' that women made and with which they furnished their homes. In addition, fine mat-making was quiet work that seemed to promote physical discipline and industry (Addo 2003). Thus, cloth production never actually ceased totally in Tonga. Queen Sālote also mandated that *ta'ovala* (waist mats) be worn by all civil servants at their jobs and by laypeople when they entered particular government buildings, as well as by all Tongans when they attended church services. This practice continues today, perhaps because, as some of my women informants have suggested, Queen

Figure 1.1. Dressed for church in Auckland: Kesaia Pulu and her great-nephew Māpili wear *ta'ovala,* while her niece 'Ema wears a *kiekie,* a woman's alternative to the *ta'ovala.*

Sālote's very *mana* (life force, sacred potency) was in her words when she decreed that Tongans dress this way.[5]

Since the mid–twentieth century, with population growth and rises in emigration, the number of Tongans who continue to exchange *koloa* as an essential aspect of their ritual lives has increased. At the turn of the twenty-first century, women in Tongan were making as much, if not more *koloa* than at any other time in their history (Kaeppler 1999a; Lythberg 2010).[6] Today there is high demand for *koloa* from Tongans in diaspora, as well as from non-Tongans, including from members of other Pacific Island ethnic groups and nations, and Western art and craft collectors and connoisseurs (ibid.). The category of *koloa* has long included handwoven baskets and scented coconut oil (Gailey 1987; Kaeppler 1999a), and today these continue to accompany the more prevalent forms of textile *koloa* in global flows of Tongan valuables. Today baskets decorated with satin and sequins and filled with store-bought perfumes and oils often stand in for traditional baskets containing containers of coconut oil. Together with commercially produced bedding—such as knitted blankets and colorful machine-made quilts, as well as loom-woven cotton and sequined fabrics—these baskets are known, by some women, as *koloa si'i* (Herda 1999). These objects play an important role in boosting the overall value and visual impact of gifts of other, more traditional forms of *koloa*.

The Place of *Koloa* Making in Village Life in Tonga

Whatever forms its globalized transformations may take, barkcloth making remains closely tied to family life and village activity in Tonga. One can roughly mark the seasons by women's *koloa*-making activities. For example, *koka'anga*, or *ngatu* assembly, usually takes place when the weather is dry. One can also mark certain ritual periods: out of respect for the dead, no beating of *hiapo*, paper mulberry bark, takes place when there is a funeral. Because *koloa* is closely connected to domesticity and women's homemaking tasks, many members of a household tend to become involved in, or at least directly supportive of *ngatu* making. Women and older girls take care of children and prepare daily meals, men and older boys work on family plantations, younger children pick up rubbish from around the household yards, and men prepare food in the earth oven on Sundays. During periods when women in a household or a kin group are producing *ngatu* intensely—for example, when there is a wedding or christening coming up for which they need to increase textile stocks quickly—men and other family members may care for small children or do cooking and housekeeping.

The production of *ngatu* typically begins with processing the main raw material: the inner bark of the paper mulberry tree (*hiapo*), a woody-stemmed plant.[7] These plants are grown by families on their plantations and are generally tended by men on their regular visits to their farmland, or "the bush." They tend to plant their trees two to three feet apart. The plants need lots of water and must be weeded regularly. The tree grows to a height of between six and ten feet and is favored for *ngatu* making when it is between two and three years old (Tamahori 1963). However, it is common for people to harvest paper mulberry bark (*hiapo*) when it is only a year to two years old (Fanua 1986:4). In families who grow their own *hiapo,* rather than buy it from the market, women may make intermittent trips to the plantation to check that the stems are growing straight. This involves breaking off the lateral stems that grow from the main stem in order to seal knotholes; fewer knotholes make for a smoother surface to barkcloth once it is completed. Thus, even before they have begun to make barkcloth, women develop an intimate knowledge of the plants whose fibers will become their *koloa.*

In the past, it was common for the activities of individuals to be coordinated such that most family members played a role in the production of these things of value. Usually, men cut the paper mulberry trees and pandanus plants (for plaiting mats) and brought the cut stems home along with the root crops and vegetable leaves that served as staples in most Tongans' island diets. Once *hiapo* plants have been harvested, only women work with them. Converting raw, harvested paper mulberry bark into barkcloth involves several technical and artistic stages, all of which required women's deep knowledge of raw materials, dyes, and patterns; and of the cultural importance of the processes whereby women convert garden products into domestic products with the highest cultural value.

Tongan women follow three main stages of converting paper mulberry from a mundane raw material into barkcloth. The stages are *tutu* (beating the bark), *koka'anga* (assembly), and *tohi* (final decorative stage), and a woman may be involved in simultaneously accomplishing each of these stages on various barkcloths that she is in the process of completing (see figure 1.1). Women refer to *tutu* as the most arduous stage, for it involves their using heavy wooden mallets to pound and soften the dried inner bark of *hiapo.* This process may take many days to yield enough raw material to make a single *ngatu* (Tamahori 1963; Teilhet-Fisk 1991). Once enough *hiapo* has been beaten and felted together to make sheets twelve to eighteen inches wide and several feet long, the women dry and store the sheets, which are now called *feta'aki.*

The distinguishing aspect of a barkcloth is its named surface patterning, known as its *kupesi,* which is applied with handmade patterned tablets that are also called *kupesi.* Before women can begin *koka'anga,* the next stage of barkcloth making, they must prepare these and other tools for both assembling and imprinting patterns on the cloth. *Kupesi* tablets are made from pandanus leaves that women reinforce with *kaka,* coconut fiber, and sew together with

Figure 1.2. Two women share the task of *tutu* in Veitongo village, Tonga.

fau, dried hibiscus bark, or with *kafa,* sennit fiber found between the dried inner and outer shells of a coconut. The raised patterns are made by bending and curving *tuʻa niu,* the midribs of coconut leaves, and securing them to the tablets by sewing them down using *kafa.*[8] Then the women have to ensure that *kupesi* have been attached to a worktable called a *papa kokaʻanga.* Since pre-contact times, women have been using long half cylinders of wood as their *papa.* These are still used, but today, it is more common for women to use a long, low, flat *papa* worktable, just high enough for them to tuck their folded legs under when seated on the ground around it. *Papa* are usually over fifteen feet long, their length roughly measuring the width of the barkcloth that women plan to make. They are usually set up in sheds called *fale kokaʻanga,* or in the shade of a large tree in a woman's yard, or in an empty hall adjoining a church in their village, thus further infusing *koloa*-making activity into the primary spaces of key village institutions.

Kokaʻanga, takes place once women have enough raw bark to make at least one *ngatu. Kokaʻanga* means "what one does with *koka*" and *koka* is the dye used during this stage—made from the pressed bark of the *koka* (*Bishofia javanica*) tree. The deep red color is rarely prone to fading, even after decades, and it is considered the basic color of barkcloth, black and white being the other two (Potauaine and Māhina N.d.). When the women—usually from the same village—produce *koloa*, they come together as cooperative women groups with their prepared *feta'aki*.

On the day of *koka'anga*, women gather their sheets of beaten bark, attach their pattern tablets to the *papa*, and sit together in facing pairs at the *papa* to assemble the two-layer barkcloth (see figure 1.2). In *ngatu* making, the lower layer is laid down with beaten bark sheets parallel to the length of the *papa*, and upper-layer sheets are pasted onto these, oriented perpendicular to the lower layer. Strip by strip, the women add the beaten bark, pasting the sheets together with glue made from half-boiled arrowroot or cassava root, or with sticky paste of boiled flour and water—whichever the women find more affordable at the time. Each time a new layer of beaten bark is laid down on the *papa*, the top of the textile is rubbed with a rag dipped in *koka* dye such that the raised pattern on the *kupesi* shows through on the surface. It is at this stage that the raw material is transformed into *koloa*, as the cloth gets its *mata*, face or surface patterning based on the (named) *kupesi* designs (Addo 2007).

Plain white borders of about twelve inches wide are left at the two sides and at the starting and finished end of the barkcloth. If the cloth being constructed is more than ten hand-measured "native yards" (called *langanga* and measuring between fourteen and eighteen inches), the borders along the length of the cloth are numbered; if the cloth is ten native yards long, the borders are decorated with specific designs, but not numbered (Tamahori 1963). As they perform *koka'anga*, the women on the "receiving" side of the *papa* worktable roll up the finished end of the cloth, resting it on their laps. When it is fully assembled, they take the long, damp textile roll to an open space like a grassy yard or an empty church hall where it can be unfurled completely and left to dry undisturbed.

Once dry, the cloth is ready for the last stage, which is called *tohi*. *Tohi*, hand painting and highlighting the designs that have been rubbed on during *koka'anga*, can take place immediately or many months after *koka'anga*. The woman who owns the cloth will usually do *tohi* on her own, or will work at it with other women and girls from her family. Using the brush-like ends of keys of the pandanus fruit, they retrace the outlines of the design that emerged during *koka* (see figure 1.3). They also add *teuteu*, smaller decorative designs to the spaces between the main designs and to the *tapa*, or uncolored edge of the barkcloth. These designs are embellishments to the main, named designs in the central area of the cloth—indeed, *teuteu* means "decoration"—but they function as extremely important aspect of a finished and visually balanced *ngatu*. A visually balanced *ngatu* is one that that has been decorated with (usually named) *kupesi* and the frequently-occurring surface background color

Figure 1.3. *Koka'anga:* assembling a *ngatu ngatu* in Veitongo village, Tonga.

of *koka,* further highlighted with darker, almost black lines rendered during *tohi* that highlight the *kupesi,* and whose borders are embellished with *teuteu* (Kaeppler 1993a). Women make the black dye, called *tongo,* by gathering the soot from burning candlenuts under a lid or pot, which they then mix with water and juice of mangrove tree roots. They sometimes add candlenut soot to *koka* to produce a rich brown-to-black dye that is shiny and water resistant (Ferdon 1988:121).

It would be almost impossible for a woman—or even for two or three women—to assemble a barkcloth alone, as the sheets of beaten bark become heavy and unwieldy as more pieces are added to increase the size of the cloth and as more dye is added for staining. During barkcloth-making season, which is typically during the dry and warm months of the year, women may meet once a week to do *koka'anga.* Tasks delegated to children at this time might include bringing work materials and meals for the women and carrying messages back and forth between the workspace and women's homes. As in many parts of the Pacific region, cooperative labor—the key to *koka'anga*—is the valued action that women perform in rendering raw materials into barkcloth (Addo 2007; Jolly 2003). Women take great pride in doing *koka'anga* work, and others respect their time and need to be in another part of the village on

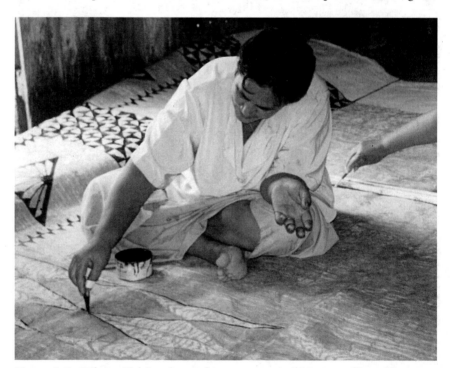

Figure 1.4. Palema Tu'alau does *tohi* on a *ngatu* in Veitongo village, Tonga.

such workdays. When working together, women transform the workspace into a site infused with *'ofa* (love, compassion, sacrifice), and the work strengthens their social bonds with one another, as well as to those to whom they intend to gift the barkcloth. That a barkcloth can evoke *'ofa* in those who encounter it is, in large part, what makes it beautiful (*faka'ofa'ofa*). *Koka'anga* is thus an appropriate context in which to express one of the highest values of Tongan society, *'ofa*.

Koloa Making in Diaspora

Just as women in Tongan villages realize cultural values through their *koloa*-making practices, the *koka'anga* also becomes a site for realizing cultural values in Tongan diaspora. Since the mid-1990s, diasporic Tongan women have formed cooperative groups for the purpose of producing forms of barkcloth with new materials (Drake 2002). In diasporic groups, women assemble the cloth when seated at a *papa* worktable, although there are often several other women who are present, but who are not seated at the *papa*. These are usually elderly women who desire to be included in this, the most esteemed stage of *ngatu pepa* production. These older women often sing Tongan songs to provide a rhythm for the work, join in the prayer at the beginning and end of a day-long work session, or help with the mixing of dyes and the passing around of materials for the cloth making.

Since rank and respect structure aspects of the *koka'anga* in diaspora, the older women provide moral support and legitimacy to the younger women's work of producing objects of value when they join in the process. The older women sit behind, yet symbolically above, the younger women who physically perform the work of *koka'anga*, and they often lead the others in beginning the work session with a prayer. The younger women receive, as "gifts," the older women's guidance and reciprocate with their own obedience and with food that they may have prepared ahead of time. In the midst of this exchange, the *koka'anga* becomes a space of *'ofa*, love, and of *tauhi vā* (caring for the space between people), which Tēvita Ka'ili (2008) has glossed as the creation of beauty and harmony in sociospatial relationships. In Auckland-based women's groups, middle-aged and "younger" elderly women fulfill their traditional roles of continuing to make the textiles by relying on the expertise of elderly women.[9] Thus, even when located far from the villages of Tonga and the plantations that yield the paper mulberry and other raw materials, women create both relationships and objects that bring *faka'ofa'ofa*, beauty, to the *vā*, the physical and social space between themselves. They also honor the mandate of Queen Sālote: that women encourage one another in textile-making skills that enhance their abilities to uphold Tongan values.

As in other Pacific textile traditions (see Ewins 2009 on Vatulele barkcloth; and Barker 2007 and Hermkens 2005 on Maisin barkcloth, among others), producing both cloth *and* the means to render that cloth aesthetically evocative of history and tradition are key aspects of how women continue to make objects that their communities consider authentic and valuable. *Koloa*, as an integral part of the Tongan aesthetic system, has also continued to support other aspects of the global Tongan social order (Kaeppler 1995:103; Young Leslie 2004). Also *kupesi* designs have been anything but static over time. Kaeppler (1995; 1999a) and 'I Futa Helu (1991) discuss some of the stylistic movements and innovations in barkcloth *kupesi* designs as reflective of notable historical moments in Tongan culture. Most *kupesi* are inspired by chiefly people whose achievements have "decorated" Tongan history. When used in diasporic *koka'anga*, these *kupesi* tablets allow the Tongan women to produce the same dark, red-brown lines that they were accustomed to seeing on the surface of their *ngatu* when using pandanus leaf and coconut fiber *kupesi* tablets in Tonga. Making *kupesi* tablets, performing *koka'anga*, and working together in groups are all processes at the core of the aesthetic standards for barkcloth. Importantly, these standards are met not only in Tonga but also in diaspora.

Making *Ngatu Pepa*

The story of *ngatu pepa* shows that Tongan tradition has been innovated not only by women in Tonga, but also by Tongan women in diaspora, and that cultural innovations flow in both directions. In the late 1980s, women in one particular village tell me, Tongan women in diaspora invented *ngatu pepa*. Today, women in Tonga also make this type of *koloa*, which employs no beaten bark at all—the traditionally crucial beating stage is entirely left out. One might ask: Given that women traditionally hammer *mana*, intention, and emotion into their barkcloth during the beating stage, what are the implications of diasporic women's conscious removal of the work that is customarily done to prepare bark for assembling a *ngatu*? How has this removal been accepted both in diaspora and in Tonga itself?

I argue that diasporic women actually use their relatively greater access to cash wealth and new materials to bolster the durability and value of *koloa* as a now global Tongan exchange valuable. Women must first source money to purchase vylene and dyes, make *kupesi* tablets, and find an accessible workspace. There is often some uncertainty, too, about whether a group of women will actually get the chance to assemble for *koka'anga*, barkcloth assembly. The means through which this goal is achieved, including the use of money and the work of preparation are part of what gives the work and its product value. In the months leading up to a projected date for *koka'anga*, women in the same cooperative work groups will often phone one another when they happen upon vylene or dyes for textile making on sale at one or another store in Auckland. Once they have obtained this raw material, some women in the group may stitch parts of the bottom layer together on a sewing machine. When *koka'anga* day arrives, they add the top layer piece by piece, orienting these pieces perpendicular to the pieces comprising the bottom layer, and pasting their surfaces to the bottom layer to create *ngatu pepa*. This is the same process used during *koka'anga* to produce what Tongan women in New Zealand call *ngatu ngatu,* or all-bark barkcloth.

Ngatu pepa is only one physical manifestation of changes in the materiality and process of making barkcloth (Addo 2007). In the 1980s, a male American Peace Corps volunteer to Tonga invented a simple machine designed to make easier Tongan women's tasks of *tutu*—the often arduous initial task of beating raw *hiapo* bark into thin, softened sheets (Teilhet-Fisk 1991). Called a *misini tutu* (machine for doing *tutu*) by the women, his design comprises two grooved rollers mounted horizontally on a wooden sawhorse. By inserting a water-soaked, unbeaten *hiapo* strip between the rollers and turning a crank on the side of the manually operated device while guiding the *hiapo* through it, one can begin breaking up the tough longitudinal fibers of the *hiapo* strips (ibid.; see figure 1.4).

Figure 1.5. Two young men use a "*tapa*-beating machine." Pieces of paper mulberry bark, thus processed, hang above them, to the right, Nuku'alofa.

When a Tongan family in Nuku'alofa demonstrated the use of the *misini tutu* for me, they ran the raw *hiapo* strips, one by one, through the device only twice; they explained that three times or more would cause the fibers to shred. Perhaps most interestingly, when I first saw a *misini tutu* being used in Tonga, it was being operated by a young man. Amazed that a man would be involved in *ngatu* making, I asked the elderly aunt of this young man what his involvement in her work meant for the associations of *ngatu* making as a women's art in Tonga. She responded that it was acceptable for him to do this since he was helping her, an older woman in his family, as was his duty. She also added that it was not as if he was sitting with her doing the *koka'anga* (assembling *ngatu*).[10] To this Tongan woman, and to others I have met, the importance of accomplishing work related to textile production—with varied materials—seems to be more important than expressly delineating textile work along gender lines in all situations.

Rather than being "caused" by the diasporic shift, the invention of *ngatu pepa* actually links women's practices in the homeland to those of women in Tongan diaspora. Besides *ngatu pepa* and *ngatu kāliko* (barkcloth made from a cotton cloth, or calico base, rather than with bark), Tongan women have tried to make a textile that could occasionally stand in for barkcloth out of other combinations of materials. In the 1990s—around the same time that women began to produce *ngatu pepa* in the Tongan diaspora—Cathy Small documented a variety of barkcloth that women in villages in Tonga made with a top layer of beaten bark (or *feta'aki*) and a lower layer of vylene (Small 1997). According to Small's informants, vylene had a similar weight and held dye just as well as beaten bark, but the greatest advantage was that women could produce twice as much barkcloth in the same amount of time and were thus able to begin meeting the demands of their own ritual needs at home as well as those of women in the diaspora. Some people began to refer to this textile as *ngatu hāfekasi,* which translates to "half-caste *ngatu*" because, like people known by the informal ethnic term *hāfekasi,* one "side" of the textile originated from Tonga and the other originated from abroad. The influence of women's experimentation thus circulates through the Tongan diaspora, and includes the Tongan homeland. Not only do women on the home islands invigorate the idea of what objects may count as *koloa,* but their innovations are linked to their ties to women in their diasporic circuit. So too women living in diaspora share with them the use of vylene as a new, accessible, and very useful material base for making some kids of *koloa.*

There are limits, of course, to how far invention and the use of new materials holds the value of tradition. Citing the inauthenticity of barkcloth made without an entirely bark base, chiefly Tongans would—for the next decade or so—continue to use only *ngatu ngatu* and other traditional forms of barkcloth to fulfill their own ceremonial gift obligations. They did, however, find *ngatu hāfekasi* useful for decorative purposes, such as for covering walls or as "red carpets," for lining the aisles of churches, and for covering the road for processions to chiefly burial sites (Veys 2009). These were occasions when only the textile's upper layer would be shown. When I first began my fieldwork in Tonga in 2000, several chiefly women, and some commoner women, told me that they did not think *ngatu hāfekasi* was "real *ngatu*." I even witnessed the chiefly woman stripping the vylene backing from the beaten bark top layer, saying that her intention was to replace it with a lower layer of bark.

But the loss of value incurred by the use of new materials is by no means uniform or unchanging. I also saw *ngatu hāfekasi* used as a "red carpet" at the wedding of the queen of Tonga's nephew in 2001 around the same time. Furthermore, despite its negative valuation by some, *ngatu hāfekasi* was quickly accepted by commoners for their ceremonial exchanges, and it is notable that these turn-of-the-21st-century innovations have been adopted with increasing enthusiasm by commoners in both the diaspora and the homeland. By about 2005, I was seeing primarily *ngatu hāfekasi* at events in Tonga and in New Zealand. In the years approaching 2010, I witnessed as much *ngatu pepa* as *ngatu hāfekasi* being presented at ritual events I attended, even though *ngatu ngatu* was still the primary form of barkcloth being exchanged at these ceremonies.

Thus, *ngatu pepa* has developed an important role in the Tongan textile wealth system. As *cloth,* it continues to be considered key in adorning physical spaces to render them able to contain the *mana* of chiefly celebrants at particular rituals, preventing the potent and harmful effects of their *mana* on commoners.[11] Moreover, I learned during a 2007 visit to Tonga that women on Tongatapu and on other islands had begun to make more and more *ngatu pepa* using vylene for both the upper and lower layers of the textile. This made paper mulberry bark available for making *ngatu ngatu,* and increased barkcloth production and augmentation. On former visits—between 2000 and 2003—I had never seen more than one piece for sale at any given time at Tongan marketplaces, but, in 2007, I was easily able to purchase several pieces of *ngatu pepa* from the marketplace in Nuku'alofa. The greater presence of this cloth in gift and commercial contexts suggests that there was a growth in demand for this textile since I began my fieldwork in 2000.

This observation is further supported by the fact that, as noted earlier, Tongan women make more of all types of *koloa* today than they ever have in their history (Kaeppler 1999b). The reason for this unprecedented level of production is a rising demand for the cloth throughout the ethnoscape. This is tied to the fact that commoner women draw from virtually all suitable material resources in their midst at a given time. Women in Tongan villages who now prefer to make *ngatu pepa* sometimes return to making *ngatu ngatu* when they are short of the cash needed to buy vylene. They might also make *ngatu hāfekasi* for similar reasons. While they are concerned to maintain a particular "look" and texture to the textiles, they are not constrained by a strict set of rules about how a traditional *koloa* should be materially composed or technically assembled. They create value by applying their womanly *mana* and their labor while experimenting with new materials, techniques augmented by use of simple machines, and new "*kupesi*" designs.

Standing Alongside, but Not Standing In For: Pragmatic Creativity

But the Tongan women whose arts I studied are not simply bringing innovations to their own sense of tradition. Instead, *ngatu pepa* results from their culturally sanctioned practice of drawing inspiration and material input from their immediate environment in what Heather Young Leslie and I have called "pragmatic creativity" (2007). We coined this phrase to describe a phenomenon we have observed to be widespread among Pacific people in their visual expressive culture: "*Pragmatic creativity*' is our term for a sense of willingness, an opportunistic investigation and awareness of the local environment, a perpetual openness to inspiration by the local, as it is applied in the production of artistic material. *Pragmatic creativity is a way of seeing, being in, and fashioning the world that is alert, flexible, pliable, open to modification, adaptation, re-adaptation*" (ibid.:12, emphasis in original). We have related the notion of pragmatic creativity to the contentious notion of "hybrid" (Young Leslie and Addo 2007). Yet, we eschewed the idea that things labeled "hybrid" should be considered debased, lesser, and inauthentic relative to the sometimes so-called "pure" forms that melded to produce them. Our argument, echoed here, is that material hybridity does not confer cultural impurity, yet often facilitates cultural continuity and creates forms that suffice for or go beyond the needs of local contexts.

My aim in this book is to use textiles as a lens to focus on people, and specifically on people engaged in nation building who happen also to be Tongans living in diaspora. I go further in thinking about these melded forms to recognize—to laud—a widespread Pacific "cultural tendency to[ward] indigenization," which I see as essential to the creation and locally-legitimized deployment of forms that incorporate ingredients from non-Pacific realms. Textiles are malleable, adaptable, semiotically open, durable, and portable, so they have the capacity to be imbued with new meanings as people deploy and redeploy them in new cultural settings and familiar cultural contexts (ibid.). That textiles like *ngatu pepa* are repeatedly deployed as gifts speaks to their value and, indeed, their value is rooted in their consummate circulation. Young Leslie and I further remark that "capitalizing on this capacity, people render textiles into socially enduring objects. Textiles endure because, and so that, their *people* endure … [and] it is precisely because Pacific textiles are re-newable—in their materiality, symbolism, and contexts—that they are durable in their sociality" (ibid.:15, emphasis added). Thus, the people who make, use, exchange, and admire *koloa faka-Tonga* such as *ngatu pepa* can continually imbue these textiles with value.

Pragmatically creative people are not overwrought with concern to con-tinue using "original" raw materials, especially if these materials are scarce. Expressive forms like *koloa* (textiles), *hiva* (song), *faiva* (group performances), and *tau'olunga* (dances), among many others, are not closed to introductions of new takes on the so-called traditional. Tongan women who make *ngatu pepa* are arguably continuing in this "tradition" of pragmatic creativity and adding these textiles to their category of treasured objects. Pragmatic creativ-ity—which leads to forms that Young Leslie and I categorize as "authentic in-novations" (ibid.)—is actually a tendency that is diffused throughout Tongan society, regardless of geographic location. It is through this particular mode of indigenizing new forms that the Tongan diaspora (and associated processes of globalization) has influenced the homeland. Having less access to fresh, whole pigs and long yams, men in the diaspora—and increasingly in the homeland, as well—often gift bags of frozen yams and frozen meat, for example. I wit-nessed a presentation of bottled soda and iced cakes to one of the monarch's granddaughters when she visited Auckland in early 2001. Commoner women who came to visit the young princess had removed small plastic bottles of soda from their original carton, laid them on large plastic trays with some cakes, and wrapped the tray and its contents in clear plastic cling film. The plastic film drew people's attention with its loud crackling and it also caught the light, adding what Fanny Wonu Veys considers to be a much-appreciated element of shininess to the presentation (2009).

These practices, which are themselves influenced by the global economic system, have taken root in the homeland as well and have done so in a de-cidedly Tongan way. Commoners who present tinned corned beef and snack chips always process onto the ceremonial grounds, carrying the offerings in their hands, and place the gifts before recipients who are as likely to be nobles and royalty (Kaeppler 1995; Veys 2009) as they are to be members of other commoner families.[12]

The pragmatic creativity that Tongans apply wherever they may live is es-sential to their continued tendency to embrace and develop new cultural forms that they mark as distinctly Tongan. This approach is related to their desire to see the Tongan cultural territory expand through transnational migration, and their duty to continue providing for relatives and engaging in exchanges that assure such material, economic, and spiritual provision. Diasporic Tongans re-create appropriate social conditions of production, employ new materials, traditional techniques, and produce culturally effective—that is, giftable—new cultural forms. They introduce things that, in formal Tongan displays, such as at Royal Agricultural Shows, would be called a "new idea" and that can at the same time quickly become everyday culture in Tonga. It is important to note that when these new material forms are included in categories of wealth, they rarely replace them outright and instead augment what already exists. *Ngatu pepa* actually add value to a woman's stocks or presentations of other *koloa*. They stand alongside other *koloa*, as an amplification to this system of ranked, female wealth objects.

Murray Chapman (1978; 1991), among many other academics, has emphasized the pitfall of applying binary oppositions between "home and away, or before-after progression from village life to cosmopolitan modernity" (cited in Clifford 2001:470). In this "standing alongside," other valuables cannot *substitute* for *koloa* permanently or entirely, yet at the same time, these other valuables are not "lesser." Even though *ngatu pepa* is one of many other forms of barkcloth that are given less than complimentary names—"half-caste" barkcloth (*ngatu hāfekasi*), and "fake" barkcloth (*ngatu loi*), for example (Veys 2009)—we should not read these labels as indicative of Tongan people themselves attaching strict notions of pure and impure to forms based on where the forms were invented, their materiality, who uses them, or the contexts in which people assign them value, as gift versus commodity, for example. Instead, by noting how and where Tongan women continue to create and gift valuables that embody what they may call "new ideas," we can appreciate a broad range of contexts wherein they augment the system of "supreme material valuables" (Arno 2005) constituted by *koloa*.

In living modern lives, Tongans' evince pragmatic creativity. One manifestation of this creativity is that they not only include non-Tongan cultural forms in existing categories of Tongan culture, but they often use them to amplify the value of "original" things in the relevant categories. The inclusion of imported and Western foods alongside traditional Tongan feast foods is an example—canned corn beef, sweet and sour chicken, and oven-baked cakes are now standards at both chiefly and commoner ceremonial feasts, but they have not *replaced* traditional valuables. Likewise, the production of plaited fine mats *as koloa* does not yet seem to have been adversely affected by the access to other forms of mats and wearable textiles that increased imports to Tonga have made available to people in Tongan villages. This inclusion without erasure is a testament to the resilience of *koloa* as a category of giftable valuables, their utilitarian value as clothing and floor covering notwithstanding.

On my most recent visit to Tonga, in December 2007, I noticed several small stores run by Chinese merchants in Nuku'alofa displaying stacks of folded "mats" about the same size as small *ta'ovala*—generally between five feet by two feet and seven feet by three feet. Some of these waist-mats were made from thin, colored plastic tubing, of about an eighth of an inch in diameter, which had been woven to create gingham (or checkered) type patterns. Others were made from treated palm fiber or from beige-to-tan colored synthetic fibers. Both types of mats were woven with the wefts parallel to the edges, in contrast to Tongan fine mats that are plaited with the wefts running at right angles to one another and diagonal to the borders of the mat itself. Tongans I knew told me that mats I saw were being sold as substitutes for *ta'ovala* and, indeed, I saw several people dressed in these walking around town wearing these "new," imported *ta'ovala* that were not so different in coloring from the diagonally plaited *ta'ovala* made from colored curling ribbon that many Tongans have long favored. Reactions from other Tongans from whom I solicited an opinion about this practice ranged from strong objection to bemusement to implicit sanction by way of explanation: these new "Chinese mats" cost only fifteen to thirty *pa'anga* (Tongan national currency, abbreviated "TOP"), in contrast to *ta'ovala* made of traditional materials that could run into the hundreds of *pa'anga*.

What is key is that the crucial practice of wearing *ta'ovala* remains intact. By shifting the materiality of these key material culture elements, Tongan women enable the continuation, rather than curtailment of traditional practices, especially insofar as they must negotiate economic constraints. That Tongans would buy and wear these obviously different textile constructions does suggest that changes in taste for *ta'ovala* are also taking place, spurred on, perhaps, by increased access to cheaper and less labor-intensive substitutes. Cluny Macpherson and La'avasa Macpherson (2010:149–151) have noted a similar trend of what they call "uptake" in Samoa, where plaited pandanus floor mats have been replaced by store-bought, reversible, brightly colored Chinese floor mats. Many Tongans, likewise, are replacing *fala*—layered pandanus floor mats, often made with colored yarn fringing—for use in their homes and church halls. However, they do not use these replacements in gift exchange.

Tongan women's continued inclusion of *fala* as gifts—even as they willingly replace plaited *koloa* as floor mats in homes and as *ta'ovala* on dressed bodies—is a testament to the place of plaited *koloa* as a cultural valuable and the role of gift exchange as communicator of material and symbolic connections to *fonua* at the most crucial, ritual times in a community. The careful discrimination between non-traditional materials in gift exchange further indexes the negotiations at play in pragmatic creativity, particularly in terms of deciding when economic factors are and are not legitimate reasons for replacement. In addition to the mats that replace *ta'ovala*, there are other "hybrid" cloth forms that are now standard in Tongan ceremonial exchange; these include machine-made quilts, knitted or crocheted blankets, and sequin-decorated baskets. These particular forms all qualify as *koloa si'i*, "little *koloa*." This is a lower-ranking, but now indispensable subcategory of fiber-based objects that women make or buy and whose gifting and reciprocation of these objects they entirely control (Herda 1999). Another cloth of mixed origin is *ngatu pepa,* barkcloth made from the synthetic fabric vylene. Like *koloa si'i* (see table 1), *ngatu pepa* is one of several different types of textiles that include non-Tongan—that is, Western—material elements and that have been absorbed into the category of *koloa* in the past few decades.

As I discuss elsewhere, *ngatu pepa* plays a role as a valuable in specifically Tongan contexts of gift and commodity exchange. Tongan women have introduced *ngatu* into the very special category of *koloa,* and have authenticated it by offering it as gifts in ceremonial exchange (Addo 2007). It is also available in venues where women who do not make *koloa* source their textile valuables, including pawnshops run by Tongans in both Tonga and the diaspora (Addo and Besnier 2008). *Ngatu pepa* is increasingly present in all of these contexts, for it *is koloa*. Like Tongan people, the value of *ngatu pepa* originates in its semantic connections to the Tongan *fonua,* its reliance on the process of *koka'anga,* and its capacity to augment the networks and connections that bolster individuals' collective identity as members of the Tongan "nation."

The Gift: Value Potential of *Ngatu* and *Ngatu Pepa*

Community lore among women in Auckland has it that the women who first introduced *ngatu pepa* into New Zealand gift exchange were persistent in their offering of *ngatu pepa* in *'efinanga. 'Efinanga* are bundles of *koloa* comprising a *fala* (fine mat) and at least one piece of barkcloth that are folded together in ways that are appropriate for gift giving. Over the course of life events in the community, other commoner women continued to gift the *ngatu pepa* on to others, and received some pieces as counter gifts. While there were some women who professed to far prefer *ngatu ngatu* to *ngatu pepa,* they also often admit to having been emotionally moved—or to have experienced *loto mafana,* "warmth of heart"—when they thought about the hard and traditional work that other women had done in cooperating at *koka'anga* to produce *ngatu pepa.* Some of these same women were subsequently willing to keep *ngatu pepa* moving through gift networks and were also able to help legitimate *ngatu pepa* by converting it into a gift, rather than regarding it as a mere curiosity or a materially inauthentic look-a-like. These women defied the "fact" that *ngatu pepa* deviated in form from so-called traditional barkcloth. Indeed, they *made the cloth traditional* by making it serve the same purpose as other *koloa*: they have gifted it to others and thereby lifted up the nation of Tonga symbolically.

Ongoing or enhanced positive social relations are of great value to people in virtually all societies. The material forms that bring about the potential for more gifts to eventuate from such relationships are thus considered powerful and desirable valuables (Mauss 1990 [1925]; Rupp 2003; Sykes 2005). A gift creates rights in obligation over the recipient, obligation that can form the basis of the ensuing social relationship. When the giver of the original gift receives a reciprocal gift, she ideally feels compensated for the loss of the original object and also feels she has a stronger, more intimate relationship with the other party. Moreover, reciprocated valuables accompany the recognition of a gifter's selfhood and "completes" him or her (MacKenzie 1991; Munn 1992; Strathern 1990).Thus, what makes Tongan women embrace a new form of *koloa* is that it has the capacity to be gifted and can be used as a tool in enhancing social relationships, and not its specific materiality or patterning. Women's love (*'ofa*) and labor embodied in an object is the root of its value, which is only realizable through the act of its being gifted. Indeed, many varieties of barkcloth and fine mats are potential commodity objects, yet their main intended purpose is as gifts for, as gifts, they generate more desirable forms of value. As long as an object remains physically intact, its quality of "giftablity"—what I call its value potential—abides as well. Selling an object does not result in as full a realization of its value potential because *koloa* retains its ultimate identity as gift in virtually all Tongan communities today.

Precisely because barkcloth and barkcloth-inspired cloth objects gain greater value through gift exchange, they may be purchased—and so also sold—for the very purpose of gifting. Making *koloa* for commercial sale is completely acceptable in Tonga and, in more rural settings—the outer islands, for example—selling *koloa* was the main source of cash earnings until remittances from relatives abroad surpassed this sometime in the late twentieth century. Few women today make all of the *koloa* that they gift themselves, and those with the financial means to buy *koloa* often stock up on the textiles, toward the occurrence of unanticipated ceremonial occasions.

The care women put into keeping *koloa* is also a factor in an object's value, and Tongan women periodically spread their *ngatu* and fine mats out in the sun to kill any mites that have crawled in, sometimes refolding them with mothballs in between the folds. If *koloa* have been well cared for and well prepared before they are gifted, it shows that the woman who arranged them for gifting truly has *'ofa*, love, for the recipients. Age and physical condition of a cloth contribute to the gift potential of a *koloa*, as old pieces are particularly highly regarded and, as some have said especially about old, named fine mats, "priceless" (Herda 1999; Kaeppler 1999a and b). Women also appreciate *koloa* with straight edges and decorative lines. With specific regard to barkcloth, straight lines, neat over-painting, and deep colors are valued, and I have heard women refer to *ngatu* with crooked painted lines and messy over-painting as *palakū* (aesthetically and morally displeasing, "ugly")—and so less valuable in gift exchange.

Smoothness and luminescence are other valuable qualities in Tongan culture (Veys 2009; see also Munn 1992). Women have specific ways of preparing *koloa* that have been stored or recently acquired for gifting at a specific event, and for the person in whose honor the gift will be presented. Before presentation, women unfurl and flatten fine mats that might have become creased when stored under mattresses or sleeping mats to ensure their smoothness. Just as *kava* bowls and headrests are polished with coconut oil after being sanded to an impeccable smoothness, so too a barkcloth is often rubbed with coconut oil before it is presented as a gift to give it the desirable shininess.

When viewing textile *koloa,* Tongan women consider these subtle, yet meaningful variations in the aesthetics as indicative of the cloth's value potential and of their own gift-giving potential: how the *koloa* they have in stock, as well as the number of gift-giving events they can participate in, potentially create moments for them to move these valuable things between people. By gifting *koloa,* women are empowered to create obligations and repay debts publicly, resulting in their greater esteem among others in the society. Thus, Tongan societies realize value—or experience that which is considered desirable (Kluckhohn 1951)—through collective and ongoing processes of creation, appreciation, and reciprocation of material and social valuables.

Traditionally, the aesthetic composition of *koloa* has been of importance primarily among elite Tongans who choose high-ranking and named patterns for gifts they present to one another (Kaeppler 2005, 1999a, 1995; Tamahori 1963). Among commoners, chiefly patterns on barkcloth are also key components of the beauty of a *koloa* that women make or gift, but the specific chiefly pattern is less important than the neatness, color, and smoothness of the "face" of the *ngatu.* For commoners, *ngatu* are beautiful for the qualities described above, and not because of the specific origin or identity of the painted designs. Yet, identifiable *kupesi* (patterns) perform the crucial task of transforming these rubbed and stained textiles into objects that Tongans of both ranks can read culturally. Another way of saying this is: commoner Tongans generally understand the language of *ngatu* designs, but are less rehearsed than elite women traditionally were in the lexicon. *Kupesi* make *ngatu* canvases for culturally readable motifs that form an allegory of key events and chiefly people in Tonga history (Kaeppler 1995). *Ngatu* are readable if they move viewers to experience nostalgia for the people and events indexed by the *kupesi;* the *kupesi* thus make the textiles into "signs of history" (Parmentier 1987).

The way in which women apply labor in the production of the *koloa* is also crucial to the value potential of the cloth produced. *Ngatu pepa* is considered valuable because women produce it from a cooperative process that they continue to refer to as "*koka'anga.*" Most groups of women I observed making *ngatu pepa* during my fieldwork were at pains to do so with equipment and techniques that were identical to those used to make *ngatu ngatu* in the homeland. They had to source materials such as wood for making worktables, and then get men in their kin groups to construct them, and they had to collect materials for making pattern tablets, *kupesi,* some of which involved waiting for relatives to send them from Tonga. These indispensible technological aspects included their emphasis on using wooden *papa,* handmade *kupesi* tablets, and prayer and reciprocity in turning the workspace into a site where womanly duty would be performed (Addo 2007). They also had to save enough money to buy all the vylene and dyes they needed for making *ngatu pepa.* Generally speaking, this entails further effort, since saving money toward a project that looms somewhere in the future is often a challenge in Tongan communities, where individuals or members of their *kāinga* (kin network) always need money for daily living costs or ceremonial obligations.

Unlike fine mats, or plaited *koloa,* which women generally do not divide up, barkcloth can be cut into smaller pieces. The size of a *koloa* influences its exchange value, which is also further conditioned by its ability to retain, or augment its potential as a gift once it has been divided or cut.[13] Some *koloa* are made in very large pieces: one historical *ngatu* was reputedly the size of a rugby field (Herda 1999). Among *tuʻa* women, the largest barkcloth is a *ngatu launima,* which is fifty *langanga,* or hand-measured native sections, long. A *ngatu launima* can be cut into pieces as small as four sections for gifting.[14] A full *launima* embodies and visually marks the immense amount of *ʻofa* and cooperative labor and time that women put into *ngatu* making. While it encodes this message in a way that no single smaller piece that has been cut from a *launima* could, cutting it into pieces yields potential economic value. Tensions between public gifting of *koloa,* which brings social or cultural value, and selling *koloa,* which brings economic value, keep women highly aware of trade-offs involved in choosing to keep a *launima* intact or being willing to divide it.

Tongan gifts typically move upward: from people who are lower, to people who are higher in rank. *Koloa* and *koloa siʻi* (see table 1) are able to materialize qualities of the recipient (Veys 2009), specifically that the recipient holds a higher rank than the giver and that a relationship with recipient is highly desired. In a kin group, a woman will normally present gifts of the largest and most beautiful textiles to the *mehekitanga*—her child's father's eldest sister, who is the highest-ranked person in relation to her child or children. *Koloa* are not only prestige goods (Douaire-Marsaudon 1998)—accruing social value for those who present and receive them—but they also bind people together in relationships of both prestige and obligation.

While Tongan valuables have become highly-desired commodities among Tongans and non-Tongans, their economic value has not *replaced* their social value. If a woman needs to make money, and has no other commodity on hand, she may cut a fifty-section *ngatu launima* into smaller pieces and sell them separately. She may cut the *launima* into ten *folaʻosi* (five-section pieces; usually sold for around TOP$100 each in Nukuʻalofa in 2000), realizing

TOP$1000 in total, or she may cut thirteen *konga fā* (four-section pieces; sold at a price of about TOP$80 each in Nukuʻalofa in 2000) for a total of TOP$1040. If she sells all her cut pieces rather than an intact *launima* (valued at between TOP$800 and TOP$1000 in 2000), she is likely to earn slightly more money, and to do so more quickly.[15] Nevertheless, because of their ceremonial importance, a woman typically prefers to keep any *launima* she already has in her stocks intact for her most important ritual obligations, such as the funeral of a close relative or the wedding of one of her children. At such occasions she will present them as a gift to the highest-ranking relative in attendance. Fine mats are almost never cut because they would fray and would be difficult to repair. To retain their high value as potential gifts—value that affects their future giver's and recipient's ability to rise in status—so they must remain intact. Social value thus trumps economic value when one considers textiles of high rank in the Tongan cloth wealth complex or those destined for highly-ranked recipients.

Finally, memory also plays a crucial role in creating value in objects, as exemplified in the way *koloa* encodes women's nostalgia for the homeland, for the social relations they enjoyed as they matured in Tonga, for their own mothers and aunts who made *koloa* while these women were growing up, and for their beloved Queen Sālote. These are memories of the past, but *koloa* are also embedded with the power to materialize women's focus on the future of the kingdom, their communities, and their families. Alisha Renne theorizes the place of loom-woven Nigerian Bunu cloth, which was formerly made by men and continues to be encoded in Bunu memory, even though it was largely replaced by cotton cloth with increasing missionization. As Renne notes, this memory also projects Bunu into the future, as "things may convey a sense of continuity through their association with the past, but may also be the focus of images of the future, underwriting processes of social change" (1998:152). Likewise, *koloa* that exist today encode memories of *koloa* that were present at key events in the past, or that now exist in stories only. *Koloa* made and exchanged today, which are linked through the potency of memory to those ancient cloths, embody women's intentions for engaging in exchange in the future.

For contemporary Tongan women, especially for those who came of age in Tonga and during Queen Sālote's reign and who are usually figures of authority in their *kāinga*, *koloa* are associated with the Langa Fonua ʻa ʻe Fefine Tonga organization and thus with moments of national pride and a monarchical mandate for modernity. Using *koloa* also facilitates women's execution of their kin-based duty to keep gifts in circulation so that as they perform *tauhi vā*, they simultaneously "maintain harmonious socio-spatial relationships" (Kaʻili 2005). To keep *koloa* circulating is to add value to, and derive value from social relationships. Thus, *koloa* making, whether in diaspora or in the homeland, whether from natural or synthetic materials, and especially for gifting purposes, constitutes *langa fonua*.

What *langa fonua*, or now-globalized nation building, and *ngatu pepa* exchange have in common is the fact that they are both highly negotiated processes whereby Tongans expand the nation and the category of *koloa* through pragmatic creativity. Pragmatic creativity is an integral part of the processes whereby Tongans maintain connections with one another, fulfill obligations to perform *langa fonua* as they move about the world, and maintain the status of the gift as a mode of sociality in Tongan communities. Moreover, Tongans negotiate the exchange of valuables in terms of their own notions of power, right, and obligation. As a result, the majority of production and exchange of their traditional valuables remains within Tongans' control—these things have not been appropriated by non-Tongans for commercial gain, nor has the system of exchange and its meaning been erased. Thus, while *koloa* is highly valued among "primitive" art collectors and enthusiasts, as well as tourists, only a very small portion of the "market" for *koloa* relies on such non-Tongan consumption. *Ngatu pepa*—with its vylene base and origins outside of the homeland—has not been of interest to Western collectors of Pacific art, save for museums interested in documenting changes in the textiles' materiality and techniques, but it has gained value as a giftable item in the Tongan system of exchange.[16] Maintaining their power and prerogative over *koloa*, commoner women have brought it into its own as a form of *koloa*, in part exemplified in the fact that Tongans all over the world now exchange it as gift.

Conclusion

This chapter has outlined the production process of the most commonly occurring type of barkcloth, *ngatu*. It also presented the "new" form of barkcloth—one that is made without any beaten bark at all—*ngatu pepa*. The focus on *ngatu pepa* as an invented form of "traditional" *koloa* emphasizes the Tongan diaspora as a site of cultural innovation and authentication. I discussed *koloa* as a specific form of material culture through which *langa fonua* is accomplished. I have situated *ngatu*, the primary form of barkcloth today, and *ngatu pepa*, a hybrid, diasporic form, in the larger category of textile *koloa*, as well as in *koloa*'s meanings and its value. Discussion of this value highlights the role of chiefly Tongans in having historically imbued *koloa* with their *mana*, or power. However, commoner women have used the outward-looking structuring of modern constitutional Tonga as their basis from which to maintain the rights to aesthetically expand the category of objects that historically constituted "*koloa*." They have introduced material and aesthetic innovations from both homeland and diaspora and have used these innovations to create new categories of *koloa* that circulate outside of chiefly realms and outside of the Kingdom of Tonga. The cosmological agency of chiefs is necessarily bound to the Tongan homeland so, for them, the Tongan homeland must be maintained as a primary *fonua*. By contrast, for commoners, the *fonua* Tonga necessarily encompasses the diaspora as well. Material culture plays a crucial role in how commoner Tongans have created their multiterritorial *fonua*. In particular, the production of *ngatu pepa* is a useful lens through which to investigate production and gifting processes whereby Tongan women in diaspora apply the ontological orientation that I refer to as pragmatic creativity to *langa fonua*, globalized Tongan nation building.

Notes

1. Heather Young Leslie's research reveals that this metaphor is further applied to the constitutive fibers of a fine mat. When Tongan mats are plaited, with the fibers placed on the ground, the wefts that lie flat are known as *fakatokoto*; those that stand up, in order to be interlaced with the former, are known as *fokotu'u*. The sexual metaphor is clear: some fibers stand up, others lie down, they interlace, and human kind is created or born. The more pairs of fibers that interlace in this manner the larger and stronger the whole that is born, and the larger and stronger the society that is created (1999:1). Textile making is a symbolically generative process and I have witnessed a few Tongan women joking about the bodily postures they adopt during textile making being somewhat illustrative of women in acts of procreation. When Tongan women plait mats, they sit on the ground, put long, thin strips of treated pandanus on the floor between their open, outstretched legs, and interlace the fibers diagonally, working outward from their bodies. The strips are called "wefts" because there is no loom, and fine mats are constructed by plaiting and not by weaving—as weaving requires a loom or some other stabilizing equipment (ibid.).

2. Women make scented coconut oil by grating the flesh of dried coconuts, placing it on metal sheets in the sun with scented leaves and flowers, and pressing and straining off the oil that oozes in the heat. They also produce baskets from treated pandanus (screw pine) leaves using fiber plaiting techniques, some of which are similar to those used for weaving fine mats. These baskets are used to hold bottles of scented oil during ceremonial presentations, so these forms of women's wealth are not just made using connected techniques, but are also presented together (Veys 2009). In contrast, both men and women make plaited baskets for carrying food, usually from fresh coconut fronds that need only be cut and are not dried or treated. Such baskets, known as *kato niu*, are mundane objects of daily life and are not considered valuables.

3. Speakers of Austronesian languages from New Guinea settled the island groups that became known as Fiji, Tonga, and Samoa; from these islands the eastern island groups of the Society Islands were settled, and their inhabitants later settled Hawai'i. Descendants of these original settlers of Hawai'i later settled the islands of New Zealand (Denoon et al. 1997).

4. Other forms of *ngāue fakame'a'a* (material treasures), such as more durable forms of male products like elaborately carved wooden weapons, are no longer deemed neces-

sary for daily use and are therefore not treasured as necessary ceremonial valuables that men must present today (Kaeppler 1999b). Carved wooden objects are more likely to be appreciated as historical objects associated with and enhancing the statuses of specific male *tufunga,* or creators, builders, constructors of artistic or beautiful things (Māhina 2004).

5. For more on divine women rulers and *mana* in the Pacific, see Kaeppler 1991 and Linnekin 1990a.

6. Annette Weiner similarly remarks on the temporal and symbolic durability of women's textile wealth in the Trobriand Islands by noting the durability of cloth as wealth, even as local people have experienced changes in national politics and material value systems and in government. She states: "throughout a history of shifting economic circumstances women's wealth has not suffered a decrease in value" (1980:276).

7. There are two main kinds of *hiapo* grown in Tonga, the *lau ma'opo'opo* and the *lau mahaehae.* The fibers of the inner bark of *lau mahaehae* are "thicker and not apt to be torn easily" and so this variety of *hiapo* is considered better for *ngatu* making (Fanua 1986:3). Such intimate knowledge of paper mulberry types is crucial to women's barkcloth expertise.

8. *Kupesi* tablets can be kept for decades and used many times. When the women have assembled all the *ngatu* that they intend to, using a particular *kupesi,* they remove the tablets and one woman in the group stores them—usually under the mattress of a bed in her house where they will remain flat and relatively undisturbed. In every generation, certain women are known for their *kupesi* making (Mariner, cited in Martin 1971 [1817]; Fanua 1986:23).

9. Among the indigenous people of the Fort Berthold reservation (American Indians belonging to the Hidatsa, Mandan, and Arikara tribes), women's quill-making and quilt-sewing art forms carry "specific ritual obligation and compensation on the part of the learner to her teacher" (Berman 2003:40). Similarly, women who produce *koloa* are beholden to honor and compensate older women who have trained or who continue to train and support them.

10. Widespread discourse about Tongan barkcloth making suggests that the *tutu* and *koka'anga* are solely women's work. I never saw a man doing any work on *ngatu* while I was doing my fieldwork in Tonga, but I did see a Tongan man doing the process of *tohi* (painting final designs) onto a *ngatu pepa* in Auckland in 2001. In the film, *Kuo Hine 'e Hiapo,* several Tongan men are shown helping their wives at work doing the *koka'anga* (Ostraff and Ostraff 2001).

11. For example Veys reports that, during the funeral rites for Tupou IV, the king of Tonga, in September 2001, a *ngatu* pathway was laid out on the road between the Palace grounds where he had lain in state for ten days, and the Royal burial site. According to photographs I have seen and reports from people who were present, the pathway comprised *ngatu hāfekasi,* at least in part. These pieces of barkcloth were used in a customary fashion to create "a protective barrier between the carriers of the casket and the ground, making the road safe to walk on once the funeral was over" (2009:143).

12. People also substitute cash wealth for *koloa* and foods, at times, but rarely do they substitute any other shared drink substance for *kava.* In both homeland and diaspora, *kava* seems to be relatively irreplaceable in ritual practices. Explanations for the apparent singularity of *kava* have presented by Françoise Douaire-Marsaudon (2002) who suggests that, in Tonga, *kava* consumption is a context for presenting other gifts,

that the *kava* ritual is a decidedly male ritual, and that *kava* is a male food (if women drink *kava,* it is usually only once, on their wedding day) and a source of male virility. *Kava* drinking is a ritual whereby "those men who occupied the position of chief took control of the symbolic production of male identity"—a crucial act of bringing (cultural) harmony into the (natural) imbalance implied by women's ability to bear men themselves, and, of course, to bear all children (ibid.:76). Men are, thus, obligated to women for their very lives, but are able to assert a sense of autonomy because only they consume *kava* in everyday realms. *Kava* also provides such a sense of rank complementarity to, as chiefs carry out the *'ilokava* (collective and ceremonial drinking of *kava* among chiefly people) for the benefit of society, using the *kava* root and other *ngāue* that commoner men produce, while their bodies are wrapped in *koloa* that commoner women have made (ibid.). Furthermore, in the myth of primogeniture of *kava,* the *kava* plant symbolizes a gift that the Tu'i Tonga (the highest ranking chief of Tonga) is eternally obligated to repay to commoner people (ibid.:64).

13. There are different attitudes about cutting textiles into pieces in Pacific cultures. Barkcloth, perhaps because it can be cut without fraying and because it can be mended and augmented by sticking additional pieces of the textile base onto the cloth, is considered less immutable once completed. As Rod Ewins explains for Fijian cases, barkcloth—whether in the original form or cut into segments—are all signs of significant social relationships. Their value does not solely lie in their size and materiality, but in people's ability to continue making these associations with one another (2009).

14. A *fuatanga*—a type of barkcloth employing a more complicated process of assembling beaten *feta'aki* sheets and a cloth form that was rare and considered more valuable than *ngatu*—would normally never be divided.

15. Prices for *koloa* have risen steadily in the last decade—almost doubling in Tonga between 2000 and 2009. One reason for this, locals whom I've interviewed believe, is because of demand from overseas relatives who "pay" with high levels of remittances. Another reason is that people in this largely non-cash economy are more desperate for money. Being made from garden products, *koloa,* as a category, is one of the few commodities that Tongans can produce without large outlays of capital. The global economic crisis of the late 2000s caused imported food prices to rise more sharply than usual, economic growth to slow to 1 percent, and inflation to reach above 12 percent (Government of Tonga 2009a). Main sources of cash for Tongan families—remittances from relatives in abroad—were also adversely affected.

16. See website for Museum of New Zealand Te Papa Tongarewa (www.tepapa.govt.nz) for information on *ngatu pepa* and *koloa si'i,* including quilts and baskets decorated with sequins and plastic flowers, collected from members of Tongan communities in New Zealand.

%% 2
Gender, Materiality, and Value
Tongan Women's Cooperatives in New Zealand

In 2001, a photograph and short article about a group of Tongan women appeared in Auckland's *Central Leader,* a regional newspaper. In the accompanying photograph, ten smiling women were seated in front of a large reddish-brown dyed textile with black hand-painted motifs of flower *lei* (garlands) and the royal seal of Tonga. The textile was mounted on the rear inside wall of the public hall that adjoined the Methodist church building where the women worshipped regularly. From its size and patterning, this textile resembled barkcloth from Tonga. The headline to the article read: "Sharing Skills and Good Laugh" (Scaife 2009). The skills were those for making Tongan barkcloth, and the laughs suggested the women's familiarity with each other, as well as their joy at being able to make, for the first time in New Zealand, a treasured form of a traditional textile. This heading came as no surprise to me: Tongan women generally relish the chance to reactivate social bonds that creating and gifting *koloa* affords them.

The women's group featured in the article was called Fauniteni 'oe Mo'ui, "fountain of truth." Using funding obtained from the Department of Labor and administered through the Auckland City council, the women produced twelve pieces of barkcloth, enough for each woman to have one piece to put toward the gifts needed for her cultural obligations. However, none of the cloths they made had any bark content—they were *ngatu kāliko,* made from calico, cotton cloth. These women had lived in New Zealand for over twenty years and would never again make *ngatu* from paper mulberry bark.

In 2002, this group produced *ngatu pepa* (see chapter 1) from vylene purchased with funds received from the Auckland City Council. They produced several ten-foot by ten-foot *ngatu pepa* whose motifs and hues lent them a similar appearance and weight to the highly valued barkcloth. The women of Fauniteni told me that they were not the first to produce *ngatu pepa* in Auckland, nor was Auckland the first place it was made; the first Tongan diasporic women to make *ngatu pepa* did so in the late 1980s, in the Tongan community of Salt Lake City, Utah, which was all abuzz over barkcloth made with no bark. *Ngatu pepa,* some said, were convincingly—some even added "deceptively"—

close to the weight and coloring of *ngatu ngatu,* the traditional and, thus far, predominant form of barkcloth being produced in Tonga.

The Fauniteni 'oe Mo'ui was one of the six groups among whom I conducted ethnographic research in Auckland. This group has continued traditional textile-making processes of assembling, staining, and hand decorating the cloth in cooperative work groups, and they retain traditional designs used by chiefly women in pre-Constitution Tonga as well as commoner women in post-Constitution Tonga up to the present. Groups like Fauniteni function as a tool by which immigrant diasporic women reproduce and sustain their own sense of womanliness and adherence to tradition. All of the groups engaged in textile production, to one degree or another, and four of them had made *ngatu pepa* within recent years, three of them using government funding to buy the necessary materials. The groups also help the New Zealand state with its agenda of being seen as investing in the cultural concerns of its immigrant ethnic minorities. To the members of *langa fonua* groups, the funding is a rare chance both to connect publicly with the state and to garner tools from outside of their own community and coffers in service of *langa fonua.*

As this example begins to suggest, *langa fonua* in diaspora works through gendered material practices whereby women bring together resources from both the homeland and the host country and negotiate a space of agency between the nation-building projects of both Tonga and New Zealand. In New Zealand, the host state has high stakes in being seen as supporting immigrants, so it periodically makes community-based art and development project funding available.[1] Arguably an extension of colonial associations between women's textile work and domesticity, such funding is meant to build on skills that the government of the majority white state of New Zealand understands to be useful for women, particularly as a means of generating income. Yet the women typically turn the otherwise salable objects into gifts. They delight in activities such as making, displaying, and gifting *koloa* that afford them a sense of accomplishment and enjoyment, especially as it furthers their cultural project of *langa fonua.*

This chapter explores how women's groups innovate their textile traditions in New Zealand and translate funding from government, local councils, and arts bodies through the language of the gift. The women desire to be recognized and to thrive *as Tongans* in diaspora. They enact these desires on behalf of their communities when they use their textiles in interactions with the authorities in New Zealand. Playing the informal role of diplomats, these commoner women reach beyond their co-ethnics in the globalized Tongan *fonua* and use the gifting of valuables—a normal practice in diplomatic relations everywhere—to develop positive relations between their communities and the host state.

Women's Groups and the Making of Value in Tongan Culture

Women's groups have had a long history in the Pacific. They were introduced by Christian missionaries in the nineteenth century (Herda 1999; Douglas 2003; Jolly 2003) as a way of extending the hand of colonial power into some of the most intimate aspects of family life (Jolly 2003:134). Both Protestant and Catholic missions relied on Western women in their ranks to convert and re-socialize indigenous Pacific women. The idiom of domesticity—child rearing, textile making, caring for hearth and home—was at the core of these Western women's socialization and civilizing projects, so missionaries' wives and sisters as well as nuns taught indigenous women sewing, embroidery, and cooking and organized them into groups affiliated with their churches (ibid.). To one degree or another, Pacific women embraced such groups, seeing in them a re-flection of their own values of sociality and creativity, and enthusiastically tak-ing up sewing, embroidery, knitting, and crochet techniques that bore some resemblance to the already highly regarded textile traditions in their own cul-tures. They also transformed the groups to suit their own desires and needs, using them to augment pre-Christian forms of sociality (ibid.).

Contemporary Pacific—including Tongan—women's groups bear the traces of these historical negotiations of religion and materiality. For example, the making of *koloa,* a pre-contact tradition, was integrated into late-nineteenth and twentieth-century Tongan modernity as a fundamental part of the bodily discipline and industriousness espoused by Methodist ministries (Addo 2003; Eves 1996). The enduring integration of religiosity and textile making is clearly indicated by the fact that Tongan women's group meetings today almost al-ways begin and end with the group's chair leading the others in a prayer before the textile-making work. Such meetings also often feature a shared meal and rotating credit activity (Small 1997).

But the group aspect of *koloa* making is not simply an add-on to the prac-tice, nor is its significance limited to such colonial tracings. Women from many Pacific societies find it impossible, undesirable, and even nonsensical to make textiles and other culturally valuable objects outside of a group context be-cause their agency emerges from intersubjective relations—women's creation of a sense of themselves through engagement with one another in culturally meaningful, collective processes—rather than from individual actions (Jolly 2003:136). Furthermore, their collective sociality and agency is crucial to the eventual value of the objects that they produce. In this sense, to invoke Karl Marx (1990 [1867]), Tongan women remain unalienated from the labor that they put into *koloa* making. Even though the textiles can be bought and sold at the marketplace, and are thus commodities, in their production phase and across their overall trajectories of circulation, they are imbued with meanings of collective female sociality—and ultimately *langa fonua*—that exceed the system of commodification through which they, at times, circulate.

Pierre Bourdieu's notion of "cultural capital" (1986) provides another way to think about Tongan women's creation of extra-commodity forms of value that are at once forms of cultural wealth. Broadly speaking, cultural capital is the accumulated knowledge and interpersonal connections that translate, through the workings of social networks, into an enhanced social reputation or status (ibid.). These "workings" are actually social transactions—the exchange of performances of one kind of expertise for enhanced respect and social status. The *koloa* that women create embody other people's positive assessment of the women themselves *and* the potential to help women realize other forms of value, including more *koloa* through gifts that others will reciprocate to them in the future. When the women exchange *koloa,* they transact both their skills (cultural capital) in textile making and material valuables. They gain material reciprocation *and* enhanced positive reputation (social capital), which, to them, are of high social *value*. And they can further exchange this reputation in other contexts in their communities, revealing the value inherent in transacting cultural capital—their skills—socially.

Belonging to particular women's groups has historically been a source of social capital for commoner Tongan women, which extends as well to commoner women in diaspora. However, the Tongan women's creation of value does not, again, function in terms of the individual woman, but in and through the group as a whole. The most prestigious women's groups in recent Tongan history have been the *kautaha*. These groups were historically part of a larger organizational structure of Tongan villages in which chiefly women held central roles, but the *kautaha* were run primarily by commoner women of senior positions in their families who produced textiles for their own purposes. *Kautaha* (meaning "company") were ubiquitous throughout Tonga between the 1920s and 1960s (Small 1987; 1995). *Kautaha* members shared plots of land specifically for growing *hiapo* and, together they also made dye, collected seaweed and fished, and hosted visitors to their village. It was prestigious for a woman to sponsor a *koka'anga* whereby barkcloth would be made for her use with cooperative labor from the women in her *kautaha,* but it also took a great deal of resources and preparation. The specific woman had to provide all the beaten bark and dye for her fellow members to use, contribute feast-like food—roast pigs and yams—and ensured that men were on sight to cook the food and to share *kava,* the soporific drink that men share with one another as an integral part of most ritual activities (Small 1997:33). Women also assembled their barkcloth using handmade pattern tablets that they themselves had made (ibid.).

Membership in *kautaha* was extremely prestigious for commoner women, and they often passed their membership down to their daughters. The value of this membership was indexed by the ways in which the work was organized. For example, textile-related work was separated from housework for *kautaha* women, and as a mode of respect for their activities the women received assistance with other household tasks whenever they were engaged in producing *koloa*. Furthermore, other people in the village provided the women with food as they worked at producing *koloa* for chiefly women. Men in their villages supported them by singing and ritually sharing in the drinking of *kava*. In addition to providing status through membership, these groups also afforded Tongan women the chance to exchange their wealth with women in other distant villages for consumer goods and, eventually, also for cash (ibid.:35). These consumer goods were useful in practical ways but they also symbolized the recipients' status as modern women, indicated their influential ties to other women in distant places, and thus contributed to the various forms of *value*—both Tongan and Western—that the women accrued through exchanges that they arranged themselves.

Social and work groups that transact as much in prestige as they do in material valuables have remained a central feature of women's active participation in Tongan national life since the early- to mid-twentieth century, when *kautaha* were especially prominent. With the growth of the Tongan cash economy in the mid-twentieth century, the nation's aims of economic development, and families' growing cash consumption needs, increasing numbers of women created groups called *toulanganga. Kautaha* all but disappeared by the 1980s, and the *toulanganga* that replaced them remain the model for barkcloth making groups in Tonga today. Rather than having a chiefly woman patron to whom they are beholden to create barkcloth, commoner women form *toulanganga* of their own volition and expressly for creating barkcloth for their specific ownership and use. *Toulanganga* are oriented toward production, rather than toward prestige and distinction as *kautaha* were. Nevertheless, membership in *toulanganga* continues to be desirable because it ensures that women will have a certain amount of *ngatu* when the work group season is over. During contemporary textile-making sessions, women also relish the additional chance to socialize, sometimes with ribald humor that is unseemly in other contexts while they work at this highly important womanly responsibility of textile making (Philips 2007; Young Leslie 1999).

Transmitting Value to "New" Textile Forms

The value of these groups does not lie only in the reification of tradition that they seem to afford women. If it did, then the use of newly introduced fabrics in *ngatu pepa* and embroidered pillowcases would diminish these objects' value. But the groups' value, and so too the value of the objects they produce, is measured by women's general desire to be associated with them, a desire that brings them together repeatedly as a collective and is expressed in and through the production of objects. The prestige of traditional *kautaha* groups that made barkcloth from paper mulberry bark lay in the value—individual social capital and collective sense of worth—accrued by women *as members of kautaha,* as much as from being associated with high-ranking or chiefly women. Because the women physically work to produce textiles, cultural capital is realized *in the women* themselves, exemplifying what Bourdieu has called an embodied form of cultural capital (1986).

In a similar way, the objects—*koloa*—can be seen as cultural (rather than simply material) capital in an objectified state, which does not lose value (or at least not entirely) when the "stuff" of which it is made changes. It is not the stuff itself, but the relationship between the stuff and the making (of *koloa,* in this case) that generates value. As Phyllis Herda (1999) has observed, the sacred potency connected with indigenous textile making in Tonga is not lost in the manufacture of introduced cloth, such as crocheted blankets and later quilts constructed from imported Western cloth, using sewing machines. Stacy Kamehiro (2007) has documented a similar association between the making of quilts and the establishment of chiefly rank in Hawai'i, and Suzanne Küchler (1999) suggests the same for *tivaivai* in the Cook Islands (cf. Horan 2012). When women in Tonga were relieved from domestic labor and childcare during periods when they were intensely weaving or plaiting *koloa,* it was due, in part, to the very sacred nature of the work they were performing. Women embody ancestors as they perform this textile work, lending *mana,* a non-earthly power, to the objects.

This potency is a basic assumption about the relationship between women and textiles in Polynesia, as Amiria Henare (2005) has explained for Maori cloak makers, Penelope Schoeffel (1999) has examined with regard to women who plait Samoan fine mats (*'ie toga*), Rod Ewins (2009) has explored for Fijian barkcloth (*masi*), and Jane Horan has done for *tivaivai* produced by Cook Islands women. Tongan women who make *koloa si'i* today with introduced fabrics embody the cultural capital—culturally valued skills and knowledge—that is their purview through association with the *mana* of (ancient) textiles and textile-related work, and so they also *transmit* this sacred potency and all of its value to the textiles they are working with, whatever their material makeup.

Herein lies the importance of women's groups and the *koloa* they produce: membership in *langa fonua* groups today associates women with the sacred potency of textiles and of the *kautaha* of old, is a context for producing *mana* and things of *mana* today, and makes both the embodied and the objectified form of *koloa* as cultural capital possible. In possessing *koloa* or, alternatively skills and resources to make *koloa* in and through these groups, women gain the capacity to enter into gift relations, to generate mana and good will, and to cement relations wherein others are indebted to them. Membership in these groups is desirable among diasporic Tongan women because of the specific form of valuable they produce—but *not* in the object as commodity—and because they provide a space where women can *embody* cultural (spiritual) value and also *generate* cultural value through both the making and eventual exchange of *koloa*.

Women's Groups in the Tongan Diaspora

Given their centrality and importance in providing women with status and value, these groups are also key institutions for Pacific island women in diaspora (Leckie 1993). Typically, women's groups have come about organically, as first-generation immigrants seek activities that afford them a chance to re-create the village relations in which they grew up. In New Zealand, Tongan women's groups' activities have also included credit rotation, teaching Tongan song and dance skills to youth, and running preschools where young children are taught exclusively in Tonga language (ibid.).[2] In Auckland, several groups of Tongan women meet regularly and work together on a variety of textile-making activities, including making *ngatu pepa*, decorating plaited mats called *kie tonga* with feathers and yarn, and embroidering pillow cases.

In diaspora, *langa fonua* groups see themselves, literally, as groups that build up the culture, and they borrow their label from Queen Sālote's original Langa Fonua 'a e Fefine Tonga. These groups "build up" the Tongan culture in New Zealand in different ways, including supporting community building among Tongans and liaising with the state to channel resources toward Tongan cultural concerns and production. Women who live in Auckland and the capital city of Wellington, New Zealand's largest cities, have set up such groups. One group donated a piece of barkcloth they created in Wellington as a gift to the National Library. Some groups produce *koloa* to sell to others, both Tongans and non-Tongans; others produce *koloa* to provide their members valuables for ceremonial gifting.

The embodied potential of making objects as gifts expands beyond *koloa*, thus textiles are not the only material objects these groups produce. Cake-baking groups, for example, are *langa fonua* groups whose members are known for sharing skills for elaborately and decoratively icing cakes (Jowitt and Lay 2002). Iced cakes—rich in fat and sugar—are another form of women's objects that are prized in modern gift presentations in both Tonga and the diaspora. Tongan women have been making them since Queen Sālote's time, when Langa Fonua promoted the acquisition and use of Western stoves for cooking and ovens for baking; these were meant to introduce women to modern conveniences that would (ostensibly) make their lives easier (Wood-Ellem 1999). Introduced items like iced cakes have remained part of the gifts given in a traditional vein at both commoner and chiefly levels since then (Veys 2009), and their presentation also moved with Tongan traditions to the diaspora. At weddings, birthdays, and christenings, it is not unusual to see elaborate setups for a dozen or more cakes decorated with flowers and ribbons that have been stacked and tiered in an elaborate display that covers an entire large table top. Most of these are given to pastors and other guests as gifts, along with *koloa;* others are divided and served to guests as part of the celebratory meal.[3]

Parallel to a point that Susan Philips (2007) makes about barkcloth-production groups in the homeland, women's groups in diaspora are important sites of reproduction of women's knowledge and gendered ideology. Moreover, like women in barkcloth-making groups in Tongan villages, women in diasporic cooperative work groups share news and reminiscences. Many of the women over sixty whom I interviewed in Auckland have a strong sense of nostalgia for the *kautaha* (special cloth-making groups) to which their mothers, aunts, and grandmothers belonged, and two had themselves belonged to *kautaha* during their younger days in various parts of Tonga. And like the *kautaha* of old, these groups plan events around which, and create spaces in

Figure 2.1. Women of the Fauniteni 'oe Mo'ui Group use discarded plastic sacking and coconut leaf midribs to make *kupesi* tablets for patterning their *ngatu pepa,* Auckland.

which their communities can congregate and connect to their own memories of Tonga in different ways. Through these events they can re-create some important village-level aspects of the homeland.

In New Zealand *langa fonua* groups, this re-creation often emerges around *kupesi*, patterned tablets traditionally used as stencils for barkcloth designs. Women of some diasporic *langa fonua* groups take pride in working cooperatively to produce the design tablets that allow them to render cloth with the same dark-brown or red-brown lines that are typical of the surface of *ngatu* produced using pandanus leaf and coconut fiber *kupesi* tablets in Tonga. Making and using *kupesi* tablets, performing *koka'anga,* and working together in groups are all processes that reinforce the idea that traditional *kupesi* and *koka'anga* are the core of the aesthetic standards for barkcloth.

While women's production of *koloa* might be seen as simply another "domestic" and so "private" activity, this distinction does not effectively describe Tongan women's qualification of space through their work. In addition to the six *langa fonua* groups of women in Auckland who made *koloa* and with whom I visited regularly in Tonga during my fieldwork, I also observed the activities of several groups of mixed gender whose members got together to socialize, to pool money in a cooperative credit scheme, and to jointly babysit their grandchildren. These groups provided the elderly people a chance to socialize during the week with age mates and to benefit their grandchildren by being with them in an entirely Tongan-speaking environment. Unless they immigrated to New Zealand many years ago, elderly Tongans may lack proficiency or confidence in speaking English, so they enjoy the chance to socialize with other Tongan speakers. Since the groups often meet in one of their members' homes it adds another layer of familiarity for the elderly members. The historical connections of such groups with domestic space (Jolly 2003) notwithstanding, the activity of the group makes the spaces, in effect, very much public, as Tongans continually scrutinize one another's activities for evidence that members of the community are abiding by "traditions." In the same way, *koloa* making is not limited to private space, but also constitutes an accessible, interactive, public space of activity and sociality for elderly women, especially, who very much welcome other members their communities to observe and admire their work and their contributions to *langa fonua.*

Recognition and Belonging: Women's Groups and Relations with the State

There is another reason that elderly Tongan immigrant women desire to build and belong to these groups: through them the women carve out spaces that virtually only they inhabit and control. In Tongan culture, many traditional practices are constructed as male centered and male empowering. Commoner women, like everyone else in Tongan culture, cannot change their rank, but they can climb a less formal and highly contested status hierarchy, mainly through association with their husbands, sons, brothers, and fathers (Doktor Korn 1974). The majority of clergy, business people, and members of parliament in Tonga are men, and town officers and landowners are always men. Women cannot own land and were only granted the right to vote in 1960. In diaspora, such patriarchal traditions continue as part of Tongan diasporic modernity, with women's roles linked to colonial projects of domesticity. The New Zealand government approaches Tongan and other Pacific women in this same mode—liaising mostly with male heads of communities and making overtures about women in development in Pacific Island communities that confine them to domestic roles. Even though women are subject to Tongan patriarchy, and others may reify their confinement to their domestic roles as well, these women tend to creatively build on their roles as mothers, sisters, and daughters. Because commoner women (especially elderly ones) are marginalized within the twin patriarchies of Tongan culture and New Zealand political economy, they welcome the chance to create publicly acknowledged spaces of agency for themselves. They craft these spaces into contexts in which they can perform *langa fonua* and positively affect their own social status and value.

These women are also subjected to the eclipsing of their meaningful ethnic specificities by the state and other mainstream intuitions and discourses that blanket Tongan practices under a generic notion of the "Pacific immigrant" (Anae 2004; Goldsmith 2003), and refuse self-determination in terms of an array of culturally specific practices and beliefs (Pearson 1990:170). Racism and ethnic discrimination also exists in New Zealand popular culture that objectifies and commodifies Pacific culture for its own gain (Anae 2004), exoticizes Pacific Islander women, and objectifies their brothers and sons as sportsmen, at best (Teaiwa and Mallon 2005) and as criminals, at worst (Fairbairn-Dunlop 2003; Loto et al. 2006). For example, Tongans are still associated with the negative reputations of Pacific Islanders, in the 1970s and 1980s, as "overstayers" of their limited term work visas in New Zealand.[4] This stereotype of Pacific Islanders has roots in articulations of state policy that have continued to be exacerbated by racist mainstream local discourse of Pacific Islanders' "cultural backwardness" and "free-loading" tendencies.[5] Strict immigration and guest worker policies notwithstanding, work practices have not always been fair either, with workers being underpaid, being made to work in challenging physical conditions, and having their passports seized.[6] There have been growing pressures on the Tongan diasporic communities whose members continue to be work-poor and education-poor and who, without retraining, face decreasing job opportunities as the market shifts from unskilled labor to more service-oriented jobs (Ongley 1991; Spoonley 2001). More recently, labor policies have been modified to favor skilled workers such as teachers and nurses among the specific quotas of immigrants from specific countries.[7]

Top-down policies like this notwithstanding, Tongan migrant families have tended to participate in the global movements of population, valuables, and information in ways that epitomize "grassroots globalization" (Appadurai 2000).[8] Perhaps nowhere is this more apparent than in the movement of remittances—cash and consumer goods sent by diasporans to the homeland. There are also "reverse remittances"—island foods, *koloa,* and other "handicrafts"—that have recently been valued at 43 percent of the value of reported remittances from diasporic locations to Tonga (Gibson and Nero 2008). As recent research has suggested (Connell and Brown 2004), Pacific women occupy a critical position in the facilitation of global flows and guarantee the everyday and ceremonial sustenance of their families. Likewise, Tongan women have historically remitted more often, and thus sometimes larger annual total sums of money than men (Vete 1995), although in recent years men's and women's contributions have become more balanced (World Bank 2006:61). Tongan women in diaspora are also gifting increasing amounts of *koloa* in lifecycle ceremonies, and these womanly valuables come to constitute important flows and "contraflows" whereby women can demonstrably engage in acts of *langa fonua* (James 1997). In addition to the textiles' value potential as gift, commodifying—selling or pawning—*koloa* afford diasporic women a quick source of cash that they often put toward ceremonial expenses and church donations (Addo and Besnier 2008; see also chapter 5 herein). In light of diasporic women's contribution to cash remittances and their growing ability to produce their own *koloa* in places like New Zealand, a more accurate accounting for *koloa* in remittances and reverse remittances would enable more nuanced understandings of the sense of interdependency between women in diaspora and women in the homeland, and how this contributes to the value and significance of *koloa* and *koloa* making.

Increasingly, the state has attempted to assess how it can help increase the quality of life for Pacific Islander women—that is, women who are members of the significant immigrant populations whose homelands are the other islands of the Pacific region (Hill 2010). It has also attempted to do so using targeted research on how to improve Pacific women's lives economically, but sometimes the studies ask the wrong questions, as in a recent study by the Ministry of Women's Affairs. In this study, 230 Pacific Islander women—referred to in the study as "Pasifika women"—were interviewed about how the state might best support them in areas such as increased job training, the chance to go into business for themselves, and opportunities to save and invest money (Koloto and Sharma 2005). Women generally responded that all of these conditions would enhance their own sense of well-being, but many also added that they were as concerned about the well-being of their families, coded in the research as "cultural upbringing and "extended family's welfare." Had the study considered more explicitly the role of exchange in the production of gendered identities and in traditional Pasifika routes to enhancing well-being, however, it might have been able to discuss a much broader range of Pasifika cultural notions about how women do indeed "save" and "invest" money and how these relate directly to the formal economy and, as Maila Stivens asserts, "often vitally so" (2005:323). As noted earlier, Tongan women in diaspora often spend their spare cash on textile valuables in part because this converts cash into a form of fungible value that relatives and friends are far less likely to ask to borrow from them. By taking a nuanced approach to what counts as women's economic activities into account, the study might also have gleaned another fact operative for Pasifika women of a range of backgrounds in New Zealand: involvement in women's groups also enhances well-being, or sense of living a life of value, because it assures more access to cash wealth through gifting and reciprocation of traditional wealth.

This 2005 study is one example of the host state's efforts to support these important aspects of Pacific people's lives and knowledge. It funds Pacific Island cultural maintenance, for example, by ensuring that Tongan language is being taught in some public schools in New Zealand today. Tongan, Samoan, Niuean, Tokelauan, and other Pacific languages are also being offered as a course of study, as are larger programs in Pacific Studies, at some top tertiary institutions. Tongan, Samoan, and Fijian barkcloth making, as well Niuean and Tokelauan weaving workshops are held regularly in schools, community centers, and museums—sponsored by both private and public institutions. The Langa Fonua group that I mention at the start of this book's introduction has received several rounds of city council funding to host workshops on barkcloth making (see figure 2.1). Museums and public galleries acquire and display large collections of material culture from these and other Pacific nations whose members, together, form a minority second in number to the indigenous Maori. After almost half a century of immigration, the birth of two and, in some families' cases, three new generations of community members, as well as ongoing relationships with members of Tongan diasporas located elsewhere, Tongans have established a place for themselves in the social fabric of the modern state of New Zealand, and women's groups have played a crucial role in this process.

Three Diasporic Langa Fonua Groups

Between January and June of 2002, I observed the activities of several *langa fonua* groups in Auckland. As I have noted, most crucial to these women and their expressions of womanliness through barkcloth making is their cooperative work, which shows them to be abiding by cultural values such as love and mutual help. As I discussed previously, *kupesi* relief pattern tablets are the means whereby women produce patterns on and encode history in barkcloth, and demonstrate important cultural knowledge. This was brought home to me when I witnessed the women of the group Fauniteni 'oe Mo'ui making these tablets using a combination of materials sourced in the Tongan islands and in the diaspora. On a chilly winter morning in June, I watched as they painstakingly copied conventional barkcloth designs onto pieces of plastic flour sacks that one of their sons had brought home from his job at a flour mill in Auckland. They cut the sacking to the size of island-Tongan *kupesi* tablets—rectangles of about fourteen inches by eighteen inches—and reinforced the edges by sewing on coconut leaf midribs that another woman's relatives had sent to her from Tonga. The sacking was used for the surface of the *kupesi* tablets in lieu of dried pandanus leaves and dried coconut tree fiber, both of which are typically used in the Kingdom of Tonga. The midribs, which could be bent and angled into desired shapes, rendered the designs in relief, so that the designs would appear on the surface of the cloth when the women later rubbed the surface of the *ngatu pepa* with reddish-brown dye.[9]

They accompanied their *kupesi*-making sessions with joyous singing and funny stories about making *ngatu ngatu* as younger women in Tonga, and began and ended their all of work sessions with a prayer led by one of the women. The Fauniteni women were all members of the mainstream Tongan Christian

Figure 2.2. Women in an Auckland *langa fonua* group do *koka'anga* to create a *ngatu pepa*. Their *kupesi* tablets are fashioned out of foam core.

denomination, the Free Wesleyan Church of Tonga; they lived and worshipped in the Mount Eden suburb of Auckland. For them duty and cultural obligations are aligned, as they see their religious virtues as being reinforced through their cloth making.

The second group whose work I was able to observe were less invested in *koloa* making as a sign of their religious devotion. This group comprised women from one ward of the Church of Jesus Christ of Latter-day Saints, or the Mormon Church in Auckland. Official Mormon church discourse in Tongan communities holds that traditional *kavenga*, ceremonial obligations, being a route to impoverishment and, in extreme cases, a form for self-promotion and (wasteful) status competition. The church, instead, practices tithing (regular offering of 10 percent of one's earnings) and promotes resistance to "traditional discourses of political authority, kinship, resource sharing, and social obligation" as practiced by members of mainstream (that is, the state Methodist Church) faiths (Gordon 1990:205; see also Addo and Besnier 2008). I was, therefore, surprised to find such a group working on traditional wealth.

When I observed their *koka'anga* (barkcloth assembly session) in South Auckland in early 2002, this group was employing novel and creative ways of making dyes and design tablets. The reddish-brown dye came from powder shed by red bricks at the construction site where one of the women's sons worked. When mixed with water, the red oxide formed a thin suspension whose color approximated that of the traditional red-brown *koka* used for staining traditional *ngatu*. To make their pattern tablets, they cut white foam-core board into rectangles of approximately twelve by sixteen inches, and used utility knives to cut out two important traditional barkcloth patterns. After attaching these tablets to the worktable, they were ready to assemble the *ngatu pepa* from sheets of synthetic vylene. As they rubbed dye over the surface of their textile the designs appeared in solid shapes of dark color, rather than in the conventional lined imprints typical of barkcloth rendered with coconut leaf *kupesi* (see figure 2.2). During *tohi*, the women used shiny black car tire paint to overpaint and outline the *kupesi* designs on the surface of the *ngatu pepa*. Even though they were using this paint in lieu of very dark brown *tongo* dye, the women said that their intention was to make the designs visible from very far away. Using very dark paint for *tohi* overemphasized the outlines, but also ensured that their *ngatu pepa* bore what they thought of as a strong resemblance to traditional barkcloth (*ngatu ngatu*).

Even though most of the women in the group told me that they had no intentions of gifting the *ngatu pepa* they would make, they were proud of their ability to make textiles with materials that involved more effort than they might have to expend were they making traditional barkcloth in Tonga. Most of these Mormon adherents were very clear about why they wanted to render traditional, named designs on their *ngatu pepa*: they intended to sell the textiles, most likely to members of the Methodist church denominations, in Auckland. Their obvious joy and pride—evidenced in their laughter and smiles that alternated with their looks of concentration and the care with which they performed all aspects of the work that I witnessed—suggested that they were tapping into something meaningful and fulfilling. This was, in part, testament to the fact that, for Tongan women of a range of religious backgrounds and in a range of places throughout the globe, textile making remains meaningfully attached to, even if removed in day-to-day ways from their world view and womanly identity.

A third group whose *ngatu pepa* making I observed came together in a more impromptu way. This group did not meet regularly and their membership was not exclusive to a particular religious group, but it was defined, for that weekend, by their close kinship relations. Two of the elderly sisters lived in Auckland and the other sister was on a three-month visit from Tonga where she regularly made *ngatu* with another group of women in her village. The other women making up the group—all of whom had lived in New Zealand for at least ten years—were daughters or nieces of the three elderly women. The women used no handmade pattern tablets and no worktable for assembling cloth. They were simply pasting vylene sheets together to form a two-layered *ngatu pepa* on the hardwood floor of the Auckland apartment where they were working. They had demarcated the edges of an imaginary *papa* using half-inch-thick rope that they had duct-taped to the floor and were using cooked flour and water paste for assembly and red-brown, store-bought dye for natural *koka*. As they rubbed dye on the surface of the vylene sheets, the braided texture of the twine below imprinted on the textile. After about an hour and a half of this adapted *koka'anga* process, the women had completed three *ngatu ngatu* of about twelve feet by twelve feet. They took each of the rolled-up textiles outside into the concrete driveway of their apartment building, unfurled them, and left them to dry in the sun (see figure 2.3). They would, they said, do over-painting (*tohi*) of designs later. They had not yet decided on the designs, but one of the women told me that she wanted *manulua*—a traditional chiefly design that Tongans share with other Polynesian barkcloth-making cultures and that resembles a pinwheel—because it would be easier to draw freehand than other *kupesi* designs. At that point in our conversation, one of her sisters interjected that she intended to use one of the children's rulers to help her draw straight lines for doing *tohi*, or the darker over-painting of lines on the cloth.

The fact that this was the only group I observed who mixed childcare with textile-making activities threw into relief a few "facts" I learned in Tonga: that *koloa* production is sacred work, that women are ideally left to do this work uninterrupted, and that caring for family members can be fit into the work if necessary, in part, because the work is ultimately meant to benefit the family. During my fieldwork I learned of only one other *langa fonua* group that

Figure 2.3. A *ngatu pepa* laid out to dry on a lawn in South Auckland.

readily mixed childcare and textile making, but it did so only in the context of a preschool that some of its members ran. In light of the fact that Tongan women's nation building was traditionally constructed around their gender and kinship roles, this seemed entirely appropriate to me. However, given the normal practice of keeping the textile-making space a context exclusively for women, I had to consider why some diasporic Tongan women sometimes mix the two. The women are members of an immigrant working-class family, many members of which are employed for long hours and rely on relatives to help out with domestic duties such as childcare. The constraints of having to do two kinds of work—childcare and textile work—led them to alter some of the normal rules of the homeland division of labor around *koloa* making in order for a family to manage financially.

Women's flexibility in shifting between a number of ideologically disparate contexts, and their devotion to executing their multiple gendered duties concurrently is again an application of pragmatic creativity, a resourceful approach in production and incorporation of "new" cultural form (Young Leslie and Addo 2007). As I discuss next, women also bring pragmatic creativity into play when they seek and use funding that state institutions make available for boosting the production of Pacific Islander art and crafts. Tongan women recipients may engage individuals who represent the state in gift-type exchange relationships in so far as it is advantageous in fulfilling their aims of being able to gift textiles and perform "tradition." The remaining sections of this chapter address how women in cooperative work groups (*langa fonua* groups) navigate Tongan notions of the gift in their interactions with the representatives of other nation states.

Receiving Gifts: Government "Arts" Funding

Whether in Tonga or in diaspora, women's associations exist to effect *langa fonua*. These associations become commoner women's direct route to people of authority in the New Zealand state and local government. Through a local funding body such as the city council, the state covers the women's cost outlays for buying materials to make *koloa* and their local transport costs to get to the group's meeting place. If the group members finance their own activities, members are typically driven to the group meetings in relatives' cars and pool money to buy resources. Regardless of how the women fund their textile-related work, others in the community usually give time and other resources to further the aims of the group. This demonstrates mutual help, *fētokini'aki,* another key cultural value that, along with love (*'ofa*) and respect (*faka'apa'apa*), is at the core of *angafaka-Tonga,* "the Tongan way" (Evans 2001). Thus, many groups continue today, despite the continually shifting attention and funding that they get from the state because, as sites of womanly knowledge (Philips 2007), they afford diasporans additional ways to bolster cultural values and nationalistic practices.

Groups like the Fauniteni 'oe Mo'ui consider funding to purchase materials for textile making to be a form of gift presented to them by a powerful entity—the New Zealand state. Visibly receiving such economic capital is highly valued by the women within their ethnic community because it is analogous, in Tongan cultural terms, with the women being recipients of gifts from high-ranking people. The state sponsorship of textile-making groups also bears echoes of the patronage of elite women in *kautaha* from the early and mid-twentieth century. As some of my informants described: sometimes a chiefly woman would call together women on her (husband's) *tofi'a,* estate, to make *koloa* for her use. They contributed their labor as a gift for which they would receive food and other valuables as well as admiration from others in the community. Patronage by elites is also considered a gift and evokes the days when ancient chiefs and the Tu'i Tonga propitiated to the gods in exchange for blessing for the entire ancient *fonua* of Tonga. Like many public transactions between commoners and elites, New Zealand state sponsorship is of high social as well as economic value among Tongans. The government representatives whom they know best—those in Tonga—are primarily drawn from the ranks of the nobility. Tongan nobles often receive gifts of money from commoners, but they rarely present money to commoners. Women of *langa fonua* groups often consider the receipt of economic capital, like the blessings of Tongan chiefs, to be a generalized reciprocation and recognition of their life's work of gifting textiles, prayers, children, and labor to others.

Langa fonua groups who seek and receive funding are a primary means through which New Zealand's decision-making authorities have come to understand Tongan women as legitimate culture brokers. Such agencies include the Department of Labor, the Ministry of Pacific Island Affairs, Creative New Zealand, the Ministry of Women's Affairs, and the Department of the Interior (Koloto and Sharma 2005). The New Zealand government is also invested in supporting under-represented groups—ethnic minorities, women, the poor, and minority artists. In keeping with its aims for leadership in the Pacific region, the New Zealand state also created several foreign aid schemes to Tonga in the early 1990s. For example, as noted previously, in the New Zealand Overseas Development Aid (NZODA) program, women in Tonga received funding to produce *koloa* as valuables that they could sell as an income earner (Horan 2002). Rather than expressly selling the *koloa* they produced through these local government-sponsored development schemes, many aid recipients preferred to deploy them as gifts in their local networks or in exchanges for other valuables from women in diaspora. The local Tongan women realized what they considered to be far greater benefit from including the textiles in existing relationships of debt and honor. That is, they used the textiles in gift exchange. While this was a result the New Zealand state did not expect, it was perfectly in keeping with the aims of Tongan modernity and with the culture of reciprocity (*fēfetoni'aki*).

Women who benefit from such income-creation schemes are also empowered to help themselves and their communities on their own terms because they do not have to pay out of their own pocket for craft or raw materials. And while the New Zealand state has assisted in this process, there is room for deeper engagement. The state's continued recognition that Tongan material priorities reflect crucial social priorities with transnational implications has the potential to further empower New Zealand's various human services institutions in achieving their aims of assisting these ethnic communities in more culturally appropriate and economically effective ways.

Exchanging Gifts: *Koloa* and Women's Representation of the Homeland

As part of the overall engagement in *langa fonua* in diaspora, Tongan women also use *koloa* to communicate to non-Tongans a sense of what it means to be Tongan. In particular, commoner women are responsible for feeding the growing demand for barkcloth in the Pacific region. In 2001, I attended an event that my commoner Tongan women informants in Nuku'alofa had been referring to, for the past few weeks, as the "*kātoanga* with Fiji." *Kātoanga* can be used to describe a vibrant, gendered "exchange institution," in which commoner women began precisely to enable themselves to exchange their prestige wealth with women who live an appreciable distance away (Small 1995). Tongans and Fijians have been engaged in relations of exchange and kinship for generations. Samoa forms the third point in an ancient trade triangle with Tonga and Fiji in which chiefly families exchanged textiles, foods, and other valuables between the islands as they forged politically astute relationships, including marriages (Kaeppler 1978a). Members of each society also sought one another out for skills such as tattooing and boat building; being tattooed and commissioning boats were both practices that enhanced the rank and political influence of chiefs (Gell 1993). Fijian chiefs and Tongan nobility continue to recognize their kinship connections during ritual times, such as when members of their families celebrate weddings or hold funerals and investitures (Kaeppler 1999b). At such events, Tongan chiefly families exchange gifts of textiles and food wealth with the Fijians, who present their own types of textiles (*masi*, barkcloth, and fine mats) and whale teeth (*tabua*).

Kātoanga, as an exchange institution, developed between women within Tonga in the early 1900s and later began to be practiced between them and women in Fiji and Samoa (Small 1995). Tongan women now also construct *kātoanga* as exchange events in which one group of women involved lives in a specific village, and the other group lives in the diaspora (ibid.; Small 1997). While Fiji continues to have strong, ongoing traditions of barkcloth making for local, ceremonial use, especially on islands such as Vatulele (Ewins 2009), Fijian women in some areas such as the Lau group, which has historical and cultural ties with Tonga, also desire to own and gift Tongan-styled barkcloth. Samoan women, in Samoa and overseas in the urban centers of the diaspora that Samoan migrants share with Tongan and other Pacific Island migrants, also desire Tongan barkcloth. Thus, commoner Tongan women who supply *koloa* to such markets recreate these ancient trade connections in many parts of the wider world.

The *kātoanga* with Fiji was held at the home of a very well-known businessman, and was hosted by his wife who had recently joined a group of Nuku'alofa women to regularly exchange *koloa* for consumer goods with women overseas. This group was not a *toulanganga or a toulālanga*, a group whose main purpose was to make barkcloth or fine mats, respectively; it was also not a *langa fonua* group. It was a group whose women assembled for exchange. The group of eleven Fijian women who had arrived the day before, were staying with relatives around Nuku'alofa or, if they were without local Tongan relatives, at a local guesthouse. On the day of the event, both groups of women arrived about two hours before the official start of the event to prepare their textiles for exchange in the large, concreted back yard of the Western-style house. The event began with hymn singing by both groups of women in their native tongues, the Tongan women humming along with the Fijians when they recognized a tune. Several of the Tongan women made short speeches to welcome the guests, and to thank God for the good weather.

The women then began to unfurl and lay out their textiles, in partnered Fijian-Tongan pairs, three pairs at a time, so that the cloths covered the surface of the concrete yard. All the women assembled viewed the textiles, remarking on their beauty. These initial unfurlings and presentations marked the stage of the event that the women referred to as *fetongi*, "exchange," and it was essential to the women *as women* for it formalized the process of recognition of the labor and skill, beauty and devotion they had imbued in the textiles they made. As had been the agreement between the two groups, the Tongan women each presented two pieces of barkcloth that each measured ten native yards in length and that were finished on their two long sides with a sparsely decorated white border. In exchange, the Fijian woman presented textiles from their homeland's traditions: one Fijian double layer pandanus mat (*pati*) with a colorful one- to two-foot-wide yard edge, one single-layer floor mat (*coco*), and one fine mat plaited from double-layer reed fibers (*kuta*) and featuring a design plaited using reed fibers that had been dyed black.

After *fetongi*, when all the pairs of women—Tongan and Fijian—had taken their turns to present their valuables to one another, the stage that the women referred to as *me'a'ofa*, "gift," began. During this stage, they would present additional wealth items. The onset of this stage was signaled by the sound of festive Tongan music that someone turned on, at blaring volume, from loudspeakers on the veranda of the house. The Tongan women danced toward their exchange partners in time with this music, holding their gift items in their hands as they crossed the open space of the yard, where each woman placed her particular gifts at the feet of her partner. From the Tongans, these gifts included brightly colored, store-bought lengths of patterned cloth, decorated Tongan fine mats known as *kie tonga*, and, from a few of the women, shorter lengths of *ngatu*—each either four or five native yards long—that had been cut from larger pieces. For their part, the Fijians presented their Tongan exchange partners with gifts of colored fabric, carved wooden bowls, and lengths of *masi* "Fijian barkcloth." Two of them presented gifts of cylindrical, molded lumps of clay that, in Fiji and at times in Tonga, is used to darken dyes for barkcloth and that sometimes are presented along with textile gifts at Fijian ceremonial events (Ewins 2009; Troxler 1972).

Cathy Small, in describing *kātoanga* between women from different villages in Tonga, has referred to this unsolicited offering of additional gifts as the "love gift," which is motivated by the "spontaneous warmth and happiness one feels on the occasion" (1995:239). She describes the presentation of love gifts as a kind of "prestige war," in which women present store-bought, imported items (often, expensive ones) to each other, such as silverware and crockery, mattresses and bed clothing, irons, stove, radios, sewing machines, ready-made clothing, and consumables like sugar, bread, powered milk, and salt beef (ibid.:240). Women in the groups whose exchanges Small observed sought to outdo one another by presenting more valuables, thus displaying what they hope others will read as generosity and *'ofa,* "love." The value of the textile initially exchanged is increased by the *me'a'ofa,* literally "a thing of love," and the value of that gift is enhanced by the dancing movements that show joy and love in the act of presentation. I contend that *me'a'ofa* is about more than prestige, but is also about *awe.* The textiles are meant to inspire awe by their beauty and size, the shininess of their "faces," and by the *'ofa* and sacrifice of those proffering them. Like the emotional pangs they evoke—whether based on an upwelling of warmth or spirit of competition—these features of the gifts and the gift givers become even more acutely *felt* in the context of the unexpectedness with which they are presented and received.

In addition to the textiles, and the words and emotions with which they were offered, dance and shared food were ways of communicating across the cultural distances between the women of the two cultures. After the presentations, and some informal performances of Tongan and Fijian dances, everyone, including the Tonga TV cameraman who had attended to record the event, sat down on the large, shady veranda to an elaborate meal sponsored by the event's hostess. There was much to celebrate and the women ate, sang, and talked well into the night, sharing stories of textile making, life in their villages, and relatives they knew who lived in each other's respective countries.

Diverting Gifts: Contemporary *'A'āhi* in Diaspora

In Auckland, the Fauniteni 'oe Mo'ui textile-making group holds *'a'āhi* roughly on an annual basis. *'A'āhi* are events hosted by groups of Tongan women—usually elderly women—who have been working together for some time to make expressive material culture that symbolizes their continuing links with their homeland. *'A'āhi* translates directly as "showing" and such displays of women's products and prestige continue to take place in Tongan villages, "during which huge areas of ground (such as the village sports oval) are covered with *koloa*" (Morton 1996:109). *'A'āhi* are modeled on agricultural shows that Queen Sālote instituted in Tonga in the 1950s as a way of encouraging healthy competition between men as farmers and between women as *koloa* makers.[10] Entrants to the competition put their most impressive *ngāue* from the past season and recently-made *koloa* out for public viewing in sometimes elaborate displays. Audiences include school children, laypeople, church ministers and chiefs.

When ministers and chiefly individuals stop at a booth, the owner typically gifts them some of the valuables on display. While *'a'āhi* are not competitions per se and prizes are not awarded, women are acutely aware that audience members are comparing their work and every woman hopes her *koloa* will be considered the best. In diaspora, *'a'āhi* are also opportunities to bring the local ethnic Tongan community together for purposes other than to celebrate a life crisis event or church donation. More importantly, they are also occasions when the women are not only in complete charge, but when the activity at hand is all about women and their products, and not directly about their extended kin groups and the presentation of gifts to commemorate a life crisis ceremony.

Among the *langa fonua* groups I studied in diaspora, women often invite representatives of the funding organizations—the state or city councils—to their *'a'āhi*. They thus transform *'a'āhi* from being sites where women represent themselves and their work to other Tongans to sites for representing Tonga as a multiterritorial *fonua* to a multicultural audience. If high-ranking Tongans were present, women would also be representing the multiterritorial Tongan nation, and would emphasize the fact that Tonganness is not only located in Tonga, but is thriving in diaspora, in part, through the efforts of women such as themselves. They believe that they reciprocate such gifts by inviting state or city officials to their *'a'āhi* and by feasting and gifting them with material gifts. However neither the women in groups nor state officials make concerted efforts to keep a relationship of mutual obligation going with one another. *'A'āhi* are sites for welcoming the state and also spaces of agency where women feel culturally grounded as they redirect wealth produced with economic resources from the state into kin-based relationships.

For their 2001 *'a'āhi*, the Fauniteni group used the hall adjoining a church where the members of the group worship. Holding the event in a community space, rather than a private home, is crucial to the construction of *'a'āhi* as events concerned with women's prestige. The women arrived early in the morning to set up the small display areas that they had been allocated by their chair; the place was busy and loud with the giving of orders and the moving of furniture and *koloa*. Accompanied by younger women relatives, the Fauniteni women brought in bundles of *koloa* that they unfurled and laid out, face up, in layers on the floor. The order of layers was important: first barkcloth was laid down, on top of which were finely plaited floor mats (*fala*); then smaller mats decorated with colored yarn fringes (*kie tonga*) and waist mats (*ta'ovala*) were placed on top of those, with baskets and braided waist ornaments added as the topmost layer. Once the objects were in place just as their makers wanted them to be, some women returned home to change into formal clothes—including waist mats—and to check on the preparation of food for the event.

They returned to the hall around 9:00 AM, an hour before guests began to arrive. During this hour, the women moved around in small groups to observe one another's work. I frequently heard the words *faka'ofa'ofa* ("beautiful") and *mālō* ("thank you") as the women recognized one another's work. During this early stage of the *'a'āhi*, I would hear women talking among themselves, naming the *koloa* by type, marveling at the objects' beauty, and pointing out to one another the textiles and baskets that they had made or decorated. When visitors from outside of the group itself arrived (including members of the women's extended families, pastors and their wives), each of the Fauniteni women stood next to her *koloa* to be able to describe her textiles to viewers. Most interacted almost exclusively with the visitors. The women stood physically close to their objects and remained much quieter than they did before the guests arrived—lending an air of seriousness to the process of interacting with others over their *koloa*—and accepted the visitors' compliments and gratitude for their work with a simple *"mālō."*

A space at one end of the hall had been set up with two long tables laden with island foods and one other table that was more neatly set up with the best foods, including two small roast pigs for pastors, their wives, and other special guests to share. After praying together, everyone sat at the tables to share the meal, still discussing and admiring the *koloa* from their seats. During the meal, music was played from a sound system; women from the Fauniteni group performed dance movements to music that was played over loudspeakers in the hall; these expressions of joy were also meant to entertain the guests as they ate. After eating, it was time for the guests to leave; the Fauniteni women prepared to see them off with gifts. They began to gift the pastors' wives with some of the objects they had put out on display. While the group had set aside specific *koloa* as a gift for each pastor's wife—a cut and folded length of barkcloth and a plaited mat called a *kie tonga*—some women chose to present other gifts such as iced cakes and additional *koloa* to them as well. One pastor's wife received a *kato teu*, "decorated basket." I later learned that each pastor's wife reciprocated these gifts with food, *koloa,* and visits to the home of the giver within a few days of the event.

The re-creation of the types of interactions that reinforce Tongan values of love, respect, mutual help, and giving freely are crucial to commoner diasporic Tongans' feeling that they have performed Tongan culture appropriately. In treating guests at the diasporic *'a'āhi* as they would high-ranking guests to a function in a Tongan village, the women honor, or "push up" (*fakalangilangi*), both their guests and Tongan culture. Commemorating village norms in transnational communities become acts of *langa fonua* in diaspora. Such acts include the *fakalangilangi* of children at their first birthday or their graduation celebration (Figure 2.4), or the bride and groom at their wedding, when these individuals are seated on folded *koloa* while others make speeches of gratitude and offer prayers for their continued health, success, and happiness.

Notably, women sometimes display recently acquired, brand new *koloa* from Tonga, which the women either requested that their relatives in Tonga send them or that they "paid for" with remittances. Exceptionally well-made

Figure 2.4. Twin brothers sit on a folded *ngatu pepa* at a celebration of their university graduation. Two women (in the background) serve *kava* to guests, Auckland.

textiles are evidence of the diligence of women in the group for having created these objects or having gathered the resources to commission them from other women in the Kingdom. Just as the Tongan women who exchanged with women from Fiji expected the latter to proffer their best work in the exchange, women who commission textiles from Tonga tend to display textiles of very high quality. Intricate discussions about the size and style of these commissioned textiles often ensued over the phone or through Tonga-based relatives of the diasporic women. Those abroad expected the island-based women to send them only their best *koloa,* as these textiles would be a source of prestige for the formers' families. The textiles also help render Tongan communities in New Zealand the *mata* (face) of the Tongan nation within that host nation. Embodied in the *koloa* is diasporic and homeland women's pride about their native Kingdom, their prestige and influence there and in the diaspora, and the beauty, uniqueness, and potency of their *koloa.*

Women's creation of value and generation of prestige through *koloa* making and gifting can be elaborated in diaspora, not only through operationalizing the valuables the Tongan community, but through the incorporation of the prestige of institutions and people local to the diasporic national site in which they live. The gifting the women engage in can be finely calibrated to the status of those from outside the Tongan community who attend events like *'a'āhi* and mitigates the outsider's lack of reciprocation. When city council officials attend the *'a'āhi,* as they sometimes do, they are also gifted with *koloa.* The women hosting the *'a'āhi* tend to be particularly excited about such visits because it enhances their prestige when *other Tongans* witness the women being respected by representatives of the New Zealand nation, but also when the women represent all that is good in Tongan culture by gifting such people with *koloa,* their supreme valuable. At an *'a'āhi* held by another *langa fonua* group in Auckland several weeks later, guests included a representative of Auckland City Council, a Tongan pastor and his wife, and the wives of two other pastors of the group's denomination. At the end of the event, women hosts presented the pastors' wives with *'efinanga,* folded bundles of *koloa* comprising a cut section of barkcloth, a small fine mat called a *kie tonga,* a six-foot length of brightly colored cotton cloth, and either a decorated basket or an iced cake. In contrast, one of the women presented the *palangi* ("white") state representative with a more modest gift, but one that was visually arresting and that constituted *koloa,* if *koloa si'i*—a colorful machine-made quilt—while another women presented him with a six-yard length of printed colorful cotton cloth.

Publicly gifting *koloa* enhances women's status among their peers, but also "gives face" to their community regardless of who the recipients are. Thus, the Fauniteni women selected their gifts to visitors carefully. The women knew that gifting *koloa*—even that which would never be reciprocated in kind—was an act of value creation ripe with the potential of heightened prestige for themselves, their group and for their community. Later, some women who were not members of the group, but who had been in attendance, explained the differences in the gifts presented to the Tongan and the non-Tongan visitors to me by saying that it would have been a "waste" (*mole*) to give a *palangi*—implying, someone who did not know or live within Tongan culture—more *koloa* than that. However, as I intimated in my discussion of the Fauniteni group's *'a'āhi,* it was clear from the discussions the Fauniteni women had between themselves in the days leading up to that event just how important the presence of important non-Tongans would be to the women, the group, and the project of Tongan community and nation building in New Zealand. They had thus chosen *the ngatu, ngatu pepa,* quilts, and *kie tonga* that they would present to them, and prepared them for gifting by carefully smoothing and then folding them, with care and precision. Even though gifts women in these *langa fonua* presented to city officials and other non-Tongans were rarely reciprocated, the audience of *other* Tongan individuals would surely understand the value of such gifts of *koloa,* adding to the prestige of the individual women and to the social capital afforded them as hosts of the *'a'āhi.*

Conclusion

The gendered identity and sense of duty among women in *langa fonua* groups hinge on their skill in making valuable objects, and their work of publicly gifting those things. Gifting *koloa,* in particular, continues to be the quintessential cultural process whereby diasporic Tongan women care for their sociospatial relationships (*tauhi vā*) and, in the interests of their kin groups, contribute to global efforts at *langa fonua,* giving face (*mata*) to their families and communities in interactions with the host state.

Through the medium of *langa fonua* groups women are further empowered to become active agents of Tongan nation building abroad through strategic inclusion of the host state and other non-Tongan entities in their nation-building projects. What I have demonstrated here is that, to such women, empowerment can take the form of translating economic resources from the host country government, through the medium of the gift, into prestige and social capital. Rather than only engaging in modernity through Western development models that primarily revolve around capitalism and monetary enrichment, the women produce a space for their culture of gifting in modern host states. In so doing, they exemplify pragmatic creativity and, at once localize their already globalized textiles in culturally meaningful ways.

Notes

1. While Australia is the largest aid donor to Tonga and to many other Pacific countries, New Zealand sees itself as having a role to "most effectively help" in developing key aspects of the Tongan economy—both international trade relationships and small business marketing skills (Foreign Affairs, Defence and Trade Committee 2005:14). In the last two decades, women have also become a focus of some of New Zealand's many overseas development projects in the Pacific islands (Alexeyeff 2008) and other nations' and international funding agencies' development projects (Cornwall 2000; Jackson 2001). Anthropologist Jane Horan's analysis of a particular New Zealand Overseas Development Aid (NZODA) project in Tonga in the 1990s reveals how aid money was funneled into local barkcloth and fine mat-making processes in order to aid women in creating wealth that they could sell or export and thus generate income for themselves (2002).
2. Heilala Preschool in Grey Lynn, a suburb of Auckland, ran for about five years. The woman who opened it was one of the founding members of the Langa Fonua 'ae Fefine Tonga 'i Aotearoa group I discussed at the beginning of the introduction. She told me that doing the preschool and the textile-marketing work took up all her time, but both were important to her. Lack of competence in native Pacific languages in second- and third-generation Pacific Islanders is a concern among migrant communities.
3. The preparation of Western foods was probably seen as a skill that could bring a woman prestige, but perhaps they also served to increase women's work, by adding to the number of different kinds of cooking that women were required to do.
4. Early morning police raids of heavily Polynesian areas of Auckland were one of the state's methods for finding, and deporting, individuals who had overstayed their work visas (Fairbairn-Dunlop 2003). Teresia Teaiwa and Sean Mallon state that "the 'dawn raids' inflicted considerable trauma on the Tongan communities, [who] were key targets during [that] period. ... They did not hold any of the citizenship privileges [that]

other Pacific Islanders could claim" (2005:209). Samoa and Niue were administered by New Zealand during the colonial era and, so people from these nations have access to more rights in New Zealand than Tongans. The Cook Islands are an independent nation in free association with New Zealand, thus Cook Islanders are entitled to New Zealand citizenship.

5. See Bedford and Didham (2001) and also Spoonley (2001). A similar discourse exists in Australia (Lee 2003) and to a lesser extent in the United States. In the US, Tongans and other Pacific Islanders are included in a generalized negative discourse about immigrants of color. They are also subject to the same stereotypes of criminalization as African American and other people of color, populations of comparable socioeconomic status in the United States.

6. Since the 1970s, employers—often owners of orchards—have actively recruited unskilled workers from Pacific Island nations such as Tonga, and often under a bond of one or two years. In 2006, a seasonal agriculture work scheme was put in place for Pacific Islanders to enter New Zealand (Stahl and Appleyard 2007). However, there have been some reports of inadequate living facilities and insufficient days of work, and thus inadequate pay, being meted out to Tongan immigrant workers under this scheme (Weekend Herald 2008a), as well as to nurses who entered under the Pacific Access Category (Weekend Herald 2008b).

7. In 2002, of the Pacific Access Category (PAC) was instituted to control immigration from the Pacific Islands and it established quotas of 250 individuals from each of Fiji and Tonga and 75 individuals from Tuvalu and Kiribati. The PAC uses a ballot system and requires applicants to secure a job offer from an employer in New Zealand before they are allowed to immigrate. In 2005, the Residual Pacific Access Category Places Policy was enacted because quotas through the PAC were not being filled. Under this newer policy, citizens of Tonga who were lawfully in New Zealand at the time would be invited to apply for work permits under the Pacific Access Category (Stahl and Appleyard 2007).

8. Family reunification for Pacific Islander immigrants has never been assured in New Zealand as it had been in Australia in the 1960s when family reunification visas allowed immigrants to help their parents emigrate from their homelands (Lee 2003). Yet, particular arrangements between Australia and New Zealand, such as the Trans Tasman Travel Arrangement, ratified in 1973, make it possible for Tongans who are citizens of New Zealand undertake step-migration in seeking employment in Australia.

9. That day, the women made *kupesi* with designs called *fata 'o Tu'i Tonga*. This design reflects the decorative lashings on traditional chiefly houses, along with the popular four-petal frangipani design. Other *kupesi* that they have made included *manulua* and *kāhoa*. These designs also constitute chiefly references: *manulua* is an abstraction of two birds and indexes, among other things, chiefly genealogy; *kāhoa* is a stylized rendition of particular flower "leis" with which Tongan chiefs have long been honored. For more in-depth historical explanations of these designs, see Kooijman (1972), Kaeppler (1998, 1995), Tamahori (1963), Addo (2004), and Potauaine and Māhina (N.d). The latter two works provide some conventional commoner ideas about the meanings of these three designs, whereas Kaeppler, Kooijman, and Tamahori draw on research aided by chiefly Tongan informants in earlier decades.

10. The agricultural shows, in turn, may have been modeled on ancient *'inasi*, or first fruits, rites in which the commoners who lived on chiefs' hereditary estates honored

these patrons by contributing *ngāue* and *koloa* towards offerings to the Tuʻi Tonga. These gifts were part of a massive redistribution system wherein valuables went up to chiefs and blessings and protection conferred by the *mana* of chiefs and the Tu ʻi Tonga were reciprocated to commoners. For more on *ʻinasi* rites, see Bott (1982), Bataille-Benguingui (1976), Martin (1991 [1817]), and Gifford (1929).

❦ 3
Women, Roots, and Routes
Life Histories and Life Paths

This chapter explores how commoner women's involvement with *koloa*, or textile wealth, articulates with their transnational family relationships and their individual life choices to produce the multiterritorial nation. The premise of the chapter is that commoner women have historically been innovators in *koloa* making, having continually experimented with new materials, techniques, decorative designs, and uses for *koloa*. Their propensity toward experimentation and embellishment with new forms has enabled these women to expand the number and types of valuables that they gift in a traditional vein, even when living in new contexts, locations, and material conditions. When commoner women present *koloa*, they index their own generative power, and the *mana* of ancestors, and the regard for *kāinga* over themselves; most importantly, perhaps, women index paths of linkage between themselves and others—individuals, ancestors, and lineages (Veys 2009). Commoner women, like chiefly women who made textiles historically, also imbue the cloths with their *mana* and prestige. They also engage in *langa fonua,* nation building, which several of my informants in Auckland defined as "something that you do to help yourself and your family with your own hands." For commoner women, *langa fonua,* like *koloa,* is literally, the work of their hands.

Since the establishment of the Tongan Constitution in 1875 and the burgeoning of Tongan migration and diaspora in the 1970s, commoner women have widened the spatial territory, and the aesthetic possibilities, for producing *koloa*. It is primarily commoner Tongans who emigrate and who have engaged in long-distance *langa fonua,* nation building, by establishing and augmenting diasporic communities. Today, almost a century and a half after Tonga's conversion to Christianity, commoner women who make *koloa* perform tasks that continue to be associated with the bodily discipline and industriousness espoused by Methodist ministries (Addo 2003; Eves 1996). Another interpretation of the value of *koloa* is that these commoner women transfer the protection of sacred beings (Filihia 2001) to their extended family members, partly by gifting these *koloa* to others in the community, and especially to people who have the power to positively influence the lives of their children (Young Leslie

2004) and others in their kin groups. Heather Young Leslie has also used the term *koloa* as a metaphor for people who have left their home islands in Tonga for other parts of the kingdom or for the outside world. These people—these *koloa*—are all the children of women who miss them (ibid.). Women attach a globalized sense of agency to their production and circulation of *koloa*, that is, they assume that, through *koloa* they can contribute to *langa fonua* in virtually any Tongan community in the world. One of my informants—a Tongan man in Auckland—defined *koloa* as "things that you take with you," suggesting that Tongan women desire to make *koloa* endure physically and to thus keep these objects indispensable to Tongan ceremonial interactions. This man understood that, by creating *koloa*, women also maintain a sense of agency over the destiny of their globalized families (ibid.).

In this chapter, I compare how three elderly commoner Tongan-born women negotiate their female roles and responsibilities to engage in reciprocal exchange of *koloa* in New Zealand. I present their experiences in their own voices, based on reflections and stories I gathered from them over the one and a half years of my formal fieldwork and several subsequent visits to Tonga and Auckland. I also include their relatives' reflections about the women. A point of resonance among their stories is the women's strong sense of obligation to accumulate *koloa* and to engage in gift exchange so that others will be favorably disposed toward their children. Engaging in exchange is something that women, especially mothers, should do *publicly* (ibid.; cf. Horan 2012). In Pacific communities, the responsibility to maintain a family's reputation falls heavily on women, who are expected to be resourceful in meeting the needs of their families (Bolton 2003; Molisa 1983). Making, caring for, and gifting *koloa* are still among the most rewarding ways in which a woman can fulfill this expectation. Immigrant Tongan women who dwell in diaspora further negotiate and augment these roles as they live in and move through the multiterritorial *fonua*.

The women, 'Ofa, Lina, and Kakala, were born and raised to adulthood in Tonga, but only 'Ofa still lives there today. Through narratives about particular moments of these women's lives, in particular places, I further demonstrate how modernization of the materiality of *koloa* is influenced by global flows between diaspora and homeland and how maintaining a fluid sense of the ideal materiality of the gift plays a key role in the women's performance of *langa fonua*. The biographical sketches I present here are by no means complete life-history narratives. I simply attempt to draw out detailed reminiscences, interweaving them to create a nuanced account of events, emotions, and ambitions relevant to the subject's life situation today. My intention is to provide a sense of how commoner Tongan women balance duty and ambition, and family lives and public personas, as they engage in transnational relationships of reciprocity through the exchange of valuables.[1]

Women as Mothers, Culture Workers, and Nation Builders

Exchanging valuables transnationally is routine for Tongan women today, because their families in both diasporic and homeland settings continue to perform rituals with *koloa,* money, and other important objects. However this is neither cheap nor stress-free. Activating kinship ties with transnational flows of wealth also leaves women socially obligated to present and reciprocate gifts on behalf of their "decentered families" (Gailey 1992), and to do so over a much wider area than one kin group, village, or city. The high costs of staging *kavenga*—the ceremonial occasions that are the site of most public exchange of *koloa*—usually exceed the money women have on hand, so much so that diasporic women may also exploit the modern fungibility of *koloa* to raise much needed funds. Many women I met during my research used *koloa* that they deemed unsuitable or unnecessary for an event at hand to secure temporary cash loans towards financing that event. They put the money toward buying food, renting public halls, booking sound systems or Tongan music bands for the event, or toward cash gifts.[2]

In Tongan families, the disproportionately larger responsibility to engage in the labor, expense, and stress of rearing children, teaching them cultural values and practices, and mobilizing resources for their advantage falls on women (Evans, Harms, and Reid 2009). One term used in the academic literature for this (institutionalized) role is "culture bearers" (Dove 1998; Rasmussen 2000). Feminist scholar Patricia Hill Collins suggests that it is more productive to think about women as *culture workers,* for this recasts our analytical focus, from women being passive *bearers* of an imagined cultural past to a critical consideration of the political economy and power relations entailed in women being *doers* or agents of culture (2006:147). In refocusing our understanding of women's cultural responsibilities on their roles in nation building, we also have to take into account how the desire for development can create pressures on women who are made to leave their homelands, or choose to do so. Sometimes Tongan women emigrate, not for their own enrichment or fulfillment, but to help their kinspeople by working abroad or by performing other tasks that help relatives to be successful at overseas work (Gailey 1992). By this I mean that women actively engage in performing roles that historically define their gender, femininity, and place in kin groups and society.

For example, Kakala, one of the women whose stories I present below, left the familiar space of her village in Tonga for New Zealand to help her sister raise her children, taking on the responsibility to assist their sisters in fulfilling their womanly duties. Besides raising children, these duties include preparing *koloa* and presenting gifts at celebratory events, as well as phoning relatives and friends, visiting them on holidays, and hosting them in her home after special church services. Michaela di Leonardo (1984) identifies such reciprocal sharing activities between women in different families as a special domain of labor among women of Italian-American immigrant families in the United States, and refers to these activities as "the work of kinship." The work of kinship also includes "the mental or administrative labor of the creation and maintenance of fictive kin ties, decisions to intensify or neglect ties, and the responsibility for monitoring and taking part in mass media and folk discourse concerning family and kinship" (ibid.:194–195). Men are integral to these networks of kin, but women create and maintain them (ibid.). In the words of Adrienne Kaeppler (1999a), women renew people culturally. As men typically cultivate and exchange prestige food—agricultural products that are sometimes known as *ngāue* or *ngoue*—men can be seen, instead, as having the role of sustaining and renewing people physically (ibid.).

The global Tongan pattern is similar in that the responsibility to gift, and to garner and organize resources for gift giving falls more heavily on women than on men. In diaspora, commoner Tongan women keep track of events in other kin groups, prepare gifts to present at them, oversee the sorting of food and *koloa* as reciprocations for gifts received, and initiate visits to those who are sick among their friends, kin, and fellow congregants (see figure 3.1). In short, women's roles as culture workers ensure that other people's cultural needs and responsibilities are met.

The three women I discuss identify themselves as mothers as well as textile makers. As mothers they bear and rear children—physically peopling "the nation" (Davin 1997), in coordination with their activities of building up the nation *langa fonua* through practices of reciprocity. As mothers—by birth and by adoption—they enter into several kinds of reciprocal relationships: one set with their children, another with extended family members (*kāinga*), and yet another with people in their communities and churches. All these sets of relationships are crucial to the women's maintenance of their status, and women participate in them in a range of ways in Tonga and in diaspora both.

'Ofa: Tradition Has its Place, and that Place is Tonga

'Ofa is the eldest daughter of a commoner family from Kolomotu'a, a neighborhood of the Tongan capital that is located on the main island, Tongatapu. She was born in 1933, and is the second eldest among her six siblings. 'Ofa's earliest female role model, her mother, impressed upon her that a woman's primary role was to care for the home, the children, and the family's material responsibilities toward the church. In 1943, when 'Ofa was only ten years old, her mother passed away. Speaking with me in December 2007 while sitting in a house she built with her husband Langi, 'Ofa told me about what it felt like in the years after her mother's death, as the eldest daughter, to be suddenly thrust into a position of family responsibility:

Figure 3.1. 'Ofa, in her house in Nuku'alofa, preparing a *fuatanga* for gifting, Tonga.

After my mother died, I did all the housework, like cooking and cleaning. My younger sister was still very small so she could not help me out until later, eh? Some years later—it was my last year of high school—our father passed away and it was up to me and Sālesi, our elder brother, to keep looking after the little ones. Sālesi was very bright at school, but he turned down an opportunity to study overseas as a dentist. When I completed school, I also turned down a very prestigious request from my school's headmistress to return there as a teacher. You see, there were a few more to care for in the household. Our *kainga* from other parts of the island—mostly from my mother's side—sent their kids to live with us in town and to go to school. There were lots of us in the old house then—the same house Sālesi lives in in Kolomotu'a today. That was the house where we lived with our parents before they died. It's not far from the Royal Palace and just two miles from here.

'Ofa and her husband Langi were married in Nuku'alofa, the Tongan capital, in 1956. They met while they were both working as Church Youth Leaders for their respective village Free Wesleyan churches. They moved to the northern island group, Vava'u, where Langi served as religious minister of the government high school. 'Ofa taught for a few years at the same institution, contributing her modest income—ten dollars per month—toward their growing family, as other Tongan women were increasingly doing in the 1960s. They eventually had eight daughters during the years in which they moved around the Kingdom for Langi's work as an attendant in the Church office. Under the native institution of *pusiaki,* or informal adoption, they also adopted two children. A young girl from a village in Vava'u became their ninth daughter; and Langi's nephew became their youngest child and only son.

Langi was a part-time preacher until he was ordained in 1976 and then 'Ofa had another traditional, work-filled role to fulfill: that of a pastor's wife. In Tongan communities, which are at once religious and moral, pastors' wives assist their husbands in ministering to a congregation. They are often gifted with *koloa* for attending life crisis events in the congregation. As a result they usually have a relatively large stock of *koloa* to use in meeting their own ceremonial responsibilities. Today, in 'Ofa's five-bedroom house in a suburb of the Tongan capital, one room is entirely devoted to storing *koloa,* as are several corners of the house's common areas. Sitting not far from the door to that room in 2007, 'Ofa recounted to me:

> Because of my mother's early death I grew up without knowing how to make *koloa.* Other girls had their mothers, aunts, and older sisters to teach them, but who did I have living here in town with all of our *kainga* in other villages? But I did try to learn *lālanga* [plaiting fine mats] a few years before Langi's ordination, while our little family lived in Vava'u. I joined a *toulālanga* [women's cooperative weaving or plaiting group] so that I could weave together with certain other

women during the day, while my children were at school. I also did *lālanga* during the evenings as well, after I had fed the family and everyone was doing their homework. I would return from the village [weaving] house with a sore back and aching hands. It was such hard work sitting on the ground, bending over, our fingers busy … but our mouths were too. We laughed and sang and told stories. I also learned about caring for the *koloa* and repairing them: adding new [wefts] to parts of my mats if they got small tears, patching torn *ngatu,* and unfolding and sunning both *ngatu* and *lālanga* every few months to kills any insects [that lived in their folds].

Thus, 'Ofa was able to acquire traditional women's knowledge and fulfill the traditional expectation that women engage in production of *koloa* in order to furnish their kin groups' ceremonial obligations. Later, as the wife of a pastor, 'Ofa was pulled into a network of exchange relationships with her husband's congregants and people from the many villages around the kingdom in which they lived over the years. Today many Tongan women stock only a few pieces *koloa* and source textiles by buying them when needed for an unexpected ceremonial occasion. Tina—their youngest daughter, said to me once:

Mum is part of an older guard of women who tend to ensure that they have many fine mats, barkcloth, and pieces of colored fabric in their homes. And because she has stuck to her guns in this way, she has been able to hold traditional weddings for all of us girls … and to present *koloa* to all of our husband's mothers and to the ministers who attended the ceremonies. And she always has some *koloa* to *foaki* [reciprocate] if anyone ever sends her something.

Even though most of her children live in other parts of the ethnoscape—in cities in Australia and New Zealand, as well as in Vava'u—'Ofa continues to care for their social relationships in Tonga by presenting her daughters' husbands' families with *koloa* at key life-crisis moments in their own extended families. In return 'Ofa expects—and has typically been able to count on—her daughter's support in the form of cash remittances from those living abroad, to those children resident in Tonga paying all of her bills, to her children's attendance at ceremonies at which she makes gift presentations, to their helping her sort and sun her *koloa* periodically. There is almost nothing that 'Ofa's children would not do for her, in part, because she has given her life, energy, and *'ofa* to them. Jane Horan refers to such love between a Cook Islands mother and her children as "domestic *aro'a*," or "the love [that] (ideally) exists between a mother and her child, but which is different than the more general *aro'a* expressed in other contexts" (2012:89). Tongan women expect nothing less from their children by way of support and eventual provision, in all realms of life: the material, spiritual, and social.

During my fieldwork, 'Ofa experienced a loss for which no amount of *koloa* could compensate. In February 2001, tragedy struck her family when one of her daughters who lived in Auckland was killed in a car accident, along with that daughter's partner and infant son. Within three weeks all of the immediate family had flown to Auckland to hold her funeral. 'Ofa, Langi, and their daughters were given only one-month visas to New Zealand, and obtaining the visas involved high fees and long waits in lines at the New Zealand High Commission. Tina had barely made it onto the airplane to New Zealand in time. The speed with which this travel and the funeral service were arranged by 'Ofa and Langi's children, who lived in Tonga, Auckland, and Melbourne, highlight how readily Tongan kin group members often cross international boundaries in order to fulfill their duty to reassemble in the interests of their family, motivated by love (*'ofa*) and mutual help (*fētokoni'aki*). As a corollary, it also suggests the high cost, numerous stressful details, and unpredictable aspects that overseas travel and ceremonial arrangements can often entail for members of a family.

Indeed, it was the stress of details that led the family to choose not to accept or reciprocate *koloa* during the funeral rites. When I interviewed them during the days leading up to the funeral, Langi explained:

> It is Malia's soul that matters now. We have to focus on praying for our daughter and on receiving visitors [who come to pray for her], not on spending time and energy at sorting and *foaki* [reciprocation] of gifts. We did not want to do that in Tonga and we do not want to do that now. Besides, our visas do not allow us enough time in New Zealand to *foaki* all the *koloa* and food that people have been bringing [to the house of their Auckland based daughter]. We will have time to *foaki* them in the future … more *kavenga* will happen. We will accept cash now because this funeral is very costly. Besides, we do not have to *foaki* the money right away.

Because of the practice of more delayed reciprocity of cash gifts, they rationalized that they could wait until future life-crisis rituals to reciprocate any money they received at this funeral. They would build up their monetary resources in the meantime. Faced not just with the tragedy of losing a child, but with the challenge of moving resources and gifts between people who are connected as kin across the boundaries of three different nation states, the old couple felt caught in a web of transnational obligations and overburdened by cultural expectations that they would reciprocate in kind all of the valuables they would receive. They made these choices motivated by their grief, and the constraints placed on them by the circumstances of diasporic existence.

As I explain in a more extensive analysis of this case in chapter 5, the repercussions of their decision to not exchange *koloa* and other gifts were serious. Many guests who attended Malia's wake with intentions to present complex gifts of cash and *koloa* were incensed that a crucial portion of their gift—the *koloa*—was being refused. Tina told me during the funeral:

> Dad stands to lose a lot of face because of this decision. Even [members of] our own *kāinga* do not understand Dad's requests for people to take the *koloa* away. But Mum and Dad are only thinking about us [their children]. Only one of us lives here in Auckland, and she would be the one who would have to finish all the *foaki* and go to all the other *kavenga* [life-crisis ceremonies] that happen after the rest of us have gone back to Tonga. And her children are small. It's just too much for her.

Tina's statement that her father could "lose a lot of face" meant that, in attempting to avoid obligations to recognize and eventually (and appropriately) reciprocate all gifts presented, Tina's family would effectively be denying the *kāinga* its reasons for existing as a set of interconnected economic units, not to mention also excusing *kāinga* members from fulfilling obligations, something many people considered a threat to a prevailing notion of "tradition" itself.

In analyzing Tina's statement, however, I wondered how her mother would be affected and wondered why Tina had not considered her mother's loss of face. After all, it would normally be a mother's responsibility to receive and reciprocate gifts of *koloa* on behalf of the family. Even though Langi made the decision to eschew *koloa* on this occasion, it was 'Ofa who would likely be subject to the repercussions of her husband's decision. When a family is unable or unwilling to accept or reciprocate *koloa,* it is the women whom others—both men and women—judge as challenging traditional ways and not fulfilling their role as women and as mothers. The burden of the gendered construction of the reputation of a family—of which women are the "face" (*mata*)—can have more negative consequences for women than for men (cf. Bianco 1991). Collins's caution about celebrating women as culture bearers takes on special relevance here because it urges us to eschew patriarchal notions that tend to restrict women's access to levels of education and public lives that are comparable to those of men (2006:147). In 'Ofa's case, she had given up opportunities to study as a young woman for the sake of raising her siblings, something for which others admired her without necessarily addressing her loss. Perhaps Tina, as a member of a younger generation, did not recognize the gravity of her mother's loss of opportunity to publicly acknowledge her ties to Malia through accepting and gifting koloa at the funeral.

But 'Ofa and Langi's stated point of view, it seemed more practical to accept cash, which would be more immediately expendable, rather than traditional valuables. They wanted to avoid developing further multiterritorial obligations at their advanced age. They wanted to follow what they considered to be tradition, but chose to focus on one aspect of this so-called tradition: prayer. I wondered if 'Ofa was going along with Langi's decision because of his role as the head of the family and former position as a cleric. When Langi spoke to me about his decision, she sat next to him and nodded at his every word, saying nothing herself. She seemed to be doing it as much out of respect for him as out of a conviction about the supreme efficacy of prayer.

'Ofa was clearly practical and flexible in her traditionalism, but she navigated her status as a woman, a wife, a mother, and a pastor's wife very carefully. While able to refuse to engage in gift exchange, she has remained conscientious about presenting and reciprocating gifts in a traditional vein, and continues to present *koloa* gifts appropriate to her relationship to others. Years after the funeral, when I spent Christmas 2007 with 'Ofa and her family in Nuku'alofa, I saw that she was the only one in her immediate family to gift a folded *koloa* to the mother of her youngest granddaughter (see figure 3.2), a fact that was all the more striking to me in light of what I knew to be 'Ofa's firm stance that prayers matter more than *koloa*. The occasion was the first time 'Ofa met the baby girl, who had been named after her own dead daughter, Malia.

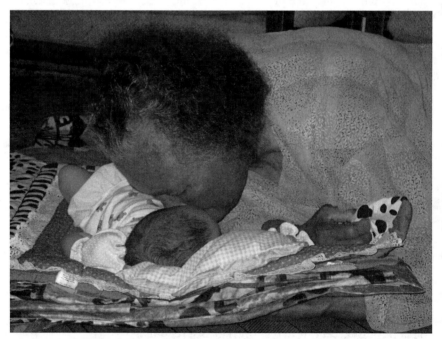

Figure 3.2. 'Ofa kisses her new baby granddaughter, who is lying on a layered 'bed' of a folded *ngatu*, Nuku'alofa.

In time for that Christmas season, all of 'Ofa's children and most of her grandchildren returned to Tonga for a family reunion. She had requested that two of her daughters ship *koloa* to Tonga, along with the large amounts of consumer goods, dried food stuffs, and electrical appliances that they had been putting aside as they planned their trip. Among the things she desired were two large barkcloths of fifty sections each (called *launima*; see chapter 1, table 1) that her two daughters based in Melbourne sent ahead of them in a crate along with the above-listed goods. She showed them to me during my visit in December 2007, while standing at the door of a room in her house that was filled with numerous bundles of folded barkcloth, fine mats, "waist mats" (*ta'ovala*), and baskets:

> One is a *launima* [fifty section *ngatu*] that I sent several years earlier, to Moli [her eldest daughter who lived in Melbourne]. But it's good to have it back since Moli did not use it and my own supply will not last forever. Even this Christmas season, there are lots of weddings and christenings I have to attend with Langi. It does not matter how much money I have—this is Tonga. I must have *koloa* to give too.

During this visit I witnessed her gifting and reciprocating fine mats, quilts, and all varieties of barkcloth (*ngatu pepa*, *ngatu kāliko*, and *ngatu ngatu*) to families in her village.

When 'Ofa's husband Langi passed away in January 2009, she was again prepared with sufficient *koloa* for his burial and for gifts to the other pastors and chiefly individuals whom she expected to attend his funeral. No one disappointed 'Ofa—all of her daughters returned to Tonga and helped her to put on a funeral appropriate to Langi's status as a well-respected clergyman who was also a member of an "older guard" of the Free Wesleyan Church of Tonga. Her task of planning for her own earthly departure completed, 'Ofa today tends to her *koloa* with the help of one of her granddaughters, putting barkcloth and fine mats out in the sun every three or four months. Notwithstanding the potential negative effects of her earlier decision not to exchange *koloa* at her daughter's funeral, she has clearly managed to maintain her family obligations until now, just as she had hoped and planned to do.

As 'Ofa plans for the future of her *kāinga*, she is acutely aware that, despite the fact that only three of her daughters live in Tonga today, their obligations to her and to others will continue long after she herself has passed away. Her main concern has been that her daughters might find it difficult to procure all the *koloa* they need from their distant places in the diaspora. "I respect our customs, but I have to look forward too. I have to *molemole* [soften] things for my own children, who work very hard ... and that is why I have already picked out my clothes for when I'm no longer breathing." Not only was she referring to the outfit she would be buried at her own funeral, whenever that was to happen, but she had also put aside *koloa* for her daughters to gift at and around that occasion. In order to ease her children's burdens in tending to their own cultural obligations—the most important ones being her own death and the death of her husband—she provided ceremonial resources for them. She knew that, through their proper honoring of her—by publicly presenting *koloa*—she would be remembered as a woman who raised her children with correct values and traditional notions of value. It is to this notion of mother in the woman that I turn next.

Obligation and Leadership

Following Tressa Berman (2003), I consider the women leaders I introduced in this chapter to embody the roles of "processual leaders"—individuals who are afforded status based on other people's consensus about the work they have performed in their communities.[3] According to Berman, in social contexts where the gift, and not the commodity or money, is intertwined with central social values, a particular kind of leader often "emerges through reciprocal social relations and community consensus" (2003:83). Often it is elderly commoner Tongan woman who fit the profile of a processual leader. Such women have the authority to flirt with tradition in such ways because they have attained the status of *fine matu'a*—a term that is used to mean elderly woman, respected woman, or mother. While they typically garner and share resources through reciprocal relationships do not simply assume some pre-assigned role as women who bear and rear children. That is, they do more than "bear" the culture. Rather, they often *work* to adapt the system of values, knowledge and practices that mediate the particular socioreligious and political economic situation in which they, their families, and communities must manage every day. As I show below, such women often take on increasing community and kinship responsibilities as they age, or as they or their husbands' or families' social status rises, as happens sometimes due to upward mobility from occupational change. In so doing they evince pragmatic creativity.

Fine matu'a often appear to be highly invested in living by rules of patriarchy that pervade their kinship and religious institutions. Yet their life stories can also help to dispel the discursive framing that Tongans often apply to their own lifestyles and experiences—as either "traditional" or "modern"—and to challenge stereotypes of Tongan social relationships as resolutely hierarchical and the Tongan homeland as culturally conservative (Cowling 1990). Senior women who were born and raised in Tonga, and about whom I write, often consider themselves to be upholders of tradition. So too indigenous women and immigrant women of color in majority white states are often broadly construed as conservative by media and other prevalent discourses. But Saba Mahmood, writing about non-liberal religious movements among Muslim women in Egypt, challenges the common use of terms like "fundamentalism, the subjugation of women, social conservatism, … [and] cultural backwardness," and their treatment of these terms as "facts that do not require further analysis" (2005:5). Similarly, I am wary of readers' possible misapprehension of what might be meant by labeling Tongan women as "traditional" or "conservative." By saying elderly commoner Tongan women are conservative, I mean that the position from which they engage with modernity—the possibilities presented by engaging with Western lifestyles and capitalist economies—is one that is preferentially rooted in older homeland-based practices, but manages to produce innovative forms. I am not suggesting that the women are backward or uninterested in embracing changes in their culture, even if many of their options for distinguishing themselves in their communities include traditional paths to leadership. I am suggesting that Tongan women are guided in their actions by an acute sense of collective expectations, aspirations, and desires that they share with other Tongans. These motivations are rooted in a worldview that sees individuals as connected and interdependent, and that rewards women for their work with effects that they can discern in the lives of others.

Tongan women share these motivations with women in other transnational communities. For example, diasporic Caribbean women tend to channel remittance monies toward education of children and caring for their elderly parents, whereas men may spend money in more "showy" ways, such as building a house in the homeland (Forsyth-Brown 2006; Ho 1993; Fog Olwig 2002). Likewise, Tongan women in diaspora certainly remit money toward caring for relatives in Tonga and also often spend a large proportion of money on the purchase of *koloa* and the public ceremonial gifting of it. Tongan women's roles can be seen as encapsulating what Bourdieu (1977) refers to as "doxa"—a set of mental dispositions—around how *koloa* has been made, presented, and reciprocated. However, here I argue for an understanding of Tongan women as culture workers, but also as agents whose roles amount to a set of diverse ways of doing culture and *langa fonua*, rather than a set of restrictions and "structures" (ibid.). Along with ʻOfa's stories, those of Lina and Kakala exemplify this understanding.

Lina: Complementarily between Entrepreneurship, Transnationalism, and Motherhood

In a transnational situation, nationalist projects are most effective in both social and material terms if actors are able to negotiate a space of recognition and political voice for their community amid the voices of other dominant or native groups. Diasporic communities thus welcome leaders who are workers for the cause of maintaining nationalistic ideals and exemplifying nation-building practices. Lina is the wife of a pastor of the Loto Tonga Church, an offshoot of the larger Church of Tonga, one of several large Tongan Methodist denominations. She also works as a liaison with the host state for immigrant services to benefit Pacific Islanders. Lina deftly switches between these roles in the Tongan community and the larger *pālangi*, non-Tongan, structures of Auckland, and she folds prestige from one role into the other roles she occupies. She also founded several *langa fonua* groups, one of which is still operating:

> The Fauniteni ʻoe Moʻui, the group at my husband's old church, and the one in Tamaki [a suburb of Auckland], I started them all in the late 1990s! I helped all of them complete their applications to obtain funding for materials and for weekly transport to and from their meeting places. It started when I was working in the area of care for the elderly in Auckland in the late 1990s. A co-worker approached me asking me if I had heard that the Department of Labour had some funds to support local community [development] projects. One area was looking to fund projects with a basis in the arts and traditional culture, so I thought about how we use song, [oratory], and handicrafts in our culture. I thought of the *koloa* making in Tonga and I formed a *langa fonua* group of over twenty elderly male and female people from my husband's congregation [as a result of applying successfully for the funds]. The group met in the church hall. The old people were happy to have something to do once a week, instead of being home alone while their children were out at work. They met to sing [Tongan songs] and to work on embroidery together. Some even brought their preschool-aged grandchildren [to babysit]with them.

Over the course of my fieldwork in 2001, I visited with Lina's group regularly during their sessions. In between singing and chatting—during which both the women and the men look after the young ones—the women would knit or embroider pillowcases.

In November 2004, about two years after I had met her in New Zealand, and several years after she had set up these groups, Lina telephoned me and informed me that she was starting another such group for the purpose of making *ngatu pepa*. I was living in Oakland, California, at the time. She said:

> Can you send me photocopies of *kupesi* [the named patterns that are applied to Tongan barkcloth during its assembly] and also some explanations? I know you read about some in books with your research. But we want only the real *kupesi,* Pingi, the ones that they used to use in Tonga. And we will also be able to explain the meanings to any

pālangi who want to know the meanings, because they are always asking and we don't even know![4]

Lina followed this with a sort laugh, and I laughed too, delighted finally to be of some use to an informant. In this conversation she positioned herself as a sort of Tongan ambassador to mainstream New Zealand and a culture worker whose labor must benefit others, not just herself. Supporting women interested in making *koloa* as a nationalistic project plays a role in the rest of Lina's endeavors. She is a mother and an entrepreneur/worker seeking to make a reasonable living for her family and to fulfill her obligations.

In the time that I have known Lina, she has had several different roles in her community and held a range of jobs. Less than a year after our phone call about the barkcloth designs, I ran into her at a Tongan function in South San Francisco, in late 2005. She had been living north of San Francisco with a relative for the previous six months, working in the area of home-based nursing care for the elderly. As she said to me that day: "I have been here working to earn extra money. It's getting more and more expensive in New Zealand, and I still have my old auntie to look after in Tonga. I have to send her money every month. This year I have a big expense—my daughter's upcoming sixteenth birthday [celebration]." Sixteenth birthdays are a key rite of passage for girls in modern Tongan culture. Methodist Tongans ideally celebrate them with a combination of a large, communal feast, dance presentations, gift presentations—including *koloa*—to the key relatives of the celebrant. The occasions afford the young women's families the chance to honor and thank members of their community for support in raising the child and to thank God publicly, as their mothers are particularly obligated to do. In addition to feasting relatives and presenting many of them with gifts of material valuables, the family benefits from prayers offered for them by pastors, and rewards them with gifts of cash and *koloa*. These can indeed be costly events that families will, several years later, follow with twenty-first birthday celebrations, which are held for both boys and girls. Aware of the considerable expense entailed, I asked Lina how much work she had to put into contributing to this expense. She responded:

> My husband gets a steady income as a pastor and we live basically rent-free in the house next to the church, but it's still a challenge to meet all of the expenses. My two sons just got married, one last year, one this year, and we put a lot [of money] into their weddings. And my daughter is not working—she only just finished high school. So earlier this year [2005] I came to live temporarily with my nephew and do some home-based nursing care for an old American couple. The pay is good and I am living with my [nephew's] family. I get Sundays off of work and I can go to church with my nephew and his family.[5]

Increasingly, it is women who are migrating out of Tonga and out of Tongan communities in New Zealand to perform relatively lucrative work (Connell and Brown 2004; Gailey 1992; Small 1997). They remit much of what they earn to families in Tonga and in other parts of the ethnoscape. As stated in chapter 2, Tongan women have remitted more in total cash and commodity value than Tongan men abroad, largely due to the fact that women send remittances more frequently, if in smaller amounts (Vete 1995). Lina presents one model whereby Tongans engage in the international labor market, while also remaining grounded and active in reciprocal practices involving *koloa* and other forms of exchange in their local New Zealand community; indeed the former facilitates the latter. These intertwined practices—travel, earning one's own money, and being successful at kin-based exchange—are all sources of prestige for a woman. However, neither such success, nor her age nor position as a pastor's wife exempt Lina from scrutiny over how she spends her money. Prestige accrues to individuals who use their cash earnings to support what are considered to be Tongan traditional concerns, such as the *kavenga* to celebrate her daughter's sixteenth birthday. Even in diaspora, people prefer being cash poor to being poor in social relations.

It would only be another two years before I encountered Lina again, this time back in Auckland, at the Church of Tonga building where her husband was a new resident minister. It was late 2007, during the New Zealand summer. I was staying temporarily in the home of a Tongan friend who lived near this particular Methodist church. One Sunday, I decided to visit the church to attend an afternoon service and possibly catch up with Lina afterward. As I approached the church from the rear, I was surprised to walk up to numerous boxes of frozen and packaged cassava (tapioca) root covering the entire back wall of the church hall. I ignored this and went in to attend the service. After the service, the church's steward announced that there was an important issue to discuss among the congregation.[6] The boxes of cassava at the back of the church, he explained, had been ordered from a grower in Tonga; the church intended to resell them for income to a New Zealand green grocer, but that establishment had recently rescinded its commitment and the church was left with a hundred boxes of the frozen produce on its back steps. The root crops, which are daily fare in Tongan homes everywhere, were slowly thawing in the summer sun and needed to be distributed quickly. At a meeting that was held after that evening's church service, one particular elderly man suggested that the congregation give the entire shipment away to other churches, free of charge. Later Lina interpreted the murmured response from other congregants this way:

> That man is *fakapiko* [tedious].... He is just trying to add wrong to wrong, and that's [unacceptable]. That's not the right thing to do here. That's not how the church is going to make a profit.... We are in New

Zealand. No one gives us anything for free. And this is not like New Zealand [was] when I first came here in the late 1970s … wages were $51 per week, rent was $25 per week for a three-bedroom house, and milk and bread were ten cents. Can you imagine? Ten cents! It's not like that anymore. … We should just take a few boxes [of tapioca root] each and sell it out to our church members. I am going to take ten boxes to sell to members of my *kalasi 'aho* … I am taking it to the families who did not come to church tonight, and I will ask them to each buy a box.[7]

It was after 10:00 PM and, although the weather had cooled down, the boxes were beginning to look wet from the thawing of the produce inside. For Lina, it was not that bought goods could not be given as gifts, but rather that in this case the situation did not merit a revaluation of the things in question. She saw an opportunity, within this context, to prevent the church from losing hard-earned money while also providing other churchgoers with useful products. Lina added, "I will take these boxes around tonight [to the *kalasi 'aho* members] and they can pay me later. That's the good thing about buying things like this from the church, because you don't have to pay it all up front." Lina took a pragmatically creative stance in this instance and rejected the option of gifting in favor of a market exchange of goods for money, made possible through the Tonga church's own informal practice of credit.

Lina also told me that night that she had recently started her own loan business wherein she makes small loans available to individuals—usually women—for a short period of time at 20 percent interest. For example, she says that if she lends $20, the borrower will return her money with $4 interest the next week; if she lends $50 today, she tends to get back an additional $10 next week. "That's a lot, eh?" she suggested, "but it's for my inconvenience."[8] She said she takes no collateral for the loans, but she stated, with a straight face and a stern tone: "They all know me, and I know them. They have to pay it back." Her borrowers' reputations are the collateral, as they could be negatively affected by any knowledge that they did not repay even the smallest loan. Financing daily expenditures and special occasions sometimes involves an intricate web of debts, loans, work, and gifts that are forged in confidence but whose terms are met with the implicit threat of negative effects on a person's reputation. Reliance on one another for social and economic capital further interconnects Tongans in their local churches and communities, and churches within the ethnoscape are further linked through commercial relations. In this process, Lina and others negotiate the practicalities and pressures of surviving in a capitalist economic system that tends to position them at the bottom, and in which gift exchange has little value. Under these conditions, *koloa* and gift exchange must be carefully engaged in and sometimes even set aside.

Lina is an extremely energetic and enterprising woman when it comes to managing her family's monetary resources, and, from the basis of her position of influence as a pastor's wife, People also seem to trust Lina. She is believed to be discreet with the highly sensitive information about those in the community experiencing difficulty paying a bill or contributing to a life-crisis event, and she uses her position as a pastor's wife to her advantage as a businesswoman.[9] She performs as a processual leader among women through diasporic textile work, through wage earning in many parts of the diaspora, and through money-lending activities, has cultivated a position of being in commercial power in her community. She has achieved this position, in part, by transgressing the patriarchal Tongan construction of women as beholden to and supported by men, be they husbands or brothers. Next, I explore the life of a woman who performs processual leadership and culture work, in large part as a mother, but without having to play the role of a wife.

Kakala: *Koloa* is Material Assurance and New Zealand is Fonua

> I was born in Vava'u [a northerly island group of the Kingdom of Tonga]. I am the second eldest of seven children—I have one brother and five sisters. They all married, but I chose to remain unmarried because, after I saw all my sisters get married, I felt it was my duty to stay and care for my parents. Our father was a pastor. Our Mum had a lot of *koloa* and when I was very young I started watching her and learning how to make and care for *koloa*. I was the one who used to sit at night with Mum and repair mats that had been torn or eaten by insects. She told me all the right combinations—how much for a wedding, a funeral, and so on—and taught me how to fold the *lālanga* [fine mats] and barkcloth in a nice *efinanga* [bundle of *koloa* suitable for gifting].

When Kakala moved from her native Tonga to the city of Auckland in the late 1970s, she worked in a canned fish factory and lived with two of her sisters who had emigrated before her. There, she raised two of her sisters' daughters, women who have three and four children each. "So," she states, "even though I never married, I have children and grandchildren." Kakala remains devoutly Christian, attending church three times a week and regularly donating to the church a large portion of her small pension and the money her grown "daughters" give to her. By the accounts of many people within the Auckland-based Tongan community, Kakala is a shining example of a tradition-conscious *fine mātu'a*. Not only does she concentrate most of her activities within the church, but she also regularly presents valuables in family exchanges and to her church—both *koloa* and cash—thus demonstrating her high regard for traditional roles and responsibilities. She teaches her grandchildren about their cultural responsibilities to mind family and attend church and she says that when she dies she wants to leave them "with the *lotu* [adherence to church] and maybe a little money." As a working-class, immigrant retiree, cash is what she is least likely to have; what little money she does have tends to be spent on buying textiles for use in religious and family functions in addition to making donations to church.

Kakala performs "tradition" by embracing modern practices and putting them into service of activities she considers her most important familial obligations. Each week, she hosts a meeting of her women's group, the Fauniteni 'oe Mo'ui that I introduced earlier, wherein she and several other women make *koloa* and socialize. Her activities with textiles also shed light on how she resolves the apparent epistemological contradictions of living a neo-traditional Tongan life outside of Tonga: she transacts in her emotions, the primary emotion being shame, *mā*. She feels *mā* when she does not have enough *koloa*, but also when she does not have enough cash, situations that often present themselves as two sides of the same coin in her life (Addo and Besnier 2008). For example, she sometimes pawns or sells some of her many pieces of *koloa* when she is "strapped for cash." She finds herself in this position—being poor in cash, but still rich in *koloa*—several times a year. She gains cultural capital—and can show '*ofa* (love) and avoid *mā*—from appearing to be *koloa* rich. This appearance—which is generally a true one, as every mattress in Kakala's small apartment has several pieces of *koloa* stored beneath it—helps her deflect the shame (*mā*) she would feel if others were to find out that she was cash poor. Thus, she is more likely to spend any cash she has on hand on augmenting her stocks of *koloa*, put it toward cash gifts, or use it to provision imminent *kavenga*. Sometimes she prioritizes paying household bills with the money, but I have known her to choose to live without a telephone connection for weeks while she is raising money to contribute to her cultural obligations. Pacific Islander families in New Zealand are often noted for being disproportionately represented among those in great debt for household expenses (Snow, Druett, and Crawford 2006), and this pattern of prioritizing cultural obligations may be one of the main reasons for this overrepresentation.

I became familiar with Kakala's life story when I stayed with her over a six-month period during the second phase of my fieldwork in Auckland, in early 2001. We talked over many evenings about her life in New Zealand: how she struggled to interact with limited English skills in the canned fish factory; how she learned to take the bus only to specific places in town that she wanted to go, such as work and the grocery store; and how, in later years, she preferred walking to a nearby grocery or convenience store to buy milk, bread, and butter for tea on Sundays—activities that remind her of being in Tonga. Hers is a story of efforts to settle into a new and larger land where she felt out of place until she was able to move to a small apartment owned by the branch of the Free Wesleyan Church where she worships three times a week. Her grandchildren visited her regularly—usually every day during the summer and several times during the week while school was in session.

Today, Kakala is in her mid-seventies, is a naturalized New Zealand citizen, and remains the coordinator of *koloa*-related concerns in her large extended family. As in many indigenous communities, certain individuals—usually elders—act as role models for younger Tongans. They take on the important responsibility of ensuring that future generations of the community are able to fulfill their families' cultural obligations through resource exchanges that benefit the community at large. Tressa Berman (2003) refers to such persons as "focalpeople." Kakala is the focalwoman of her family; all of her sisters, nieces, and daughters consult her when they need to arrange *koloa* for a *kavenga* in Auckland. But she gives more than just advice; she keeps a stock of *koloa,* as her mother did, which she uses toward her own or her female relatives' ritual needs. She does this "for free" but feels this culture work is reciprocated with gifts and monetary support from her younger kin and other community members. These gifts both mark and strengthen relationships of debt in which she is entangled, and through which she accrues social capital within her wider kin group and her community. Through these gifts, Kakala embodies a mother—indeed, she emulates her own mother. And this is one reason other she commands her relatives' esteem.

Kakala has done the "culture work" of raising two of her nieces and one of her nephews. As a childless, unwed, older sister, Kakala's had the right to request to raise the children of a younger sibling. The practice of *pusiaki* ("adoption") affords women who are unmarried a chance to raise children and to gain the special status reserved for women as mothers, but it is also, at times, an economic necessity for the child's birth family, who may not be able to afford school fees and other childrearing expenses. She told me in 2001, as we sat in her living room:

> After our parents' death, I asked my youngest sister, Linitā, to let me raise two of her daughters. And I asked her to sponsor my immigration to New Zealand, this was in 1978. While Linitā worked, I looked after the girls, Sia and 'Ana. Linitā had a very hard time—she worked very long hours in a factory after moving here and sending for her daughters to join her from Tonga.

A woman wishing to secure the free labor of a female relative to care for her children will normally approach her own sister, especially if the latter is younger, rather than any of the children's paternal aunts. This is because, in

Tongan culture, sisters outrank brothers and men outrank their wives, so a wife's sister is lower than the requesting couple and, thus, unlikely to refuse the obligation to help her sister. One advantage of such arrangements for the woman raising the children is that she often secures rights as the children's "mother," a form of status that paternal aunts are not shy about pursuing. By this token, a few years later, Kakala asked to raise her brother's son, Sione. If requesting to adopt and raise children is the privilege of a woman's elder sister, it is even more so the right of the father's sister, the person who, according to Tongan ranking principles, is in the genealogical position of *fahu,* or "above the law," in relation to the child. *Pusiaki,* this institution of informal, kin-based adoption has also facilitated out-migration from Tonga. According to Christine Gailey (1992:60), during the early years of Tongan emigration to places like Auckland, emigrating families tended to leave their children in the care of the wife's sister until they were able to send for their children, often years later.

As in other Pacific Islander communities (cf. Horan 2012) mothers hold an unparalleled position in Tongan societies: as the people who teach children to be Tongan, they are endowed with society's greatest responsibility, are highly respected, and are expected to maintain this respectability through gifting (Young Leslie 2004). When she became an adoptive mother, Kakala acquired the rights to receive gifts, and the obligation to reciprocate them. During the life crisis celebrations of her two adopted daughters and her adopted son, she, along with the children's birth mothers, would continually be recognized. Both Kakala and the biological mothers of these children received gifts at the girls' weddings and twenty-first birthdays.

Kakala's sense of obligation towards her adopted children and of having been enriched both socially and materially because of these *pusiaki* relationships is very strong. She continues to engage in reciprocal relations that benefit 'Ana, Sia, and Sione, even though they are now adults with their own children. For example, at 'Ana's youngest child's first birthday celebration in Auckland in 2001, 'Ana requested that the pastor of her church give a formal blessing to the child, but it was Kakala who presented the pastor with a textile gift of a fine mat [*fala;* see chapter 1, table 1], a four-section *ngatu,* and a decorated *kato teu,* a basket filled with store-bought toiletries.

In mid-2009, Kakala made a formal presentation to her adopted son, Sione, and other representatives of the church for which he is a pastor in Niuatoputapu, one of the two most northerly islands in the Tongan archipelago. She made the presentation at the end of Sione's short visit to Auckland to raise funds and to buy building materials for the construction of a new church on his island. Sione received the textile gift—a barkcloth and a plaited fine mat with colored yarn fringe—on behalf of his wife, whose role it was to care for and reciprocate these gifts in the future. In normal remittance behavior, cash and consumer goods move from diaspora to homeland, whereas *koloa* is usually gifted or transferred in the opposite direction. In a relatively rare transfer of textile wealth from diaspora to homeland, Kakala recognized her abiding ties to Tonga, showed deference to a child she helped to raise and who is now her senior in the hierarchy of the church, and conveyed *koloa* through him to Tonga.

In addition, Kakala's material orientations map onto geographical orientations that connect her to Tonga through Sione and through her own brother who lives in the capital, Nuku'alofa. As Sione's "mother," Kakala is expected by others in her community to be humble about her son's achievements, glorifying God instead of accepting praise for herself, and she does this symbolically through her gifts to God and to Sione. With her gift to Sione's church, she added to her reputation as a woman who embraces her traditional womanly responsibilities by engaging in exchange for the benefit of others. Discussing this gift the next day led Kakala to reflect on her life in New Zealand:

> I am very lucky to be living in New Zealand—all of my family is here. With all my sisters here, and all their daughters, and some of those have daughters too, we have three generations, a *hako fefine* [a group of women who descend from the same matriline]. One of my nieces and her daughter are in university studying to be teachers and another one works a big job at that customs office at the airport. We used to struggle, all of us, but now things are better. And the girls can even afford to pay for my airfare to Tonga at least once every two or three years. In the first decade of the 2000s, I returned to Tonga more often than I was able to in the 1980s and 1990s. I love going to Tonga, but I have a good life here, with all of the sisters here and the church in New Zealand as well.

Analysts such as Helen Lee (2003, 2007), Richard Brown and John Connell (1993), and Christine Ward Gailey (1992) have explored identity and attachment issues for Tongans and other Pacific Islanders abroad. The notion of split belonging to only one place—homeland or "hostland"—is not always a familiar idea for all elderly Tongans whom I have met and interviewed. For example, while elderly people in Kakala's congregation usually cite their *fonua*, the land they "come from" as Tonga, many of them have also answered "both places" or "partly here, partly there" when I ask them whether they feel that they most firmly belong in Tonga or in New Zealand. One elderly man I interviewed about his emotional attachment to Tonga and New Zealand said: "my family is here in New Zealand, but my heart is in Tonga." Likewise, Kakala perceives New Zealand as a land that is her home—even if it is not her ancestral homeland—and as a land that, for her, constitutes a meaningful articulation of people and place. She stated: "I think we Tongans have done a lot to *langa fonua*, to help ourselves, here in New Zealand, but Vavu'a [where Kakala was born] and Tongatapu [where her brother currently lives] are my *fonua* also … some of our *kāinga* still live there and our parents are buried there. That is why I go back to Tonga when I can—I am from that *fonua*." Her use of *"fonua"* here could be interpreted as both land and placenta.

In addition, Kakala claims to be deeply loyal to Tonga and to Tongan institutions, such as the church. She returns to Tonga periodically for Methodist church conferences as well as holidays, but she has no intentions of returning to Tonga permanently. She expresses ambivalence about Tonga, even as she espouses it as her homeland. I once asked Kakala if she would ever return to live in Tonga. Her reply was:

> What for? … Everyone in my family is here, except for my brother who has his own family in Tonga, in Kolomotu'a [a suburb of the capital, Nuku'alofa]. Already one sister is dead and she is buried here. I want to be near her and my other sisters for as long as I can. That means I am here to stay. I get lots of good things from here too. … Life in Tonga is good, but who would look after me if I went back to Tonga? My *pusiaki* are here in New Zealand, and their children. I am here because they are here.

Such answers reinforce the notion that *fonua*, the articulation of the meaningful place and people, conditions diasporans' attachments to both Tonga and the diaspora in complex ways. Diasporans actively transform a new homeland into a *fonua* through their fulfillment of responsibilities through *koloa* exchange, as well as through institutions like *kāinga* (extended kin group) and church to which these exchanges contribute. For practical reasons, Kakala actually prefers to live in the diaspora and does not intend to return to the Kingdom of Tonga to live permanently. Her closest kin are diaspora dwellers, and she can also receive more adequate healthcare and can better finance her religious and kin-based duties in diaspora. Her response above underscores the tensions wrought by the political economy of family and religion on people's sense of "loyalty" to a given nation-state. While diasporans relish visiting Tonga and maintaining contact with kin in the homeland, the material and social conditions that help people feel at home in diaspora also result in a somewhat fraught relationship with the idea of return migration (Connell 2009a, 2009b; Kingma 2006; Liava'a 2007; Maron and Connell 2008; Schoone 2010), even when it comes to *koloa* exchange. Thus for Kakala, New Zealand is perhaps the crucial node in her multi-territorial Tongan *fonua*, as it affords her expanded possibilities for engaging in exchanges that help her maintain a particular level of prestige while also maintaining proximity to family and other relations.

Gender, Place, and Wealth in
Transnational Identity Constructions

'Ofa, Lina, and Kakala have nurtured three large global kin groups and have contributed to the collective *langa*, "building up," of a multiterritorial nation. While they fluidly cross national borders in fulfilling their kin-based roles and responsibilities, they distinguish between the forms of valuables that are appropriate for exchange in specific communities and nation-states comprising the multiterritorial Tongan *fonua*. 'Ofa maintains that part of Tonga's distinctiveness as the homeland is that, while cash is acceptable, *koloa* is indispensable in exchanges there. To her, using cash as ceremonial wealth in diaspora is more acceptable than not using *koloa* in Tonga. However, 'Ofa has also had to navigate gendered expectations and the pressure of tradition in the diaspora because she has had to attend several important ceremonies in New Zealand and in Australia. My analysis of her history is not merely centered on how she performs *langa fonua* in diaspora, but on how she performs or embodies the role of woman and, especially, of mother by being pragmatically creative. This includes her deploying modern valuables like money in gift exchange and to access synthetic raw materials to make *ngatu pepa*.

Like Lina and Kakala, 'Ofa is a woman dedicated to upholding traditions, but she has expanded the territory over which she can source *koloa* and applies pragmatic creativity in executing her cultural roles. A pragmatically creative approach grounds her role as a processual leader in her community. In particular, 'Ofa seems to demonstrate her loyalty to Tonga as a homeland by continuing to dwell there, even though her daughters, on whom she depends for income, live overseas. However, she keeps particular nodes of diaspora central in how she manages materially and symbolically to maintain a Tongan identity. Thus, multicentricity is also integral to her identity.

All three women show some preference for keeping the wealth that they brought into the family by maintaining relationships through gift exchange in the form of *koloa*. In one sense, this is a way of displaying their wealth, since large stocks of *koloa* indicate that one is entangled in a robust network of relationships of debt with other people and, thus, provide some sense of one's influence over others. At the same time, keeping wealth in non-cash form forestalls requests for money, because relatives who cannot discern how much cash a person has are less likely to ask to "borrow" money.[10] Kakala's story exemplifies another way in which commoner women apply pragmatic creativity in doing *langa fonua*. In this vein, she renegotiates the diaspora as a place of tradition through her work making *ngatu pepa*. Finally, Lina's continual mobility and multicentrism—the simultaneous orientation to different spatial locations—reflects a traditional mode of social orientation for Tongans and other Pacific Islanders (Francis 2009; Hau'ofa 1993; Ka'ili 2008). At the same time, her multicentrism is also necessitated by the modern political economy of global labor markets.

So these women's life histories are as much about how exchange helps them to participate in modernity as they are about the women's desire to maintain practices that others will recognize as "traditions." Kin-based activities seem to conflict with more modern practices like commodifying traditional valuables and participating in global labor. Indeed, while doing this research, I often felt that my informants' identities embodied ambiguities and contradictions. For example, Lina's many community-based duties as a pastor's wife contrasted sharply in my mind with her money-lending practices. She seemed to depart most markedly from the traditional female role of being a continual supplier of gifts and someone whose husband would provide for her. She even traveled abroad, leaving her husband to do his ministry without her daily support, during which time she was also out-earning her husband.

Commoner Tongan women have always been at the forefront of overseas travel (Gailey 1992) and pastor's wives are no exception among Tongan women who must shift, in fluid ways, between their statuses as wives, mothers, sisters, and daughters. The apparent contradictions between these prescribed female roles and women's daily modes of meeting responsibilities are closely tied to their embeddedness in local and global economies that do not discriminate between these various roles that women play in their kin groups and communities. Indeed, as Dorinne Kondo (1990:47) states, women's lives are often "mobile sites of contradiction and disunity." I prefer to think of elderly diasporic commoner women I have met as accommodating roles that have a certain "fluidarity"—a term Teresia Teaiwa (2005) uses to index processes of creating contexts for solidarity that also incorporate fluidity between multiple social roles and social situations. I would add that "fluidarity" applies also to people moving between geographic locations while nurturing relationships across those spaces, and doing with no small degree of adaptability to the challenges entailed in navigating differing material, social, and political contexts.

A feature of this current global moment is that huge numbers of women participate in global labor movements that enable them to earn additional money for their families' livelihoods (Trager 2005). Such women often willingly shoulder the responsibility of becoming entangled in relations of debt and obligation that stretch over long distances in order to perpetuate "traditions." However, they do not always benefit directly from their own labor. They do the hard work of making and sourcing valuables, and of distributing gifts and reciprocating them often quite selflessly, but with little material reward. So, unfortunately, family and cultural pride can also provide "proof" of a woman's role as a culture bearer, thus limiting her agency. In this sense, the experiences and concerns of diasporic commoner Tongan women parallel those of third world and diasporic women globally, for across cultures and socioeconomic classes, women who are attentive to their kin-based spatial relationship regularly participate in the global economy with their families' well-being as a goal. Indeed their roles in their often patriarchal native societies ensure that they continue to be the people who ensure the well-being, education, and future prospects for their kin, which often means that they spend money earned in the diaspora on people other than themselves. This basic inequality in the lives of women who thus devote themselves to their families, and who are called to do so by "tradition" needs to be acknowledged, even when the women in question embrace their own sacrifice with pride and love and gain no small amount of prestige therefrom.

Conclusion: The Role of Tradition in Transnational Tongan Modernity

The case studies offered in this chapter capture some of the crucial ways in which commoner Tongan women are able to nurture transnational kin groups through *koloa* exchange and related practices, obligations, and relationships as these are affected by the conditions of diaspora. These three women's stories illustrate that diasporic women are able to move between the demands of their multiple social roles, which so often also includes moving between far flung places. The women have contributed to a confluence of monetary and kin-based exchange networks that stretch between homeland and diaspora in order to finance their obligations in any one part of the multiterritoria *fonua*, negotiating traditional expectations and the exchange of *koloa* in the process. They have often done so using *koloa*—or the value inherent in their association of *koloa* with other things of value—to meet the economic and social demands of modern life.

This chapter also explored how such women perform traditional Tongan gender roles despite what, in their culture, might be perceived as limitations of being unmarried or dependent on men who themselves make relatively marginal earnings in both homeland systems of exchange and global labor markets. Earning money through textile-related work provides the women with monetary resources that they, and not men, control. Women often channel money toward other pursuits that they believe will improve their and their families' standard of living; among these are travel costs to visit relatives and donations to church. For commoner Tongan women, however, earning money also seems to involve subordinating their own ambitions and desires. Like other women from developing countries in diaspora, so much of the daily struggle during their younger and middle-aged years had been around making ends meet by participating in an impersonal labor market, and they have often made their own health, education, and leisure secondary to the needs of the family. As elderly women, mothers, and grandmothers, however, commoner women have the time and have developed a type of traditional reciprocal resource base and enhanced social connections to put into motion a preferred form of wealth, *koloa,* whereby they can also perform *langa fonua.*

Regardless of physical location, living lives ensconced in and embellished by *koloa* is not only something that commoner Tongan women are required to do, but that they can do, and that they often prefer to do, to help themselves and their families thrive. Together, 'Ofa, Lina, and Kakala's stories afford us expanded ways of thinking about women's agency in the spatial relationships constituted by family, about how place does not always map neatly onto the location of "traditions," and about the role of movement and fluid orientations to place in modern identity constructions. Their multicentric orientation is not simply a byproduct of their particular experiences of modernity; it is actually a result of their maintaining traditional connections, doing the work of kinship, and strategically executing their role as culture workers and as mothers.

Notes

1. In *Between the Folds: Stories of Cloth and Lives in Sumba,* Jill Forshee (2001) weaves together eloquent and moving histories of a community whose late-twentieth-century economic survival economy is highly dependent on women's production of handwoven and dyed textiles called *ikat.* Using her informants' life-history narratives, Forshee is able to construct images of local exchanges, affiliations, and textile aesthetics on Sumba, an island in Indonesia, and the ways that these forces intersect with local politics and global circulation of ikat.
2. In a recent survey conducted by the New Zealand Ministry of Women's Affairs, 230 women of Pacific Island ethnicity were interviewed in order to inform policies and projects to improve economic development of these ethnic communities throughout New Zealand. Tongan women seem to have been the majority of the survey respondents. Thirty-eight percent of respondents said that they "took out a loan either from a bank or a finance company, to cope with financial difficulties" (Koloto and Sharma 2005:5).
3. Berman (2003:82) distinguishes between processual leadership (aligned with ceremonial leadership)and categorical leadership (a form of political leadership) as the two main forms of informal political positions that she recognizes in American Indian tribal politics. Processual leadership is also a feature of Polynesian societies, where generalized and balanced reciprocity strongly shape daily economic relations and are integral to how people live their modern lives.
4. As discussed in chapter 1, many commoner women today are less invested in the specific histories and meanings of the *kupesi,* or designs, on *koloa,* even as they remain devoted to the production and aesthetic enhancement of the textiles with new designs and alternative materials.
5. For many reasons, Tongans find it prestigious to visit and live in the United States, even temporarily. See Helen Lee (2003), who refers to the United States as a preferred destination. See also chapter 2 in this book. Living with relatives while performing

temporary work in the diaspora is a fairly common practice because it allows the visitors to save on rent and other expenses, and affords them more disposable cash to remit to relatives elsewhere. An important aspect of *anga faka-Tonga* is to interact meaningfully with kin members—indeed, to put one's family, and its members needs and interests, before oneself—thus migrant Tongan individuals often prefer to work in places where some of their kin group members live. Kin also help new or temporary immigrants to settle into a new town or country, and introduce them to neighbors, friends, and fellow congregants. Some Tongan churches also provide assistance with finding housing and work.

6. An important role in Methodist church congregations is that of the steward. In Tongan congregations, the steward is normally an older male congregant who is already well off financially and whose work it is to see after the non-spiritual affairs of the congregation, to coordinate the activities of church groups, and to ensure the general upkeep of the church building.

7. *Kalasi 'aho* is a group comprising four or five immediate families who belong to the same congregation and whose primary responsibilities include arranging their constituent families' annual *misinale* (periodic lump-sum cash donations to the Methodist church) presentations.

8. The signing of loans by Tongans, using their cars, appliances, or even homes as collateral is common in both New Zealand and in Auckland (Snow, Druett, and Crawford 2006), and I have met very few Tongan families whose members have not, at one time or another, engaged in this low-level, high-interest borrowing in the face of a sudden, high-cost obligation. Being unable to source money when needed to finance traditional obligations is an extremely shameful position for a Tongan family to find themselves in. Moneylenders and pawn shops who make cash available at high interest rates like 25 percent make exorbitant profits off immigrants like Tongans who are unlikely to be lent money by banks or who find walking into an institution designed for and run by Westerners to be daunting. Similar businesses dot the landscape around Nuku'alofa in Tonga (Addo and Besnier 2008).

9. A pastor's wife is usually as revered as the pastor himself, because of her husband's status in the community. The status and *mana* (spiritual power) associated with this iconic couple render them somewhat apart from congregants, even though they are all commoners (van der Grijp 1993). Members of the congregation rarely approach a pastor's wife to ask for favors or to *kole pa'anga,* "ask for money," as they might a friend or relative. By the same token, a pastor's wife may be the guest of honor at a congregant's ceremonial occasion, such as at the *'a'āhi* (display of *koloa*) that I mentioned in chapter 2, but , unless it is her family's event, she will rarely be "down in the trenches" preparing food or distributing gifts at the end of the ceremony.

10. Ilana Gershon's research among Samoans living in New Zealand and California (2001 and 2012) and Parker Shipton's work among Gambians (1995) present two other ethnographic cases of people in recently monetized economies who find empowerment in concealing the amount of money to which they have access.

🎵 4

Gender, Kinship, and Economics
Transacting in Prestige and Complex Ceremonial Gifts

The obligations inherent in the bonds of family are the reason that Tongans engage in the often complex and challenging processes of financing kin-based exchange, now under conditions of a globalized world largely controlled by capitalist exchange. Anthropologist Ilana Gershon (2007) calls for a reconceptualization of the scale of diaspora, suggesting that diaspora is not simply happening on a global or regional scale, but also at the level of family. Diasporic communities develop because people move or relocated between different branches of a kin group, a reorganization of family across national borders. In this chapter, I build on Gershon's conception of (Samoan) diaspora as a change in family scale and, sometimes, in the relations that comprise family (2007), to address the crucial role of maternal *kāinga* (extended family) in the multiterritorial Tongan nation. I analyze the amplification of gift exchange that typically results from people organizing and executing kin-based ceremonial events in a dispersed diasporic territory. As I have argued in preceding chapters, rather than curtailing the practice of traditional-style rituals in favor of Western forms of expression of kinship and community, living in diaspora affords agents a chance to intensify certain aspects of how they perform Tongan tradition and to participate in global nation building. Since one of the key acts of tradition and nation building is gift exchange, and since increasing numbers of Tongans live in or are being born in diaspora, gift exchange has become a more multicentric process—one in which more people are interacting as co-ethnics via networks that comprise more people and encompass more places.

From the perspective of Tonga and the Tongan diasporic communities I studied, nation building involves the intensifying and widening of material exchanges, political allegiances, and social and other bonds between ethnic Tongans, regardless of geographic location. Here I concentrate on the role of exchange in Tongan nation building, where nation building can be defined as the expansion of the spatial relationships over which Tonganness, and in particular Tongan kinship, is practiced globally. I suggest that, despite where they were born, where they are located, or how frequently they visit the homeland, Tongans in diaspora preferably negotiate their belonging in the nation through *multiple* forms of exchange. These include sending remittances; gifting valuables; socializing children into Tongan culture; hosting relatives from Tonga for what can often be long visits; and sending children to the homeland for school holidays, to be exposed to "the culture," or to be educated in the infamously "strict" disciplinary regime of Tongan schools (Lee 2009b).

The series of short case studies that I investigate in this chapter illustrates how people can contribute to *langa fonua* by the exchange of ceremonial gifts within and between their kin-group members. I explore how a nation—a "site" that does not necessarily exist as a contiguous space, but that is nevertheless objectified in processes of nationalism—can continue to be actively constructed and augmented by people of multiple generations, in dispersed locations, using material culture. Like the elderly first-generation women introduced thus far, members of the second and 1.5 generation in diaspora embrace a range of options to express and explore their allegiance to tradition and to the homeland. In particular, I highlight how they connect and reconnect with others through kinship bonds and social obligations that people actualize through the gift, focusing on the exchange of what I have called complex ceremonial gifts of *koloa,* prestige foods, and cash. The gifts are most often exchanged in the context of *kavenga,* which literally means "burden." These obligatory kin-based life crisis rituals are sites for cultivating reciprocal obligations between Tongans, as well as fostering acts of *langa fonua* and generating feelings of allegiance to Tonga. The *kavenga* I examine here are a traditionally styled wedding, a first birthday, and a church donation event, all of which are formal contexts for the flow of gifts between family, Tongan friends and neighbors, and the church (through the clergy)—three of the most important social institutions in Tongan culture.

Commoner Women and the Tongan Family in Transnational Perspective

The *kavenga* I consider in this chapter highlight a system of kinship ranking whose history and meanings have been heavily debated in recent anthropological literature. Christine Gailey's history of Tonga (1987) is a detailed consolidation of the extant written sources on Tongan kinship and its historical relationship to the formation of the modern Kingdom of Tonga. Prior to sustained European contact in the early nineteenth century, the kin-based system of exchange was pre-eminent in Tongan society and social relationships were controlled by notions of rank. Sisters ranked above brothers, elder ranked above younger, and husband ranked above wife, but mother's kin ranked above father's kin. Kinship codified the rules, and roles, of production within which commoner women were entitled to call on resources from their brothers

(Kaeppler 1971). Gailey argues that, through this ranked sibling system, commoner women had long been advantaged in kinship. They became disadvantaged in the emerging capitalist state formation of the mid- to late-nineteenth century. After Taufa'ahau I created and ascended the Tongan throne in 1875, certain chiefs of hereditary estates who were loyal to this monarch, and who associated with his foreign allies, were redubbed nobles and granted control over particular tracts of land that included villages and their inhabitants. With use rights to land being consolidated in the strata of society that eventually became known as nobles, control or ownership of the means of production became synonymous with rank above commoner status (Lātūkefu 1974).

Commoners continued in their role as workers but with an important change in women's status, especially when monogamous marriage became tied to property and land rights that were granted only to men. Meanwhile women continued to "possess" their *koloa*. According to Gailey (1987), because women's rank within families remained ambiguous after European contact—that is, women's high status as sisters was in tension with their lower status as wives—it was to the advantage of both members of the nobility and men of commoner (*tu'a*) rank to "demote" commoner women to the status of mere workers in families. With the encroachment of a capitalist market in the early nineteenth century, wage work, whether for men or for women, according to Gailey, was eventually codified under the rubric of *ngāue* (work; men's wealth) and thus, was not associated with women's power and influence (*mana*) in the way that *koloa* had been before (ibid.:205). Kerry James has strongly criticized Gailey's position, arguing that Gailey has conflated work and ownership of labor and asserting that commoner women retained a strong sense of ownership over their own labor and the material products of that labor even when circumstances prevented them from continuing production (James 1988). Therefore, especially after "emancipation," neither men nor elite women could have presumed to have rights to textile *koloa* that commoner women were making. Whereas Gailey suggests that women today regularly perform *ngāue*, James suggests that women's identity continues *through koloa*, which is a category of treasured objects *because* they are generated by women.

My ethnographic evidence supports James's claim that commoner woman have persisted as the owners of *koloa*, custodians of the important cultural knowledge in relation to these valuables, and defenders of their gendered rights to the value of the objects through the complex system of reciprocity within which the women exchange them as gifts. A key point in my argument throughout this book is that, despite the historical changes in Tonga's religious-political system and the challenges of living in modern capitalist consumer states today, commoner Tongan women were *not* transformed into a class of people whose *identity* was defined by reproducing the nation—through child bearing, for example—or by alienating their labor. Indeed, commoner women have continued to affirm their identities by retaining important cultural knowledge and exclusive rights around *koloa* even while they have moved to other places and engaged in other economies to work for the good of their families. Thus, *koloa* have remained the unique purview of Tongan women and the embodiment of women's *mana* in ritual contexts. *Koloa* encodes "what one values" (Herda 1999:149), and women value their *mana* and womanliness. In the following section, I highlight the efforts to which diasporic Tongan women often go to ensure that they have "the right" *koloa*—adequate combinations of appropriate forms of textiles—to exchange publicly at a kin based celebration.

Tonganness, Value, and Prestige in the Gift

A major feature of being a successful agent in the political economy of Tongan ceremonial exchange is the ability to allocate one's family's resources between immediate sustenance, current and imminent gift-giving needs, and potential reciprocations. In Tongan household economics, different types and schedules of reciprocations are considered appropriate for different material forms of gifts. Gifts of long yams, pigs, frozen meat, and other important food items are usually reciprocated almost immediately, as are gifts of *koloa*. The reciprocations may be equal in value to the initial gift or they may be somewhat smaller. In either case, the reciprocations accomplish one major role of the gift in Tongan culture: to recognize the work, labor, love, and generosity of the presenters of the initial gift (Ka'ili 2008). Gifts of cash are reciprocated on a more delayed schedule and typically not until members of the gifting family are observing their next life stage ritual event.

This practice of differential reciprocation of cash and traditional valuables persists in the Tongan diaspora, and the demand for *koloa* is increasing throughout the Tongan ethnoscape. Indeed, *koloa* exchange allows diasporic Tongan women to have unique forms of influence over people beyond their immediate kin group, village, and island. Access to and knowledge of how to gift *koloa* are forms of cultural capital that Tongan women convert into respect and status in their communities through exchange.

Yet, modern valuables matter as gifts, too. Knowing how to gift modern commodity objects is also a source of respect and status, as is appearing competent in use of those objects. However, buying expensive items to give away—and even purchasing the relatively cheap toiletries that women include in their decorated baskets today—is not within every woman's easy reach. It requires disposable income, of which commoner Tongans generally have very little, given the economic structure in most of the places they live: low wages, high costs of living, and the many *kavenga* that arise for them. I contend that the uncertainty of being able to demonstrate modern competence in this vein is part of the reason that numerous homeland- and diaspora-based Tongan women are generally unwilling to entirely embrace Western genres of valuables in lieu of *koloa*.

Commoner women have a history of "Tonganizing" non-Tongan valuables such as store-bought cloth and bedding, machine-made quilts, and knitted blankets (Herda 1999), and Western toiletries using them to augment their handmade traditional-styled textiles for ritual presentations. This simultaneously displays their pride in being Tongan and their right and capacity to augment the size, value, and aesthetics of the category of objects that they consider to be the supreme Tongan valuable: *koloa*. There is value in maintaining *koloa* as their quintessential gifts *and* remaining its main definitive purveyors. Thus Tongan women continue to produce *koloa*, and are also instead creating and introducing "new" forms, such as *ngatu pepa*. These "new" textiles would have been impossible to develop without the kin-based network of women who were continually thinking of ways to increase their access to *koloa* in diaspora and homeland communities and who sent materials like vylene (Addo 2007) and completed textiles such as quilts (Herda 1999) to support the textile work of kinswomen in their villages of origin in Tonga.

Weddings: The Gift and Gendered Identity

Traditional-style commoner weddings are seen as upholding Tongan traditions and are modeled after contemporary chiefly weddings, in which *koloa* plays a central role. For instance, commoner women typically dress the bride in their families' best and oldest *koloa* or display these textiles while they or others present speeches at certain points during the marriage celebration. As they do in chiefly ceremonies, these *koloa* embody the history and the power of the lineage through which they have been passed down (Kaeppler 1999). Maternal and paternal relatives both have a responsibility to ensure a happy and materially secure future for the celebrant to whom they are related. In Tongan kinship terms, people who are related to the celebrant through his or her mother's kin group are considered lower in rank than the celebrant, while those on the father's side rank above him or her. This ranking system affects the form, size, and symbolism of gifts presented at the wedding, as does the notion of how a gift giver's status may change when she is known to have presented a gift of particular value at a *kavenga*. This is, not least, because being able to affect a person's standing in the community is crucial in a system where, despite rank, prestige can be enhanced by the respect and *'ofa* that others show to that person by, for instance, proffering ceremonial gifts.

In the wedding I consider here, women of the bride's mother's matriline (*hako fefine*) were compelled to use gifts to recognize traditional differences in rank between themselves and the groom's mother and father, and their respective *kāinga*. While gifts do not affect actual rank, they can symbolically raise the esteem of the gifters in the eyes of others. Because they presented their gifts publicly, the women of the mother's matriline were effectively able to mitigate their low status vis-à-vis the groom's kin. This further highlights givers' material advantage in accruing prestige, and material and social obligation from others through the gift.

Kin-based obligations to uphold and secure the bride's standing are important even in preparation for the wedding. Parents whose daughter is about to get married tend to hold much stock in being able to demonstrate their confidence in her suitability as a bride—especially with regard to her having remained a virgin, having the skills to run a home, and being able to manage the daily affairs of a family. Despite the fair number of Tongan children who tend to be born out of wedlock in Tongan communities inside and outside of Tonga, the ideal of a girl's virginity being highly prized continues to be upheld. The public discourse is that a girl should not "shame" her family and "break her mother's heart" by engaging in pre-marital sexual intercourse, even though many do. Those who do may well be forgiven if they *do* get married, and a wedding provides a context for a mother's setting in motion gifts of *koloa* to indicate her (renewed) support and love for a daughter. It is a mother's duty to care for and watch over (*tauhi*) her daughter and to encourage her to maintain her virginity until her marriage. By this token, *koloa* encodes associations with the bride's procreative power: women's bodies produce offspring, their work produces children with culture and also produces textiles, and children and *koloa* are a woman's dearest treasures. Indeed, children are sometimes referred to as *koloa,* which can be parsed as things of value produced by women (Young Leslie 2004).

During my fieldwork I was often told that the girl's side usually "loses out," or presents more gifts to the groom's side than it receives at the rituals involved in commemorating a wedding (see also Young Leslie 1999). This statement mirrors some discussion of other "losses" that ensue when a daughter gets married: her labor—devoted to both household tasks and making *koloa*—and her child-bearing capacity are "lost" to the groom's family. The idea that a bride's side loses value in marriage exchange might be seen as an acceptance of the negative reciprocity that seemingly exists in Tongan gift exchange: it involves the investment of a great deal of value, even if there is no equivalent return of value. But this imbalance hinges on the inequality in the kin system, in that the bride's maternal kin perceive themselves as having an obligation to "push up" (elevate in status) the girl who represents them among her new affines (Young Leslie 2004). Indeed, the bride's relatives often bring to the site of gift exchanges extra barkcloth, fine mats, store-bought bedding, and patterned fabric so that they might be sure to augment their gift if it does not meet or exceed what the groom's kin appear to have brought to gift. This "pushing up" (*fakalangilangi*) of the recipient kin group is a material act: in elevating the relative status of the groom's *kāinga* by giving more gifts, the maternal side seeks to secure their reciprocation in the form of love and protection for the bride and her future children among the groom's family (ibid.). The large gift also symbolically raises the esteem of the bride in the eyes of all around, showing her—and thus her family—to be worthy of love and respect from all assembled.

Another aspect of gift exchange at Tongan weddings concerns the house and valuables of the couple. In the agrarian economy of Tonga, where men inherit rights to land, the groom and his family usually provide the house, while the bride's family sends her to her new abode with as many of the necessary furnishings of an adequate home as they can provide. Ordinarily, a bride's natal family will purchase, at the very least, a bedroom set to start the new couple out in their home. However, it is not uncommon for them to load up a truck with a dining table and chairs, a living room suite, crockery sets, even a washing machine, and a certain amount of *koloa* to deliver to the groom's or the groom's parents' house on the night before the wedding.[1] Members of the bride's extended family—both maternal and paternal—assemble outside of the house and process, sometimes dancing, into the house, each with an item in his or her hands. They gift the items, deliver speeches, and stay for refreshments. This tournament of value is a thinly veiled challenge to the groom's kin to present material wealth on the wedding day. Kin and friends gathered around to witness the delivery of the bride's "trousseau," and when people recount the wedding, they always discuss this pre-marriage delivery.

Part of this delivery process emulates the practice among *'eiki* (chiefly or royal) Tongans of supplying certain kinds of textile *koloa* folded in a particular configuration labeled "the marriage bed" (see figure 4.1). These *koloa* are customarily added to other mats on which a wedding couple would spend their first night together after marriage. Today, commoner brides' families present *koloa* that is also called the "marriage bed," *mohenga mali*, to the groom's family, in addition to a Western-style bed.

During the early months of my fieldwork in Auckland, I attended the pre-marriage festivities of a soon-to-be-wed commoner couple that included preparations of the marriage bed. The night before the formal Christian marriage ceremony at a local Tongan Methodist church, I watched as two plaited mats and a folded black-painted barkcloth (*ngatu 'uli*) of a length of ten hand-measured "yards" were placed on the floor in the couple's new townhouse to comprise the marriage bed. The couple would not actually spend their first night together on this arranged marriage bed of *koloa,* which took up practically the entire floor space of the tiny master bedroom in their new townhouse. In a layering arrangement typical of Tongan inclusion of traditional and modern

Figure 4.1. A Tongan noblewoman instructs commoner women on folding *koloa* for a *mohenga mali* (marriage bed), Kingdom of Tonga.

forms, they would sleep on the Western-style bed that the bride's maternal kin brought in and had assembled right on top of the bed of *koloa*. The wooden legs of the Western-style bed were thrown slightly off-balance by the deep layers of soft, yielding traditional textile below.

Not only was this remarkable to witness—why two beds, one might ask—but it also illustrated a particular symbolic practice of layering. As I have argued elsewhere (Addo 2003), the Tongan practice of wrapping or layering textiles either on the body or when heaping them on the floor for presentation as gifts, can be read as a material translation of ideas about rank: wrapping the body in waist mats (*ta'ovala*) that have been layered over Western clothing positions the more powerful textile forms on the outside, where they can help contain the *mana* of the wearer's ritually charged body (ibid.; see figure 4.2). Likewise, in bundles of textiles readied for gifting, more highly ranked textiles are often layered on the outside of lower-ranked forms, as in the folding of a barkcloth within a fine mat such as a *fala paongo*. Layering *koloa* on the ground also have the effect of *fakalangilangi,* "pushing up" that which sits on top of the textiles, enhancing its status and making it the focus of everyone's attention. In her work on plaited *koloa* on Ha'ano Island in the Ha'apai region of Tonga, Heather Young Leslie (1999) describes how parents enhance the status of their children whose first birthday they are celebrating by seating them on folded

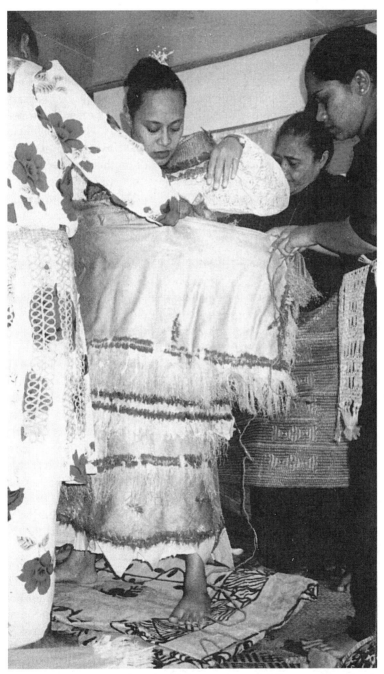

Figure 4.2. Wrapping a bride in several outer layers of fine mats or *ta'ovala*. She also stands on a folded *ngatu*, Nuku'alofa.

koloa. Adrienne Kaeppler (1999b) describes in similar terms the elevation of a bride and groom who are seated on a dais of folded mats in a chiefly wedding and also the placement of the casket of the late Queen Sālote on twenty-three named fine mats. The layering of the bed on top of *koloa* effectively elevated the status of the Western bed to a valuable appropriate for Tongan gifting. Also, as it does for an envelope of money resting on top of folded *koloa* when both forms of wealth are gifted publicly, the *koloa* draws attention away from the "foreignness" of bed resting atop the Tongan cloth.

The strategic and prominent placement of *koloa,* even when it made the bed unsteady, suggests the *'ofa* (love) of the bride's mother and her *hako fefine* to members of the groom's *kāinga*. *Koloa,* more than any other form of valuable exchanged at a wedding, is fundamental to the *kavenga* in that it attests to a Tongan woman's commitment to fulfilling her gendered and kin-based duties as a mother. The groom's family bears the economic responsibility of raising the children, the married couple typically reside virilocally with the man's parents or in their village, and the new bride and her children will usually attend the groom's family's church. The bride's family, for their part, and particularly her mother, must guarantee the bride's value as a mother and wife. As a future mother of children from the new union, the bride is assumed to have learned her mothering skills from her own mother. By contributing resources toward outfitting her daughter as a proper wife, the bride's mother, typically with the assistance of her natal family, shows in material form that she is highly invested in her daughter's performance as both a wife and mother, and has therefore also taught her daughter well.

Maternal *kāinga* is not only or necessarily a line of material inheritance, but is instead always one of value, with the particular features of nurturance and solidarity in social *and* economic senses (Young Leslie 2004). Due to the kinship-ranking system, it is to a mother's social advantage to present *koloa* that recipients and onlookers will consider beautiful, and of high quality to the groom's father's eldest sister, or all of his sisters, who will be the highest ranked relative(s) in relation to the daughter's future children. But the value that gifting accrues for both giver and recipient is not primarily material. Instead, things deemed suitable to a particular special context are often referred to as *faka'ofa'ofa,* meaning that the value of the forms in question lies in their ability to materialize and inspire *'ofa,* which is an appropriate response to things that are pleasing to the senses and the sensitivities. The bride's mother and kin customarily facilitate the public presentation of the gift, and thus the public recognition that the bride's *kāinga* is unwavering in their support of the young woman. The following case study highlights how one woman's maternal *kāinga* financed and staged an extravagant wedding for her, and consequently "pushed her up" in a variety of ways (ibid.).

"Like Legs on an Octopus": Kinship and *Kavenga*

'Ana hugged and kissed me when she picked me up at the Auckland airport on 26 December 2001. Speaking quickly and excitedly, she said:

> Welcome home, Pingi ... but too bad you did not make it before Christmas. ["Elina's"] wedding was great ... but we all worked so hard that we sort of ignored Christmas. We just sat around Olivia's [her eldest maternal aunt] house and ate and slept. ... I tell you my mum is lucky that she has six sisters, although one is dead now ... they are all like legs on an octopus ... when you see one of them you'll see them all together helping out. ... I do not know what they will do when another one of them dies.

'Ana is one of Kakala's "daughters" and it was her aunt Talanoa—Kakala's sister—whose daughter had just got married. As we drove toward Kakala's house where I would stay for the next few weeks, 'Ana excitedly described the dancing and feasting on the wedding day, the unusually large amounts of *koloa* her aunt Talanoa gave away to members of the groom's family and how lovely her cousin, the bride, looked.

Because I had missed the wedding events, Talanoa, the bride's mother, made a point of showing me a video of the gift presentations that she made to members of the groom's *kāinga* at the three days of formal wedding celebration for 'Elina. The first was the *fa'alealea,* a joyous, joking celebration that sometimes doubles as a sort of delayed engagement celebration. It took place on the evening before the wedding, but a few days after presentation of household goods, which I will discuss below. That evening, Talanoa and members of her maternal *kāinga* presented *lei* made from candy strung with ribbon and colored cellophane wrapping that they had stayed up the night before making themselves in one of Talanoa's sisters' living rooms. They presented the *lei* to everyone who came to the *fa'alealea,* and made Elina sit on the lap of her one of her paternal aunts, who was in the ceremonial position of *fa'e huki* ("mother who raises one up"—a member usually, but not always, female of one's maternal *kāinga*). Her fiancé did likewise, seated on the lap of his *fa'e huki*—a man from his maternal *kāinga*. Then everyone watched as Talanoa presented some of the *koloa* she had prepared for the groom's family along with formal speeches and prayers.

This part over, the women on 'Elina's side let out loud ululations, and pulled her fiancé to his feet. At the *fa'alealea,* the bride's family controls the proceedings, and will typically accost the groom and other men in his family. Indeed, a key scene on the video came when one of 'Elina's female cousins threw her fiancé into the swimming pool at the back of the house. Everyone—

both on camera and off—roared with laughter as they watched the young man swim to the edge of the pool, pull the crumbling candy *lei* from around his neck, and accept the towel that another of 'Elina's sisters offered him. This sort of clowning can be construed as a ritualized challenge to the authority of the husband's side (who, again, normally occupy higher rank). Clowning at rituals—often of a suggestive and sexualized form that is not at all encouraged in daily public interactions—is a long-standing, if temporary, leveling mechanism in Pacific societies (Hereniko 1995). The evening's antics ended when everyone shared a large, late meal of meat, boiled root crops, potato salad, cakes, and soft drinks.

There would be two other days of formal celebrations. The first was the marriage in Talanoa's Methodist church with the bride and groom dressed in Western wedding gown and tuxedo respectively. The photographs of this event were packed with people, as the twenty bridesmaids and groomsmen squeezed into the frame after the ceremony for photographs; there was also a video of the event. This ceremony would be followed by a large reception in a rented hall in South Auckland. There were several wedding cakes, only two of which would be carved for guests; the others would be gifted away. Six pastors were invited as special guests and seated at a table at the head of the room for the meal at the reception. The other wedding observance would be the "First Sunday" when the couple would appear at church for the first time as a married couple, dressed in formal Tongan attire of very special waist mats over stitched white clothing. No *koloa* would be exchanged on the First Sunday, but as the bride's mother, Talanoa would treat the entire church congregation to lunch at a nearby buffet restaurant, thus ending the formal period of her presentation of wedding-related gifts.

The Source and Value of Gifts

Talanoa smiled as she described the gifts of cloth, pointing at them on the screen and naming the people who had gifted them at the wedding. She remarked that, now that the wedding was over, she had begun to reciprocate or "answer" these gifts, a process called *tali holo* ("answering the flow [of gifts]"). She was doing so by taking *koloa* and food to the homes of those who presented her with *koloa* at the wedding; she had begun doing this within two days of the wedding celebration. She explained that receiving gifts from friends and kinspeople before the wedding is their way of helping her meet the expenses of feeding guests and preparing gifts for key members of the groom's side. She would completely answer the gifts over time, by gifting more *koloa* and food, and also some money, when these same friends and more distant relatives would celebrate weddings and funerals in their own immediate families.

Talanoa also told me that, over the course of all the wedding events, she had given away NZ$100,000 worth of *koloa,* cash, and other goods to her daughter's future sisters-in-law. When I remarked that this was a very large sum of money and asked how it felt to amass that much wealth, only to give it away, she beamed and said, "It was a lot of work and I spent a lot of money … but, oh, it was worth it." As I listened, I learned that she did not spend this money all from her own pocket. She had saved some, but she had also spent time in the previous year-and-a-half receiving and collecting a fair proportion of this money from friends and relatives who had owed her a reciprocation over the years. She had also relied heavily on her own sisters and other members of her maternal *kāinga* to finance and put on this wedding. Besides helping Talanoa plan for the wedding, her four sisters had all donated large amounts of cash as part of their sisterly obligations to her *kavenga* and, especially, for *kavenga* that center around her daughter. Talanoa's youngest sister gave $1000, her second youngest sister gave $1000 and her eldest two sisters and a female cousin gave a total of $1000. Her son also gave her some money and thus contributed to the gifts of the maternal *kāinga.*

'Ana had rightly said that the senior generation women in this maternal *kāinga* were connected and interdependent, like "legs on an octopus." Each woman's gifts were imbued with the power to affect the others' abilities to accomplish gendered duties, family duties, and to help assure further spiritual protection and positive social reputations for their shared kin group. At the same time, Talanoa was not obligated to reciprocate these gifts she received from very close *fāmili* members, but she did reciprocate some of their support and good will with *koloa.* I was at her sister Kakala's house when Talanoa and her son drove up with a Samoan-styled *kie* mat—its fibers darker than those of Tongan *kie* mats, indicating age—to present to her. Kakala mentioned this reciprocal gift many times over the next few weeks, to anyone who visited or called, emphasizing that Talanoa had given her this gift "because of 'Elina's wedding." The *'ofa* between herself and Talanoa and her *'ofa* for 'Elina were implied in this brief explanation, as was Kakala's family's increased prestige due to the wedding that many described as *faka'ofa'ofa.*

At the time of 'Elina's wedding, Talanoa was sixty-five years old and had been resident in Auckland for over twenty years. In mid-2001, she made her first trip to Tonga in over five years, in order to ensure that she was well provisioned for her daughter's marriage. She was the wife of a deceased pastor in the Free Wesleyan Church of Tonga, the daughter of another, and the granddaughter of a famous nineteenth-century Fijian Methodist missionary to Tonga. Even before traveling to Tonga to obtain what she called "the best *koloa,*" she had arranged large amounts of textile wealth that she either commissioned from Tongan women in the islands or that she asked relatives in Tonga to purchase with funds she had been sending to them. During this trip, Talanoa also visited with her maternal and paternal relatives, and with her late husband's relatives, across their respective villages. "All they could talk about was the wedding!" Talanoa told me. Obviously, they held a lot of stock in the event and considered it of high value. Their reputations would also be affected by how well Talanoa could use gifts to show her love and gratitude to both God and kin.

Talanoa said that just when she was leaving Tonga, some of these relatives presented her with gifts of other *koloa faka-Tonga*. These were primarily reciprocations from debts that these relatives owed Talanoa for gifts and remittances she had been sending them over the years. Presumably to keep these relations of obligation going, or because she was bound by further obligation—such as to her brother, who lived in Nuku'alofa whose house she always stayed in when she visited Tonga—Talanoa presented some of these people with what she called "small gifts" of cash. "It was just my way of helping out … something you're supposed to do when you go back for a visit to Tonga," she explained to me when I asked if the small cash gifts were further payment for the *koloa* she had ordered ahead of time. As she and I chatted, it became clear that even these small, inter-family exchanges had the potential to further obligate these homeland kin to lend their support to 'Elina's wedding and to future *kavenga*. Talanoa was secure in the knowledge that she could have asked a relative to send her extra *koloa* or feast foods if she needed them as the date for the wedding drew nearer.

Finally, 'Elina also made a contribution to her own wedding by buying several living room sets from her own earnings and savings. She said that she had a duty to help her mother keep up the reputation of their family. 'Elina was able to forego some of the home furnishings that, in other circumstances, her mother would have provided as part of her trousseau because her middle-class Tongan-New Zealander fiancé's home was already fully and richly furnished—he was a semi-professional rugby player. Instead, Talanoa presented furniture suites, *koloa,* and cash gifts (of about NZ$2000 each) to three of the groom's sisters who lived in Auckland. The two sisters of the groom who lived in the United States received more portable gifts of *koloa* and cash. These gifts—especially the gifts to 'Elina's affines who live in the US—are evidence of Talanoa's sense of family as a multicentric web of relationships spread across several parts of the diaspora. Through her gifts to them, Talanoa felt a greater assurance that these women, who would be the future grandchildren's highest-ranking relatives, would respect and protect her daughter and any children she would bear.

The effects of gifts to affines in a bilateral kinship system such as Tonga's can be read as both material and symbolic. In their form—money and consumer goods—they are embodiments of modernity; in their interpretation, they encode tradition. In terms of value, what matters in the gifting of these household items is the buying, as much as the gifting, of items that represent modernity. As I suggested in chapter 3, coupling consumer practices with, or discursively coding them into acts of traditional gifting, may be seen as creating contexts in which others legitimate a woman's desire to engage in modernity and to distinguish herself in additional ways. While tradition holds discursive sway in Tongan gift-exchange practices, acts of tradition are not devoid of references to, or engagement with the materiality of modernity.

The fact that members of Talanoa's community would reflect on the gifts in discourse and memory was also highly instrumental. The event, and the gifts that constituted it as a site of value, marked her as a conduit of large amounts of costly and globally dispersed valuables. The capital Talanoa spent on these gifts constituted social capital—influence on others such that she could call in debts they owed to her, economic capital—the cash she had saved or funneled towards the wedding, and cultural capital—the sense of hew knowledge around how to manage all of these responsibilities such that the wedding itself came off with the right balance of material, spiritual, and emotional elements. Her expenditure of these other forms of capital were, in part, reciprocated by her accruing of social capital in the form of her enhanced reputation in her community. I interpret her statement that "it was a lot of work … but it was worth it" to be an assessment of the labor, carefully planned interactions, and machinations that it took for her to garner debts, save money, buy and transport furniture, *koloa,* and other valuables, and to keep track of the accounting of all of these valuables. In "spending" $100,000 on gifts for others around her daughter's wedding, she had played the role of a conduit for valuables that she estimated amounted to this sum. What is more, she had played the role as a conduit of Tongan values: into her execution of the wedding event, her kinswomen, friends, and family had put their hopes for the perpetuation of Tongan values in the world today.

The acts of gifting related to the wedding served as articulations about value, and specifically Talanoa's sense of the worth, or value, of her own actions. As David Graeber states, where gifts create and maintain social relations, value can be described as "the way people represent the importance of their own actions for themselves: normally as reflected in one or another socially-recognized form" (2001:47). I read Graeber's meaning to be that the value of a gifted object encompasses the gift giver's sense of the worth of her presentation of that gift assessed in cultural terms, or in the eyes of others. Thus, it is worth examining the idea of "worth" that Talanoa espouses in her statement above. Both she and her daughter 'Elina knew that their community—both local and global—was expecting them to perform their duties as commoner women of high religious social status, and they felt that they had to make it a "big wedding." Their and their kin group's reputations were tied up in the gifts that Talanoa would present at her daughter's wedding. The more guests whom she could feed and present gifts to, the more she could show her love to

God and kin, and the more others would value the wedding as a sign of this love— all of these things would enhance her particular status as a commoner of distinction. So, in saying "it was worth it," Talanoa was making a statement about value. She knew that the worth of her expenditures would be realized as she continued to receive gifts and other forms of material support from her community over time. This material valuation aside, she was already realizing the symbolic value of her actions—a particular sense of fulfillment—because she had kept up her maternal family's name both by gifting appropriately and by marrying her daughter to an eligible young man and in a manner befitting someone of her status in community of Tongan commoners.

Space, Time, and Value in the Diasporic Ceremonial Gift

In analyzing Talanoa's motivations in giving such costly gifts at the wedding, we need to consider the role of diasporic space, along with the role of time, in gift-exchange strategy. The exchange of the ceremonial gifts actually began months before the three formal wedding rituals I outline above, encompassing multiple nodes, or established communities in the ethnoscape. Talanoa also received most of the contributions that her kin and friends in Auckland would make to help her finance the wedding long before the actual wedding day. These gifts—called *holo*—were delivered to Talanoa's home on the Monday and Tuesday before the wedding. She described these gifts as having two purposes: they were customary at a wedding and they symbolized love and compassion from the givers, of whom Talanoa said, "they feel *faka'ofa* to [sympathy toward] 'Elina … because her father died already." Some relatives who lived abroad and could not attend the wedding arranged for *koloa* or envelopes of cash to be presented on their behalf by representatives who lived in or had traveled to Auckland.

Talanoa told me that gifting to the groom's sisters—the paternal aunts to the couple's future children—was crucial to her in particular, and that through these gifts she was upholding "tradition" and of "doing things the right way." As indicated above, I offer a more instrumental interpretation: as the future children's highest-ranking relatives, the aunts are also the people who, culturally, should have the greatest prerogatives to make decision in the children's lives. It was therefore important to appease them with gifts (Bott 1982; James 1997; Filihia 2001; Kaeppler 1971; Rogers 1977; Young Leslie 1999). Moreover, by presenting these gifts for which she seemingly expected no material return—wanting only the devotion of her future grandchildren's paternal aunts—she engaged in what Bourdieu (1990) might call the work of time. Bourdieu draws parallels between the gift with a challenge to someone's honor in Berber society: neither can go unanswered without loss of face to the recipient. The response is bigger than the challenge or the initial gift and has the effect of keeping the initial challenger or gift giver indebted to the other party. Bourdieu further suggests that the strategy of allowing time to elapse between receiving and reciprocating is "intended simply to neutralize the action of time and ensure the continuity of interpersonal relations" and further obligations (ibid.:107). Talanoa hoped for a lifetime of support for her future grandchildren from their paternal aunts. Thus, she gave as generously as she could, effectively "neutralizing" or laying hold of the time that would elapse before such grandchildren were born, even as she challenged these women to do right by those very future grandchildren.

By gifting valuables that would travel over great geographic distances, Talanoa also worked across the space of family, widening the circle of obligation to which she would traditionally have been entitled. She widened the geographic scope of her kinship bonds as a way to transcend space, which is a phenomenon of the multiterritorial Tongan nation that emerges through diaspora (see Gershon 2007). The creative use of the resources from different economic and cultural environments across the diaspora also demonstrates the importance of space and location in Tongan relationships and culture.

Second Generation Dilemmas in Life Ceremony Observances: To Gift or Not to Gift?

'Elina's first cousin 'Ana was singular among the women of her *kāinga*. She generally withheld money gifts from the church, and she did not attend church with her mother, aunts, and two sisters. Moreover, though she contributed money, time, and labor toward putting on 'Elina's wedding in late 2001, 'Ana had a history of not contributing to the church obligations of senior women in her family. For example, she did not contribute to the gift that her aunt—who was also her adopted mother—Kakala, made to a visiting pastor (described in chapter 3), even though others in her family considered it an important moment of pride for their family. At first, I thought 'Ana's refusal stemmed from the fact that she had recently stopped working as the night manager of a video shop and might have been strapped for cash; I had actually heard her telling her mother and aunt, the previous week, that she and her husband had "no money" after paying her household bills and buying her two older children some new clothes for the summer. However, she later told me: "I'm not going to give [the pastor] money and food and *koloa* just so he can pray for me more than the others. And my Mum and aunties think they'll all get into Heaven faster that way. Well, he's supposed to pray for everyone. That's his job."

Increasingly, there is a discourse in which Methodist Tongans express hardship at regularly being able to afford the large cash gifts required of them

for church donations called *misinale* (Besnier 2011). In diaspora, some mainstream church members say outright that they refuse to remit cash (Lee 2004).
Tongans in diaspora are primarily working class and many of them have at
least one family member who is a relatively recently arrived immigrant, and
who thus has neither the local cultural knowledge nor the opportunities to
become a viable economic contributor to household costs and church obligations. In New Zealand, about half of Tongans live in state housing, and
one-third of them receive some form of government aid. The demands of the
church pose huge challenges to these families' pockets and a number of FWC
members in New Zealand are voting with their feet by shifting denominational
affiliation to non-Tongan churches.[2]

'Ana and her husband have followed this pattern. They were both born
in Tonga, but raised from a young age in New Zealand. As they needed all
of their spare cash for raising their three children, they tended to be careful
to spend their money primarily on necessities, saving some for emergencies
such as the basic costs of funerals, and only rarely contributing to large donations such as the annual Tongan church *misinale*. Soon after their marriage in
the early 1990s, this young couple began attending a mainstream Methodist
church—one with a majority *pālangi* (non-Tongan) membership where there
was no prescription to donate in the amounts that are considered minimally
respectable in Tongan Methodist congregations.

They perceived this move as allowing them to restructure their commitments, while affording them greater control over their budgets and their
time. It is one of several strategies for articulating traditional economic activities with the kinds of behavior needed to cope with the financial and social
challenges of living in a post-industrial consumer society. Diasporans who
switch denominations for this reason are also likely to disengage from remittance sending. Breakaway Tongan Methodist churches have been developing
since the 1980s, usually because of some political disagreement with the main
Church in Tonga (Brown and Middlebrook 2001; Makisi 1992). These newer
Methodist churches tend to maintain *misinale* gifting, however. Such gifts are
crucial in shaping the flow of resources between people in different transnational communities and, thus, to their sense that they are building a multiterritorial nation, a space over which they can engage in Tongan practices and
realize Tongan values. As with all institutions, these flows are, in one sense or
another, out of specific individuals' control.

Yet 'Ana attempts to exert her own sense of influence over the outflow of
her earnings. She claims that she never sends money specifically to relatives in
Tonga, although she is sure that some of the money she gives to her mother
and other senior women in her kin group in New Zealand gets remitted to
Tonga. Here she admits to her own inadvertent participation in remittance
sending of the kind Helen Lee (2009a:17) calls "indirect transnationalism"—

when parents request money from their children and then send that money to the homeland as part of a gift for another purpose. Lee (2004) analyzes the implications of even subtle changes in amounts of remittances, and in another work analyzes second-generation Tongan diasporans' decisions about remitting, or refusing to remit directly (2009b). The reasons for the latter often stem from a sense of disconnection from, or discontent with how Tongan elites are running the kingdom or spending its money and how "rich" clergy seem to be getting off the donations from their mostly poor congregants. While such opinions do not result in large recorded numbers of 1.5- or second-generation diasporans switching denominations per se, they could, over time, have serious effects on the political economy of the Tonga's politico-religious system.

Being affiliated with both the *pālangi* (mainstream) and Tongan (Methodist) churches afforded 'Ana a chance to avoid the expectation that she would annually present *misinale* to the church. While she avoided spending more money than she felt she could afford on costly *kavenga,* she said she "always attended the important family things," that is kin-based events that her maternal *kāinga* held at the Tongan Methodist church near Kakala's home. So, while 'Ana's approach to gifting money was seemingly non-traditional, it is also a reminder that remittance sending is a highly contingent and negotiated process.

Kāinga, Gifts, and "Face" as Second-Generation Concerns

Certainly Tongan individuals like 'Ana may assume the agency to act individually in gift presentation and reciprocation, but they also often desire to be associated with gifts that their *kāinga* present collectively. The collective concern and responsibility to ensure material and social continuance of kinship is still an important motivation for Tongans' participation in the global economy and the means whereby they realize the value of their work in this system. In Tongan communities, both mainstream and marginal churches play a key role in weaving together the threads of what Peggy Levitt calls a "moral economic fabric" (2009:1228), facilitating the public gifting of both ritual gifts, like those presented at the wedding above, and one-off gifts, like the one that Kakala presented to 'Ana's pastor on New Year's Eve.[3] Yet it is important to note that, as a 1.5-generation member, 'Ana's way of dealing with her family responsibility to do the work of kinship, to finance group gifts, and to remain a practicing Christian involves a confluence of strategies that might be described as reweaving some of this fabric's threads. Having been "socialized directly and indirectly into the asymmetries and disjunctures inherent in the transnational social field," as Levitt (ibid.:1231) says of members of the second generation, 'Ana engages in a form of wealth negotiation for each event. Even though she and her husband attend the *pālangi* Methodist church together, she continues to negotiate her own channeling of wealth toward her natal, or maternal, kinship purposes.

Indeed, natal kinship ties continue to greatly influence a Tongan individual's willingness to contribute to gifts, even when that person also has newer kinship affiliations. As noted previously, women marry into their husband's family and often worship in the same church congregation with them, but they also maintain very close material and emotional ties with their sisters and their sisters' children. They thereby ensure the proper execution of ceremonial obligations, which are embedded in kinship relations. This was the basis for Talanoa's confidence that she could execute a large, expensive wedding for her daughter, its high costs notwithstanding. In addition, Talanoa and her sisters felt that they had to continue to uphold their reputation as members of a deeply traditional and devoted family, so they presented gifts valued over and above those they expected to receive at the wedding. Like other commoners, diasporic Tongan women gain much capital—both materially and in terms of prestige—by doing the exhausting work of staging a large, kin-based celebration.

These networks are both the reason and the means through which a woman works to finance such obligations: by maintaining relationships in the network, she can potentially garner more resources for gift exchange; and by publicly exchanging gifts, she incurs the material obligation and implicit support of others and strengthens her status in the networks. Prestige is her reward; it is a form of social capital that a woman accrues by transacting with her community in ways that affect her reputation. The transactions take place through her public gifts. *Koloa* do embody value—materials, history, and work, as well as womanly *mana* and motherly *'ofa*—but public gift transactions with *koloa* also afford a woman social capital, and here is where the value potential of the textiles lies. Before a textile is gifted it has the potential to distinguish its owner; but once presented as a gift, a textile affords the giver social capital. In the presence or retellings of others, this capital can be further transacted for cultural capital that becomes encoded into the giver's reputation, as well that of her kin group.

An important point about capital, underlined by Bourdieu (1986), is that it is often (only) recognized in a social system as legitimate competence, because people's actions are valued as symbols of the actors' innate social value in particular contexts. Indeed, Tongans will normally attribute competence in gifting as arising as much from emotion as from competence. They see properly executing traditionally styled *kavenga*, and presenting appropriate combinations of food, cloth, and cash in a complex gift, as an expression of a woman's *'ofa* (love), thus perpetuating a discourse that makes the emotion *'ofa* the source of properly executed—or carefully calculated—acts that embody tradition.

Tongan observers also critically monitor those whose group members do not contribute to collective kinship gifts or who do not attend events. Showing up is itself read as a sign of support for *kāinga* and community, as well as a sign of devotion to Tongan tradition; failure to show up, literally or figuratively, indicates failure to invest time and *'ofa* in performing one's Tonganness and is considered shameful. "Shame" (*mā*) is an emotion that Niko Besnier and I have theorized as being the motivating force behind gifting (Addo and Besnier 2008; see also Besnier 2011), and it can be mitigated if one publicly gifts valuables at an event. As Besnier notes (2011:255 n.4), *mā* operates in tandem with another dominant emotion, "love" (*'ofa*). The threat of being judged *mā* certainly gives one pause if one is considering *not* gifting toward one's *kavenga*. A person and her *kāinga* are judged "shameful" (*fakamā*) if she fails to make a presentation where others expect it of her. Her shame is attributed to her being ignorant of custom or, worse yet, to her ignoring it. Alongside this monitoring of gifting competence as a valuable characteristic, there are also some situations in which competence can lead to jealousy. While they will certainly view generous gifting as a sign of the kin group's material fortune, Tongans are also always on the lookout for those who "cross the line" between devoting enough resources to exemplify *'ofa* and spending more than is necessary or than they can afford. Tongans see this over-expenditure as a sign of the giver's desire to show off or be uppity (*fie lahi*) (Besnier 2008), emotions that also incur *mā*. The person who is so judged is regarded as unconcerned with the Tongan way which involves not showing others up. Thus, the tension between *'ofa* and *mā* must always be managed in gifting.

There are numerous ways in which the family's reputation can be affected at such events. Second-generation youth members often stand in groups socializing outside the main hall where the event is taking place. For them, it is enough to be seen, but not directly involved unless someone in their kin group needs help with a specific task, such as carrying in large bundles of *koloa* or cases of food during an event. Their presence, a visible contribution of support, adds to the family's public image, to the extent that not having numerous family members present to perform even these simple, yet publicly witnessed tasks, can foil the efforts of a senior kin-group member. However, the financial contributions of second and 1.5 generations are even more important, as it is even more shameful when the family does not have enough money to donate at an event. Because these later generations often outearn or outnumber first-generation members of their families, their cash contributions are currently the mainstay of diasporic Tongan ritual events. Warnings about decreases in remittances notwithstanding (see Lee 2009a and b, for example), analysts will have to monitor changes in overall spending patterns—including the financing of public ceremonial events and the sending of remittances—to fully substantiate claims about changes in the intensity of second and 1.5 generations' allegiance to the homeland.

Mother's Love and the First Birthday Gift

The daily economics of 'Ana's life, and not just her ceremonial expenditure, are affected by her self-identity as modern and independent, and as a daughter conscious of kinship obligations and invested in her mother, aunts', and cousins' happiness. Her abiding sense of family obligation means that, even though she had a history of trying to follow a non-traditional path of individual capital accumulation, she could often be prevailed upon to contribute to church in indirect ways. She felt a sense of fulfillment whenever she provided material and moral support, in the process of marking crucial ritual moments in her maternal *kāinga*. Around deeply important ritual events that stand to benefit the entire kin group, even fiscally conservative Tongans may quite willingly express the principle of gifting with which they were raised, especially if it conditions their standing as parents—and 'Ana was a mother. Indeed, when 'Ana's youngest child reached his first birthday, 'Ana volunteered to gift cash to the church in order to ensure the receipt of blessings for her immediate family, and she embraced her aunt's and her mother's more traditional way of commemorating this life ceremony through gift exchange.

A child's first birthday is one of the first and most important of commoner Tongan life-transition events (Young Leslie 1999). Agnatic kin relate to the child according to whether they are on the child's father's side or mother's side. They often send gifts of cloth and cash to high-ranking family or community members in the child's honor and to ensure spiritual blessings for that child. Sometimes, gifts received by the child's parents in honor of a birthday are redistributed and put toward gifts for clergy. The reason typically given for this redistribution is that it further helps to ensure "social and spiritual well-being" for the child (Evans 2001:133; Young Leslie 1999).

So when 'Ana's infant son Samuela turned one year old in early 2002 she seemed willing to follow the principle of reciprocity (*fēfetongi'aki*). She explained her temporary change of opinion about giving gifts to the pastor like this: "I'm lucky Samuela was born healthy and has had a good first year. He deserves a blessing as he has his whole life ahead of him. That means that it's time to take him to the pastor." The significance of the maternal *kāinga* in facilitating life transitions arises again here, as 'Ana embraced this act of "public mothering" (Horan 2012) and unquestioningly and gratefully supported her mother's and aunt's efforts in securing blessings for her child. 'Ana had made a choice to engage in an exchange of cloth and cash specifically because she could secure a culturally crucial blessing for her son while acting in solidarity with the rest of her maternal kin. 'Ana's particular complex religious convictions are also highlighted here. Even though she and her husband eschewed regular attendance at their parents' Tongan Methodist churches, she retained positive associations with the worship practices of her maternal *kāinga* in the context of her children's spiritual well-being.

On the weekend that little Samuela turned one, 'Ana, Kakala and Kakala's sister Eva—the baby's biological grandmother—and their family dressed him in a brand new outfit, and took him to be blessed by their pastor at the pastor's house behind the church. Representing their *kāinga,* the three women presented the pastor with their gifts of a cut piece of *ngatu* (provided by Kakala) and a $100 cash gift in *sila pa'anga* (an envelope of money, literally "enveloped money"), provided by 'Ana. Coincidentally, another family was also there with their one-year-old son. They too had come for blessings from the pastor. 'Ana had said it was to be a private ceremony, but several relatives from each child's *kāinga* were present, many milling around outside near their cars. The ceremony was a short one: the pastor blessed both children separately—essentially telling them each "may God bless you and make you strong, healthy, and obedient children"—and then he prayed for them together, his hand on both boys' heads. After leaving the pastor's house, 'Ana smiled almost continuously and kissed the little boy as she held him close, saying to me, "I am so happy Samuela got such a good blessing … it's because [the other one-year-old boy's mother] was there with her boy too … it meant Samuela got double the blessing he would have got we had come by ourselves." Kakala smiled, too, and it was clear why. By implication, Kakala also received a blessing through the public recognition that she had nurtured 'Ana as a child, shaping her into the woman she had become, and making it possible for her to bear and rear three children in the Tongan way.

For the children of migrants, the public recognition gained by participating in such events results in feelings of pride and sense of belonging to the family, ethnic and church community, and to the multiterritorial Tongan nation. These are palpable rewards for fulfilling their responsibilities in kinship to uphold the family's social obligations and reputation (Gershon 2007; Lee 2003; Hong and Pyong 1999) and to provide both children and opportunities for their elder relatives—people to whom they owe their lives—to be publicly recognized and honored. Even when members of the 1.5 or second generation living in the hostland express ideas about ceremonial gifting that depart from those of their parents—often expressing their own participation as personal choices to which they are entitled—they remain painfully aware of how their choices affect their parents' and elders' sense of self-worth or value and of how public gifting and reciprocity present inherent avenues for enhancing this sense of value. They can also justify to themselves that they are being good parents as well as good children—showing *'ofa* and affording others the chance to show *'ofa*—if they make the "right" choices to help their elders accrue prestige.

On Spiritual Rewards: Gifts with No Material Reciprocation

In chapter 3, I mentioned Kakala's voluntary gift, in early 2008, to a pastor from a northern island of the Kingdom of Tonga, who was on an extended visit to her congregation in Auckland. Bestowing gifts on guest speakers at her church is nothing unusual for Kakala, as she regularly volunteers to prepare a formal gift for a congregant who gives one of the many opening-year sermons to her church as part of her congregation's New Years' services. At the beginning of 2002, I also witnessed her presentation of a complex gift of food, cloth, and a cash offering for one such speaker. She told me that the gift helped ensure blessings for the church congregation and, especially, for her *kāinga* (see figure 4.3). For this, Kakala had saved $500 from her winnings over several months in a weekly cash pool she was involved in with several other Tongan women. She also contributed some *koloa fakatonga,* and her five sisters each donated some foodstuff such as tinned corned beef and eggs. Two of her nieces also transported the *koloa* from her house to the nearby church hall for the presentation. It was a time of pride for their family; everyone pitched in. All of Kakala's sisters, their children, and grandchildren were present, seated in various corners of the church hall, as if to show support for her from all sides.

The complex gift of money, food, and *koloa* that Kakala presented was an embodiment of the worth of her actions to the community and to the ultimate judge of all human actions, God. Her actions defined her as more than a Tongan individual and a Christian; they defined her as a woman and a gift giver. The specific importance of her actions lay in the fact they could be culturally decoded, by others in her community, as a sign that Kakala had engaged in the cultural principle of reciprocity (van der Grijp 1993) and that they were witnessing this action. Interestingly, Kakala received no tangible gifts in return for her gifting. However, the pastors who prayed aloud that evening repeatedly asked God to "bless Kakala and her *kāinga*" for her exemplary act of devotion to God and to the Church. Indeed, Kakala believed her act established a direct connection to God. As a spinster and therefore also as a virgin, according to common understanding, she described herself as a woman who has "devoted her life to prayer or church" (*tauhi ki he lotu*). In response to the clergy's pronouncements about her generosity and exemplary womanliness, Kakala said out loud *fa'afetai,* her voice choked with emotion. The term *fa'afetai* suggests her general gratitude for the opportunity to present, as she said, such a "small gift." After the event, when onlookers commented on the beauty of the *koloa*

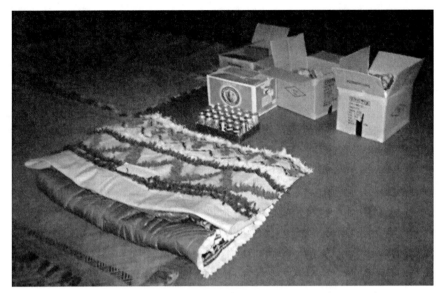

Figure 4.3. A complex ceremonial gift of *koloa*, money (in white envelope on top of *koloa*), and food (in boxes to the rear), Auckland.

she presented, she simply stated, "it was [my] duty" (*ko e fatongia*), or "it was [God's] grace" (*ko e kelesi*).

The reciprocation, in other words, was given to her in and through God's presence. But she could not convincingly experience this presence on her own. In Tongan communities, church ministers are placed in the position of mediators, or "bottlenecks" between God and people (Evans 2001:142). As discussed earlier, clergymen (*faifekau*) are responsible for invoking the blessings of God on a congregation and on the *kavenga* events of families in that congregation. Because status among commoner Tongans is fragile and contested (Besnier 2008), laypeople—specifically women—are empowered to transact in particular forms of value, one of which is perceived closeness to God. They can gain this closeness by making public gift presentations to church ministers, whose role it is to intercede on behalf of parishioners to God. Like their homeland counterparts, diasporic Tongans seek blessings for their families from church ministers to ensure this connection to God's material or spiritual blessings of good health for themselves and their kinspeople. They also desire the enhanced status, positive social value, and cultural capital that the pastor's recognition brings them among the congregation. They reproduce this capital, in part, by "investing" their material resources in ceremonial gifts, key among which are complex gifts of *koloa*, cash, and food. Diasporic Tongans often make difficult economic decisions—putting off paying bills, losing telephone service, and so on—to ensure that they can make the appropriate presentation of these gifts. They additionally expect that future gifts they receive will offset the costs of initial gifts that they themselves present—an aspect of the instrumentality inherent in the gift. Yet there is something more—a value addedness, if you will—bestowed along with a gift by the way the giver presents it and by how the giver perceives its consequent reciprocation. This value addedness can be thought of in terms of Bourdieu's theory of capital.

The mechanism whereby capital accrues to the giver of a gift in Tongan culture is always a social one—it relies on the complicity of others. Intrinsic to Bourdieu's theory (1986) of capital is the interpersonal and negotiated nature of that capital—whether economic, social, or cultural. So an individual can only build up her social capital—sense of respect and honor that others associate with her—if others who share the same system of value recognize and validate her actions in the wider group. Social value can accrue to a person from gossip—for example, about how long the blessing went on—because such gossip can be regarded as indirect praise for that person's acts of apparent generosity in the community. Of course gossip can be maliciously generated about those who give beyond their means—they will be labeled *feilahi* or *fie'eiki* (pretending to be like chiefs), at best. They must strike a delicate balance between over-giving and under-giving and perform their generosity appropriately. The performative aspect of the gift is an important part of its efficacy or value because it supposedly reveals the giver's true feelings and true nature. All aspects of Kakala's comportment that night added to the material value of her gift—speaking from a seated position in a voice that wavers and cracks with emotion, performing a *fakatapu*, or honorific opening to a speech made in public, being self-deprecating about the obviously high value of her gift in the speech, and, later, deflecting compliments with responses of humility. The ministers' thanks, blessing, and repeated mention of Kakala's name during prayers that evening at church also bolstered the value she had already derived from presenting the gift.

The week following Kakala's gift presentation, the pastor thanked her again, this time at the beginning of the Sunday church service. This public statement of gratitude from the pastor compounded the recognition Kakala received from congregants and from God, and, in short, it meant the world to Kakala. She later told me how happy she was to have had the opportunity to lose (*mole*) such a large amount of money for God. Paul van der Grijp (1993) reports on a similar response from members of Methodist congregations in Tonga who presented gifts to the church. These people felt a strong sense of reward both in the form of spiritual blessings from God and the admiration of people who witnessed or heard about their presentations. Van der Grijp observes:

> All the participants in our case study of gifts to the church replied that they were "very pleased" to be able to give. They often explained this

by adding: "The more we give, the more we get from God." ... "We want to show other people in Taoa that we give a great deal of food, because God has given us very many gifts."

The relationship with God ... is not only mediated by the ministers, but also by the attention of other people. ... By giving a lot ... to the ministers, which is *seen by other people* ..., one acquires prestige in the village and possibly *power* ... too. The generous faithful are thus repaid twice: by God and by [the respect of] their fellow villagers (1993:208–209; emphasis added).

In discussing the event with me, Kakala never mentioned the praise of the pastors or the obvious admiration of the people who had witnessed her gift that night. She simply stated that the New Year's gift was her *"fatongia,"* duty. Her use of the term *fatongia* captures the public nature of the enactment of her duty and its encapsulation of larger institutions such as the church, government, or nobility. In contrast, speaking about her sisters and daughters, she often used the term *'ofa*—a sense of obligation that emanates from emotional connectedness to another individual or to a group such as *kāinga*. Gifts to church ministers, government officials, and chiefs incorporate these more distant institutions into the obligations embedded in more intimate relationships between people related as kin. Demonstrating a connection to such institutions is a form of cultural capital (ibid.). Securing the opportunity to present such gifts—as Kakala has done annually for many years—is something valuable and desirable precisely because being witnessed and remembered by others imbues the giver with greater esteem among more people. Once again, with gifting, performing the principle instantiates the reward.

Conclusion: Time, Space, and Exchange in the Tongan Diaspora

With diasporic populations now rivaling and surpassing homeland-based ones in size, an important feature of the organization of Pacific diaspora operates through space and time. As I have analyzed here, Tongan diaspora can be enacted through families and across generations. More specifically, the temporality of the gift, as in the time of presentations and reciprocations, is integral to the material and symbolic perpetuation of Tongan society and culture. The theoretically endless cycle of gifts and reciprocations through which people engage over time and space with one another is a way of continually creating their society, or nation. Given the monetary challenges of funding gifts in the diaspora, this is true in both the material and symbolic senses. Through the varying schedules of gift reciprocation—immediate or immenent reciprocity for food and *koloa* and delayed reciprocity for cash—diasporic Tongans make ends meet around an uncertain schedule of resource use for both daily and ceremonial life. Even younger generation members in diaspora, who may choose not to engage in particular aspects of gift exchange, and who might oppose the material expenditures that go into a complex ceremonial gift, cannot deny the benefits that will accrue to them and their children in the future. Parents who are especially generous can expect that their children will receive bigger gifts from others, benefitting in turn from the warmth of heart that giving engenders. This is a major aspect of the work of time in the (transnational) Tongan gift.

The Tongan diaspora persists over space and time, powered by the discourses, hopes, fears, and expectations of families. The traditions that ground the political economy of identity—and in this case, the identity of women and kin—in both the diaspora and the homeland, are also traditions that ground the nation. In this chapter, I have discussed how Tongan diasporans negotiate the costs and politics of ceremonial gifting by choosing among multiple kinds of valuables and among a range of opportunities to be seen in public as gift givers, and by calibrating the timing and size of reciprocations. This negotiation affords diasporans a chance to develop and maintain their relationships with other people, especially old and new kin (as in the case of a wedding), but also pastors and other high-ranking members of the community. Fulfilling the obligations both to give and reciprocate valuables is a source of value for Tongan individuals and kin groups. The gift's value is generated out of the human context of who prepares it, who is present when gifts are exchanged, how gifts are reciprocated, in what form they are reciprocated, *where* each of these processes takes place, the timing of reciprocations, and even the esteem in which community members hold the presentation of the gift and its giver both during and after the exchange. Indeed, it is through the development and maintenance of social relations enhanced by gift exchange, and through sourcing (transnationally) the valuables that are to be gifted, that Tongan women, in particular, build the multiterritorial nation *as* value. To fulfill their obligations through gift exchange in new places is to maintain old and build new social relationships, thus contributing to *langa fonua*.

Notes

1. This would depend on whether the groom still lives with his parents or not. Unmarried Tongan young people generally live with their parents. Sharing a home space with one's parents after marriage—either in one's house or in theirs—is as much an economic necessity as it is a "duty" of Tongan children.

2. Denominational switching is neither uncommon nor new among Tongans. Elites have engaged in this practice in the past as a matter of political expediency (Rutherford 1996) and women usually switch at marriage to worship in their husband's churches (Gailey 1987). I know one woman, in Tonga, who was raised Catholic and who attended her husband's Methodist church for fifteen years. After her husband's death, she resumed worship at the Catholic Church, seemingly without missing a beat. Switching to newly arrived denominations is increasingly popular in Tonga. In particular, the Mormon church, with its requirement of tithing 10 percent of a person's or a family's monthly income, has seen its numbers rise in the past few decades among Methodist Tongans, who have desired to shake themselves loose of the more burdensome obligations of *misinale* and other competitive, regular donation practices. Incidentally, most of the pawnshop owners I interviewed in 2001 in Tonga, in collaboration with Niko Besnier, were recent converts to the Mormon faith (Addo and Besnier 2008). Other denominations that promote tithing and individual accumulation and gifting of money, and that diverge from the Tongan practices of financing both *kāinga* and church interests are the Seventh-day Adventists and Assemblies of God. Due primarily to Methodist Tongans' denominational switching, these churches' numbers have also been growing in the past decade in Tonga (Besnier 2011).

3. See Gordon (1990) and Ka'ili (2008) on Mormon Tongan communities.

Cash, Death, and Diaspora
When Koloa *Won't Do*

The use of money as gift continues to transform gift giving in Tongan life-stage rituals, occasions at which families present both women's valuables—textiles—and men's valuables, such as long yams and pigs. Indeed, several Tongans I have spoken to predict that money will eventually replace *koloa* as a ceremonial valuable, especially in diaspora, and some of these informants perceive some advantage to this scenario. They note that cash is less cumbersome than large pieces of *koloa;* it takes less time and labor to transport than traditional wealth; it carries important symbolism as a modern valuable, indexing spiritual devotion and acting as a sign of migrant family success; and, compared to *koloa,* cash is immediately useful in the capitalist market contexts with which virtually all Tongan rituals are entangled today (Addo and Besnier 2008; Besnier 2011; Small 1997). Nevertheless, as I have been arguing thus far and as other research strongly suggests, Tongan women show few signs of decreasing their production of *koloa* (Kaeppler 1999a; Teilhet-Fisk 1991; Young Leslie 2004).

This chapter explores some of the tensions around contemporary Tongans' incorporation of cash, or state currency, into ritual exchange alongside traditional valuables, even as textiles remain embodiments of Tongan women's power in kin groups within wider society. I note that there can be noticeable repercussions for families who seem to eschew *koloa* in favor of cash wealth in their rituals. For example, during 'Ofa's daughter's funeral—a ritual that took place in diaspora and that I began discussing in chapter 3—the family requested that people who came to mourn with them present money rather than *koloa.* This occasioned discussions among the community on the problematic aspects of refusing to engage in *koloa* exchange. I analyze this series of events for the ways it throws into relief the differences between contemporary diasporic Tongans' gifting and reciprocation of money and *koloa* in ritual contexts that epitomize tradition.

Valuing Money as Tongan Wealth

For two centuries, Tongans have been integrating money into calculations and expressions of wealth alongside traditional valuables. To understand money as Tongans use it in the diaspora today necessitates understanding *koloa* in its most important role as a form of Tongan (traditional) gift, and the ways in which Tongans' ideas about *koloa*'s value have come to articulate with or elide ideas about the value of money.

I have asserted throughout this book that there are few forms of material culture for Tongans that are imbued with the same symbolic import and spiritual potency as *koloa* (Addo and Besnier 2008; Young Leslie 2004; Kaeppler 1999b).[1] The notion of *koloa* delineates a particular, extremely special form of ownership, or relation between the possession and its possessor. Traditionally, among chiefly Tongans, textile *koloa* were considered "inalienable possessions" (Weiner 1992). Such objects have high symbolic density and, thus, convey key messages about the possessor's rank and rights to hold certain societal positions. They served as icons of the owner's family history, or personal exploits and achievements, and as such, they were—and still are—too valuable to alienate from the possessor by being gifted or sold. Indeed, when others know that the object exists and is in the possession of a particular person, there is a reverence—Annette Weiner calls this a "difference" (ibid.)—for that person's unique power to maintain ownership of the object, or to resist exchanging it. Adrienne Kaeppler, in particular, has described the significance of inalienable *koloa* in chiefly Tongan culture: chiefly families have exclusive rights to own, display, and wear the fine mats (*kie hingoa*), typically at their own distinguished families' ceremonies of investiture and other rites of passage. Such events often have national, or at least regional or village, significance and cement elite Tongans' connections to ancient people renowned for notable exploits in history. Stories about the origin of these cloths are intertwined with the history of the kingdom's greatest heroes and where no origin story exists for a cloth, it is as if these objects have existed since the beginning of time: the time before human beings, when only deities existed (Godelier 1999). Needless to say, these are sacred objects and are not to be parted with easily, if at all.

In homeland and diaspora alike, commoner women's textile *koloa* are symbolically dense for other reasons that have been explored throughout this book. The textiles are "heavy" with the associations that their owners have maintained over time with chiefly women from the past; with specific other individuals or groups, including ties with kin and chiefs; with memorable events and specific places; and for some women, with weaving and barkcloth-making houses in their villages. Yet in contrast to long-standing *koloa* often worn and exchanged by elites, these individual cloths are somewhat interchangeable. A woman rarely despairs of having to alienate a particular textile *as a gift* to another Tongan as long as she is confident that the recipient shares her sense of obligation to reciprocate *koloa* or food or some other (similarly) weighty object or valuable. In addition, rarely do women regard *specific* items of *koloa* as irreplaceable. Indeed, one could offer a commoner Tongan woman several things that would make her part with a particular textile: another textile of the same category, some other form of textile, such as the fine mats the Fijian women exchanged for Tongan barkcloth in the *kātoanga* I describe in chapter 2, a gift of money, or an outright monetary purchase of the cloth. In other words, specific pieces of *koloa* are replaceable, within the construct of the gift-exchange system. What is *not replaceable,* however, is the *koloa* system itself—the (women's) labor, kin-based connections, production and exchange processes, particular aesthetics, textures, scents, and associations that the textiles hold for Tongans, especially associations with the Tongan homeland.

A system is a complex whole formed by interacting and interrelated elements—people, objects, environment, and ideas. The *koloa* system, as a material embodiment of the Tongan cultural system, affords people a way to communicate the depth and character of their feelings toward others through specific exchanges of particular textile *koloa.* It is the relationship that is created and sustained, and the *koloa system* that signifies it, that is irreplaceable. Likewise, one will not find a Tongan who will easily part with the *idea* of their Tonganness, whether or not that person professes to live by so-called "Tongan traditions" (Evans, Harms, and Reid 2009). The value of Tonganness to which people are so attached is vividly embodied in a textile or bundle of textiles (*'efinanga*) that has been folded and readied for gifting. Such a bundle embodies the Tongan cultural values of layering and of gifting, and holds great value potential—a great sense of worth translated into social recognition and the material reciprocation that will result from its subsequent gifting. *Koloa,* therefore, might be considered inalienable to Tongans' notions of themselves.

My informants frequently used the statement "our *koloa* is like your money" when explaining to me, as a non-Tongan, why their *koloa* is valuable. I interpret this to mean that Tongans (in many cases probably, quite accurately) consider money to be the valuable that Westerners value most highly, and, thus, seek to accumulate. Considering that the cash presentations I am concerned about in this book continue to be ubiquitous among diasporic Tongans, and still take place *along with* presentations of traditional valuables, I am led to ask: why do Tongans say that their cloth is like Westerners' money, yet they gift and reciprocate these two categories of valuables *so differently?* Following Weiner (1992), I suggest that *koloa* bestows on the Tongans a sense of their cultural system's uniqueness, or "difference." They thus maintain a culturally assumed and essential difference between modern state money and "traditional" money.

Anthropologist Andrew Arno has argued that traditional money sometimes constitutes "supreme valuables," which can only represent themselves (2005). While Arno uses the example of Fijian ritual whales' teeth, the claim applies to *koloa* as well. Similar to Fijians' cultural rationale, nothing can stand in place of *koloa* and prestige foods for Tongans; these can only represent themselves. For Tongans, money is ranked below *koloa* as a ritual valuable. Again, this is because, relative to other categories of objects in the world, these objects are inalienable from Tongans' notions of themselves, whereas state money is specifically associated with the post-contact, non-indigenous realm. These objects, and for many only these objects, can fully materialize Tonganness and its exceptional value for Tongans. Given this basic assumption about the objects and their value, I use this chapter to focus on what happens when individuals decide to exclude *koloa* from their ceremonial exchanges, and temporarily substitute cash in its place. I do this in an effort to analyze the value of cash in the aspects of Tongans' modern lives that they continue to consider their "traditions." I highlight the economic and social challenges of gift exchange in diaspora, the implications of addressing these challenges by attempting to limit ceremonial gifts to cash, and the consequences of deliberately delimiting the categories of the valuables exchanged in such a context.

My analysis allows me to return to the already noted concern shared with me by Tongans of diverse generations, in both the homeland and the diaspora: that money will eventually replace *koloa* as a ceremonial valuable. I argue that, thus far for diasporic Tongans, cash is actually not equivalent to *koloa* because cash on its own is not endowed with the generative quality that *koloa* embodies. Instead, cash and cloth *together* have become repositories of value that potentially allow Tongans to continue building their society and nation across both the diaspora and the homeland.

Koloa, Cash, and Modernity

Like many people from developing nations who profess to be deeply concerned with maintaining their traditions, Tongans are simultaneously heavily invested in the ideology and practice of modernity (Besnier 2011). While money signifies modernity and enables people to access its material trappings, traditional valuables enable a particular and prized form of sociality—gifting in a traditional vein. Tongans thus embrace both traditional wealth and modern (state) currencies in their local systems of exchange. Examining the ways that Tongans deploy either state or traditional wealth in some contexts, yet incorporate both forms of wealth in others, is a way to make clear how Tongans link certain valuables with particular cultural origins and purposes in their system of value.

As Marshall Sahlins discusses, many contemporary Pacific peoples—and other "others" who have been marginalized by the fraught global histories through which the West has been empowered—perceive themselves as legitimately having the right to choose which valuables they should involve in their own particular cultural and economic transactions, and how they will use them (1988). That is, people maintain a sense of agency in how they both exchange valuables and express their sense of their own modernity within their indigenous homelands. Here, I suggest that the conditions under which members of a gift society would substitute cash for traditional valuables include the specific materiality and value of objects and how these objects are associated with other contexts for cultivating pride or augmenting status. The choices people make about which valuables to present or prefer as gifts afford them a sense of agency in how they live culturally meaningful and/or traditional lives in their current social, geographic, and political-economic contexts. Having and taking advantage of choices is key to displaying competence at modernity; being modern is not a question of completely overhauling traditional processes, but is about strategically adopting modern ways and valuables into an ongoing cultural system of "traditional" meanings and values. So it is with Tongans who have adopted money into virtually all aspects of their traditional exchange system, but for whom money is not a "supreme valuable."

The concomitant use of *koloa* and money in Tongans ceremonial gifts is not an unusual situation in the Pacific. Indeed, for at least the past two decades, analysts of state currencies and their roles in contemporary Melanesian societies have posed the question: Why does cash seem to be replacing traditional valuables, but without eclipsing them (see Akin and Robbins 1999)? David Akin and Joel Robbins answered this question by examining how local people attribute value to both modern money and traditional valuables when exchanging them as gifts. They compared what they called contrasting "modalities of exchange"—that is, whether valuables were exchanged as gifts or as commodities—and concluded that money, while useful as gift, was still associated with a general modality of commodity exchange. In contrast, traditional and local forms of money were associated with both modalities of commodity and gift, rather than commodity or gift alone.

Similarly, as traditional Tongan wealth, *koloa* straddles the modalities of gift and commodity. For women who gift often or primarily using *koloa*, adding money to a gift enhances a sense of willingness to embrace modernity while performing tradition—Kakala, from chapters 3 and 4, is one such example. Like other Pacific women today (see, for example, Van der Grijp 2003 on Uvean textiles as gifts and commodities), Tongan women who gift *koloa* also use money to purchase *koloa* at some point in their lives. There is also a long-standing practice among them to sell *koloa* for money when in need of quick cash.

My informants often told me that money was hard to come by and hard to keep around because they find it so easy to gift, spend, lend, or lose. Such an elusive and confounding valuable, while being widely commensurate, is not one that all Tongan people would rely entirely on as their main means of exchange. Compared to money, *koloa* is harder to lose physically; so, continuing to present traditional valuables such as *koloa* and prestige food allows for the possibility of enhancing the social connections that increase status, and also affords people time to accumulate cash resources for future reciprocations. Money may be versatile, but *koloa* is just more *reliable,* as some of my women informants explained.

The differences between the ways in which Tongans typically reciprocate cash and *koloa* point to the existence of a cultural notion that cash and *koloa* are fundamentally not interchangeable: *koloa* is reciprocated with *koloa,* in part immediately, but cash is almost always reciprocated in a delayed fashion. The sequence of events and enactments of the principle of reciprocity that obtains in gift exchange would be "thrown off" if Tongans should cease to present *koloa* and other forms of traditional wealth. As explained previously, when a family is invited to a celebration, it typically presents a complex ceremonial gift of *koloa,* cash, and prestige food to the host. Those who receive the gifts on behalf of the celebrant's family begin to reciprocate immediately with speeches of thanks. Parts of these speeches are delivered publicly and sung prescriptively with a rising tone on the penultimate syllable: *malo 'ē koka'anga* ("thank you for making barkcloth") and *malo 'ē lālanga* ("thank you for weaving").

A second stage of reciprocation takes place within a day or two of the initial presentation to the family hosting the *kavenga.* The family reciprocates *koloa* and prestige foods with other pieces of *koloa* and various foods, such as choice portions of cooked pork and other feast foods from recent celebrations. Finally, the host family will reciprocate the cash part of the gift equivalently at the guest family's next life-passage event, where that family becomes the host. It may take months or even years for such a reciprocation of the initial gift to occur, and so the reciprocation of the cash part of the original gift constitutes a form of "delayed reciprocity." The staggered form of reciprocation is advantageous to the recipients of the initial gift because they can recognize the initial gift with a partial reciprocation in the form of cloth, food, or both, and still gain some time to amass the cash resources needed to reciprocate the earlier cash gift.

The inclusion of cash in the gift and its delayed reciprocation also means that *koloa* and other non-cash valuables are essential to maintaining reciprocity. Without these other valuables, hosts would have nothing to reciprocate at the time of the event, perhaps a reason for the persistence of *koloa* alongside cash gifting. I suggest that the initial reciprocation of food or cloth in this sequence is as much a recognition of the recipient's intention to reciprocate the cash part of the gift—a promissory note in the form of an immediately consumable valuable—as it is a form of reciprocity in itself. If people broke with convention and eschewed the gifting of non-cash valuables and so offered no initial reciprocation, those who presented the initial gift might lose faith that the rest of the reciprocation—the cash portion—would be forthcoming.

Faith in the system of exchange—and in others' commitment to continue contributing to that system—is bound up with Tongans' expressions of their own uniqueness as kin and as Tongans.

The Value of Labor in Gifts and Reciprocations

As I described above, gifting *koloa* and prestige foods elicits immediate reciprocations, which include public expressions of gratitude toward the gifting family and some form of in-kind material reciprocation. Both bring honor to the gift giver's kin group. At both homeland and diasporic ritual events, one still hears "thank you for the barkcloth," "thank you for the plaiting of mats," and "thank you for the food," but not "thank you for the cash." What is being recognized as valuable is partly the labor involved in the gifting. Valued labor is not that of the wage laborer, but of people who labor at traditional work—cloth making and food growing or preparation. Through their vocalizations of gratitude, recipient families validate men's and women's labor and love specifically, and recognize those implicated in the work required to prepare the gift. Just as Tongans assume that an individual's actions reflect the sentiments and labor of their kinspeople, so too the material form of the gift reflects them as well. The material form of cash reflects less highly on its presenters in part because it does not embody a valued form of labor, which is labor put toward the making of traditional objects.

Furthermore, just as material valuables represent more than their mere physical forms, so too people who play the role of presenters of material gifts represent more than themselves—they represent those who labored to make or produce the objects and those who prepared them for gifting. Those represented are often members of their *kāinga* (extended family) or, in one way or another, are members of Tongan *kāinga*, writ large. In other words, receiving gifts necessitates recognizing the gift giver's *kāinga* and, by extension, all Tongan *kāinga*, past, present, and future. In effect, what traditional valuables represent when presented and reciprocated is the multiterritorial Tongan *fonua*. What is at stake in exchange is Tongans' unique identity, their sense of what makes them, and no one else in the world, *Tongans*. The gifting of cash does not—and cannot—produce this inestimable form of value.

Gifting cash exclusively in ritual situations has other disadvantages in modern contexts. The suddenness with which the need to gift cash often arises, even under conditions of delayed reciprocation, demands that people keep cash on hand, or, as is more often the case, find cash quickly by liquidating belongings, working longer hours, or "borrowing" from others. Even on unexpected ritual occasions, such as funerals, being unable to accumulate enough valuables—in this case cash—to gift or to reciprocate can lead to a certain loss of face. Likewise, being unable to reciprocate gifts—whether cash or traditional—can have detrimental effects on a family's status. For a host of reasons I will explain next, funerals are particularly crucial sites for exploring the high stakes for Tongan identity embedded in people's choices about ceremonial gifting of cash and *koloa*.

Gifts and Funerals

In the anthropology of the Pacific, funerals have been largely analyzed as moments of tradition in which agents are forced to adjust to the challenging influences of modernity. Scholars studying funerals in the Pacific have focused on the ceremonial significance and cultural efficacy of material culture (Addo 2009; Kaeppler 1978b; Young Leslie 1999), role delineation (Kuehling 2006; James 2002), rank (Kaeppler 1971; Bott 1982), ritual states and keening practices (Sinclair 1990; Kaeppler 1993b), and gift exchange (Kuehling 2005; Evans 2001; Van der Grijp 1993). In such situations, people tend to be in highly emotionally charged states, and ceremonial duties are ideally executed through unquestioningly carrying out ritual roles. As in almost all Tongan ritual contexts, gift exchange ordered by kin-based roles is a defining aspect of funerals. Exhaustion and stress are often said to arise from the prescriptions that the bereaved family feed all visitors at the wake and that they reciprocate, in kind, all gifts of food or *koloa*. Ideally, no expense or trouble will be spared in a funeral because the ritual is the last time that the deceased will be surrounded by a large number of kin and, during it, everyone will be engaged in recounting his or her achievements (Kaeppler 1978b). Funerals are times when the reputation of the kin group is also brought to the fore and it can be affected by how the family deals with gifts presented at the ritual. Properly executing these roles constitutes a crucial form of value, so that any failure to reciprocate a gift, whether immediately or at the prescribed later date, adversely affects the reputation of the recipient and dishonors the giver.

At funerals, a gift of textiles, called a *teu*, is typically presented to the bereaved funeral hosts by a group of women, usually themselves members of a nuclear family. Each textile is borne by a woman in her outstretched arms, and one of the *koloa* carried by these women will usually have an envelope containing the money resting on top of it. Each woman lays the particular piece of *koloa* she is carrying at the feet of a male representative of the receiving family. Before the next group of women brings in a subsequent *teu*, the cash given by the previous group is usually removed to another room, along with *koloa*, to be counted and noted along with the name of the gifting family.

Before the funeral, friends, co-workers, and kin members often bring gifts of food to the grieving family's home, presenting them along with prayers and sometimes with cash and cloth gifts. While some of these gifts may be used to sustain the bereaved family during its many days of preparation before the funeral, the food is often used to feed the mourners who come to pay their respects on the night of the wake. During funeral preparations in Tonga, very little farming or fishing—and certainly no textile production—would be performed on estates and villages. In an agrarian economy such as Tonga, food is drawn from other families' daily provisions, and it may be for this reason that gifts of food and cloth are usually reciprocated in kind soon after the funeral and burial—it ensures the continued sustenance of gifting families, even as they contribute resources to the grieving one. To refuse a gift of cloth or food is seemingly to leave unrecognized another family's sacrifice and generosity. Moreover, while the form of the gift has its own value, this form is meaningless without the actions whereby it is presented and later reciprocated. While accepting money upholds prevalent notions of tradition, money (a modern valuable with a generic form) given in lieu of *koloa* (objects of unique form combining tradition, *mana,* and women's labor) can be read as a defiance of principles of reciprocity, which include properly acknowledging a gift one receives with reciprocations of appropriate forms offered at appropriate times.

To some extent, commoners have the prerogative to decide to reciprocate only some or even none of the gifts brought to a funeral (James 2002; Kaeppler 1978b), but this is something few Tongans would actually do. As practices affording esteem in traditional ceremonial exchange have become totally enmeshed with Christian worship and notions of tradition, Tonganized forms of Western religion have provided ways for both commoner and noble families to distinguish themselves by giving and spending money in public arenas. In the 1920s—fifty years after Tonga had been established as a Christian kingdom—Edward Gifford recorded the lengths to which Tongan families would go to ensure that they reciprocated gifts appropriately. Citing an example of wedding gifts exchanged between the bride's and groom's sides in Nukuʻalofa, Tonga, he wrote: "In accomplishing [a] return the distributor often stripped his own house of all its possessions, counting the social prestige of his family of greater value than his material property. If he should fail to complete the traditional remuneration to all concerned, his unmarried sons and daughters and the progeny of his married children lost face and might consequently fail to contract desirable marriages" (1929:193).

Bereaved families frequently feel great anxiety when deciding how to finance a funeral and to perform an ideal ritual send-off for their deceased relatives. Making gifts of cash in the context of life-crisis rituals also assures continued prosperity for kin groups. For the families of Methodist ministers, the fact that the form and timeliness of a countergift delivers a message about one's regard for social rules and kin-based roles (James 2002) is especially important because clergy are expected to exemplify Christian virtues and any related Tongan traditions in every aspect of their lives. Thus, when a particular retired Free Wesleyan Church minister decided to reject gifts of *koloa* while accepting cash gifts at his daughter's funeral, it was a cause for great concern for many in his community.

When Gifting Matters More than The Gift Itself

In chapter 3, I noted that during my fieldwork in Tonga (2000–2001), 'Ofa's family, with whom I had grown very close, tragically lost a daughter and her infant child in a car accident in Auckland. The status of 'Ofa's husband Langi as a recently retired minister in the state church came with expectations that he and his family would exemplify Tongan traditional practices in their most ideal form. But as I also described in the previous chapter, after the death of his daughter, Langi ran the risk of censure by publicly requesting that mourning gifts be presented in the form of money and that no gifts of *koloa* be brought to the family home in Tonga or to the wake in Auckland. This decision very much went against the conventional grain of gift exchange and was detrimental to Langi's good name as well as to the reputation of his family. Within three weeks of the deaths, all but one member of the immediate family who lived in Tonga flew to Auckland to host the double funeral. I flew with them, and here I present an analysis of the gifts exchanged at the funeral.

Before leaving Tonga for Auckland, the family had made preparations and announcements in order to pre-empt mourners attending the funeral burdened with gifts of *koloa*. These announcements were made on radio and by word of mouth in Tonga and in Auckland. Tina, Langi and 'Ofa's youngest daughter and my close friend, was concerned that refusing *teu* at a funeral from other branches of the *kāinga* might be seen as a breach of proper Tongan behavior. She explained:

> Dad stands to lose a lot of face from this funeral … but we have no choice. We can't afford to fly Malia back [i.e., repatriate her brother's body to Tonga] and have the funeral here. It would cost so much. We would even have to get people coming from New Zealand and Australia to bring some of the food if we were going to have it at home [in Tonga]. It's better to do it [in New Zealand] … and Mum and Dad decided last night not to take any *teu* … any *koloa* … because it would just be too hard for us to have to do the *holo* after the funeral. And we will be lucky if we get a month on our visas to stay [in New Zealand]. If we bury Malia in New Zealand … Sona [her sister] can look after her and visit her. We'll all visit her when we can. I know I will want to.

From my discussions with some people who attended the funeral, one perception of the family's choice to forgo all *koloa* exchange was that the family was trying to shirk tradition; another was that it was just inevitable that, with the increasing use of cash in gift exchange in both Tonga and in the diaspora, money was finally beginning to show signs of replacing *koloa* in ritual presentations. Langi later told me that his family was willing to take the risk of losing face in order to minimize the logistical challenges and the monetary and cloth wealth costs of reciprocating the gifts in the traditional manner. Furthermore, the funeral was for both Malia and her young child. As each belonged to their respective fathers' lineages and therefore to a different *kāinga*, potentially twice as many gifts would come in. Accepting only cash gifts would mitigate Malia's family's obligations to immediately reciprocate numerous and costly gifts to members of two kin groups.

Despite the family's request, on the night before the wake, many friends and relatives in New Zealand gave Tina's family *ngāue*, food mostly in the form of store-bought frozen meat and root crops. Some of this food went toward a light meal prepared for visitors at the wake. Moreover, on the night of Malia and her baby's wake, the family was gifted with several traditional presentations of *koloa*. In the dim basement of a large Free Wesleyan church building in Auckland, I listened and watched intently as the spokesperson for Tina's family announced his thanks for the gifts and subsequently relayed the family's decision not to accept *koloa* this time. On hearing this, one member of a particular family of presenters picked up the envelope of money and handed it to the representative. The women visitors who had brought in the *koloa* picked up the textiles that they had already presented, and left the hall. Later, a relative of Tina's mother's brother through marriage, a woman named Teuila who lived in Auckland, came in carrying part of a *teu* consisting of three pieces of barkcloth, two decorated mats, and several pieces of printed, store-bought fabric. Malia's family's spokesperson thanked her family with a short, formal speech and then asked them to remove their *teu*. However, Teuila stood and took each of the *ngatu* with either a fine mat or length of cloth folded up inside, and presented one to each of the three men from Malia's *kāinga* who were seated in front of her, thereby making them the token gift recipients. The men all showed their acceptance of the gifts by saying "*mālō*" (thank you), and then Teuila and her [family] group stood and left.

I was confused: Why had this woman not heeded the spokesperson's request to take the *koloa* away? Why had the men accepted the *koloa* she was so insistent on giving to them? Two of Malia's sisters who had been seated nearby took Teuila's textiles into another room and later analyzed Teuila's motivations this way: "She was being generous. It's like she just wanted someone to take the *koloa* from her, like if you offered me [some] chocolate and I didn't want to accept it, but you were going to give it away anyway, so you offer it to the person sitting next to me." Another sister said: "She was showing that she was *liongi* to [ritually lower than] the [spokesmen] and the others with him."[2] This second response reveals the operation of roles at the funeral, rank being the principle governing who must gift, who must receive, and who must reciprocate. Sensitivity to her own role and ranked status permeated Teuila's sense of right and proper actions at this funeral and so she proceeded with her gift presentation. I believe that the gifting woman was fully aware that the spokesmen—who, while members of the immediate family in mourning, were also fully aware of the value of *koloa*—would not refuse the *koloa* if she gave it to them. It was one way of saving face for herself, as well as doing something with the *koloa* that elevated her status.[3] Teuila might also have been asserting her own right to be recognized as a gift giver, especially since the anomalous structure of the funeral meant that she would not be receiving any immediate material reciprocation.

Annette Weiner's analysis of Trobriand Islands' gift exchange offers us another way to think about Teuila's insistence on bestowing her *koloa* on representatives of the bereaved family. Weiner described certain objects as inalienable possessions (1992). For example, Trobriand Islands men hold the most chiefly *kula* shells while circulating shells that have little symbolic density, or value as historical objects (1994). These lesser shells can be bought with money, given or sold to others, and are sometimes copies of other well-known, named valuables. Weiner also remarked that, among Trobriand Islands women, the most symbolically dense objects are not old objects associated with specific ancestral lines or cosmologies, but newly made banana-leaf bundles that women distribute at mortuary feasts. These objects are of great value to women, but they *are* exchanged. Likewise, among commoner Tongan women, some of the most symbolically dense cloths can, and ideally *should*, be exchanged. Teuila's textiles were important to her, not simply because they were traditional wealth, but because having them afforded her a chance to do what she thought was appropriate at this time: to present a gift to the grieving family. Thus, when she was asked not to gift the *koloa*, she did not comply because she felt it improper—unTongan, if you will—to gift *nothing*.

Koloa and the Focus on Tradition

Sitting in their daughter Sona's living room in Auckland after the funerary rites were over, Langi and his immediate the family, calculated that he had received NZ$8,800 in condolence gifts from visitors to the Auckland funeral. The family recounted their uses of the money among themselves one late night in Auckland, before leaving to return to Tonga. This sum did not even begin to cover their initial outlay for their airplane tickets to Auckland, the expense of feeding the hundreds who attended, the price of funeral plots for their daughter and grandson, or the cost of countergifts (constituting cloth and store-bought food) to the six or seven Methodist ministers who visited during the night of the wake and to the one who officiated at the burial. There was not a penny of the money left; there was also no *koloa* in Sona's house in Auckland because the elderly couple had not wanted to accept any.

This was an unusual position for Langi's family to be in, for they usually engaged in relatively high levels of exchange of traditional wealth in Tonga. Having spent almost fifty years working as a minister in the Free Wesleyan Church, Langi had been presented with numerous complex gifts of *koloa*, prestige food, and cash over the years, and 'Ofa was renowned in their village for the large room in their home that was a storage place for *koloa*. But here they sat with no valuables at all because they had chosen to focus, not on things, but on prayer. Of course, they believed that celebrating the funeral in diaspora afforded them some leeway in how they dealt with gifts and reciprocations, but, as Tina had said earlier, they also felt a certain loss of face. The loss was especially acute for 'Ofa who could not demonstrate her *'ofa* (love) for Malia with the same intensity and symbolism that she had celebrated that daughter's wedding in the early 1990s, an occasion when 'Ofa had exchanged large amounts of *koloa*. As if to mitigate against the loss of opportunity to exchange cloth at the funeral, 'Ofa resumed her participation in traditional exchange, seemingly without missing a beat, by preparing and proffering *koloa* (see chapter 3).

In their communities, Tongans continually debate the moral value of choosing to act in ways that have come to be thought of as embodying "tradition," and many Tongans continue to exhibit a fierce passion for what has been called orthopraxy—the performance of particular rites that are considered to define a ritual (Watson 1988). Orthopraxy refers to culturally prescribed behavior, whereas orthodoxy, its counterpart, is a disposition that instead requires "consistency and continuity in belief" (ibid.). Using this author's logic, Tongan religious belief and ritual practice historically fall somewhere on a continuum between the two concepts. In the case of contemporary funerals, orthopraxy becomes evident in the curtailment of normal daily practices: no barkcloth is beaten in villages, there is at least a one-night wake when the body is on display, relatives come to view the body and kiss the deceased goodbye, and families typically exchange large amounts of cash and traditional gifts (see figure 5.1). However, there is also a sense of orthodoxy whereby Tongans, as Christians, adhere to the liturgical teachings of their various denominational faiths and foreground prayer, church attendance, and faith in God to take care of the soul of the departed. Seemingly attending to different aspects of the death ritual—the material and the spiritual—both contexts embody elements of what Tongans today call "tradition."

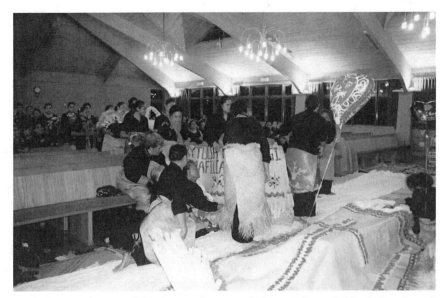

Figure 5.1. Relatives of the deceased present *koloa* at a funeral. The *koloa*-draped coffin is visible on the right, Auckland.

When Langi declared that his family would only accept money as funeral gifts in Auckland, many people questioned his respect for both *anga faka-Tonga and* for the church in which he had been a minister. In order to avert stigma in his efforts to temporarily remove *koloa* exchange from the funerary exchanges, Langi had to render new practices acceptable to the community by framing them as achieving the same results as those that are considered traditional. On the one hand, Langi had to appeal to a sense of orthodoxy— adherence to notions of faithfulness and the efficacy of prayer (Ferraiuolo 2006; Watson 1988). On the other hand, however, his decision to only accept cash seemed to depart from other aspects of Tongan culture, such as prescriptions to exchange traditional valuables. Because he eschewed accepting the usual gift offerings of *koloa,* he had challenged people's expectations for orthopraxy.

In her work in the ethnology of Tonga, Kaeppler states that "the traditional and new are nowhere better demonstrated than at funerals" (1978b:198). I would add that traditional and novel practices can also be meaningfully redefined and rearticulated in such ritual events. The constraints of time and location at work in satisfactorily completing a funeral involve not just the inconvenience of distance and expense, but also throw into relief the very meanings of tradition and modernity in culture. They also reveal globalized kinship to be highly economic forms of relationships, but of the kind that are shot through with emotion, negotiation, and power.

Economic considerations were clearly central in the case of Langi's daughter Malia's funeral, affected the whole family before, during, and after the funeral, and had an impact on people like Teuila and others who proffered gifts. As anthropologists of Tonga and Tongan culture have been stating for decades, for commoners, the most economically and socially marginal citizens, identity is also forged through the negotiations of the specific material choices people face amid prevailing fashions, material constraints, expectations based on rank, and aspirations within a community (Korn 1995; Marcus 1983; Small 1997; Young Leslie 2004). From this perspective, these decisions, along with the multicentric actions whereby Tongans in the diaspora and the homeland rework tradition and modernity, count among the processes of nation building that continue today over diasporic space. However, patriarchy in Tongan families also abides in nation building, so it was not surprising that 'Ofa did not seem to challenge Langi on what seemed to be *his* decision to exclude *koloa* from their diasporic mourning for Malia. Teuila was one woman who was not daunted, however.

Teuila's insistent gifting of her *koloa* raises the question of what is at stake in ritual giving for Tongans everywhere—not just those still living in the homeland. It was giving, and not just giving *koloa* that she was intent on. Going beyond the usual role of *koloa* as a crucial material presence at rituals, the textiles are an important index of cultural appropriateness, as evidenced in the complex emotions that arise when people try to access the value embodied in their valuables through money. A short example about pawning *koloa* in diaspora will help me elaborate.

Pawnshops: Gifts as Commodities and Kin as Customers

Known as "loan companies" (*kautaha nō pa'anga*), pawnshops are ubiquitous in Tonga. Their number has been growing steadily in the past decade. They are very popular because their loans can be obtained instantly; they do not require the same long waiting period as requests for loans from banks or for relatives to wire money from the diaspora. At the beginning of 2001, when Niko Besnier and I first began researching pawnshops and pawning in Tonga, we identified about twenty scattered throughout Nuku'alofa and nearby villages (Addo and Besnier 2008). At the end of 2007, when I again visited Nuku'alofa, there were at least twice this many shops. All of them accepted *koloa,* while only a minority of them accepted electronics—such as television sets—because of the low resale value of such items (see figure 5.2).

Diasporic Tongans frequent a few specific pawnshops in Auckland that resemble those in Tonga. These businesses are usually small, one-room operations where customers offer their *koloa* in exchange for a relatively modest loan (between NZ$50 and NZ$500) that they must return within a month, at 25 percent interest. Customers who cannot pay forfeit their *koloa*. The pawnshop owner normally sells the *koloa* in such cases, often for more than the loan is worth, thus recouping the money lost on the loan, plus some interest. While Tongans need money for ceremonial occasions that can fall anytime during the year, everyone is under pressure to obtain money at set ritual times. So the pawnshop business is seasonal, but most brisk, for example, during the weeks leading up to Christmas and before annual donations to the various churches in May and September.

Some pawnshops are highly localized in Tonga or Auckland, while others operate across borders and oceans. For example, Pasifika Pawnbrokers, the largest and most popular Tongan-owned pawnshop in Auckland, has been operating for the better part of a decade in the Mt. Eden suburb of Auckland. The couple who own this pawnshop operate an ambitious transnational business in forfeited goods: the wife travels regularly to cities in the United States and Australia, taking the forfeited *koloa* items with her to sell to other diasporic Tongans, and turning a profit even after meeting travel expenses.[4]

Kakala's obligations at the end of 2001 provide an example of the kind of pressure that leads Tongans to pawn their valuables. Kakala's resources had already been drained by Christmas and by her niece 'Elina's wedding (see chapter 4), but Kakala also took on the obligation to present a designated gift to the

Figure 5.2. Two women employees take stock of the *koloa* at a *kautaha nō pa'anga* (pawn shop), Nuku'alofa.

speaker who gave the closing sermon in her church on New Year's Eve: a piece of *ngatu*, a *kie tonga* fine mat, a brightly colored quilt, a NZ$500 money envelope of her own money, and several boxes of store-bought food. This *kavenga* drained all of her cash resources and, early in January, she had to pawn some *koloa* to make the NZ$130 she needed to pay some overdue household bills. When I drove Kakala to the Pasifika Pawn brokers in January 2002 she did not at first reveal our destination, choosing instead to characterize the trip as a social visit; the business owner is Kakala's first cousin's daughter. It was only upon arrival that she diverted us to the pawnshop, where her niece greeted her warmly.

While her niece's assistant located her *koloa* in the well-stocked storage room at the rear of the building, Kakala asked about the other woman's family, but did not mention the family wedding that they had both attended a few weeks before. When the assistant brought her *koloa*, Kakala quickly paid her money, kissed her niece goodbye, and told me it was time to leave. From there we headed for a post shop, where Kakala paid her phone bill and part of her electricity bill.

What is striking about this encounter is Kakala's apparent anxiety to keep it "socially minimal" (Bailey 1997) and end it promptly. This contrasted with the leisurely pace, the serving of food and tea, formal speech making, and sometimes closing prayers that characterize most visits, including those with a material purpose. The shame of being monetarily poor and of having to alienate traditional valuables that the short visit embodied was aggravated, for Kakala, by the involvement of family members in the transaction. In addition, Kakala seemed to be worried that others would see her "selling" *koloa* to be inappropriate when she had so many imminent *kavenga* at which she needed to gift them.

As in many other places in the Pacific, business and family mix uneasily in the context of Tongan pawnshops. People with money and the power to harness signs of modernity by, for example, starting businesses such as trade stores, have little protection from requests made by their kin for credit and for gifts or loans of money (Van der Grijp 2002). Refusing to lend or gift money to kin often reads as rebelliousness against the gift system in which kin not only are obligated to share wealth and windfall gains, but also have the right to call on kin for resources. Kakala's adopted daughter later interpreted the pawnshop interaction for me. She said that Kakala did not feel like she could save face in public for several reasons: she was low on cash, had forfeited her precious *koloa*, and also had to abide having a niece who was profiting from her misfortune. Nevertheless, Kakala's other nieces tell me that the old woman returned at least once more to the same pawnshop that year, which suggests the level of her need, since she had to again endure some loss of face in front of her niece, the owner.

Diasporans like Kakala, who never visited a pawnshop while living in Tonga, may now do so from time to time in diaspora. One reason is that the geographically dispersed way in which Tongans inhabit Auckland's urban landscape means that they are away from the prying eyes of relatives. Another is that it is one other way of managing the competing demands of living in a modern, post-industrial society while continuing to attend to one's traditional economic and social responsibilities. I should note that pawning *koloa* is not an example of alienating *koloa,* as a category of valuables, because it is done with only a minority of *koloa* that is in circulation. Commoditizing *koloa* at the pawnshop may not be a traditional use of such objects, but pawning particular items of *koloa* does help to facilitate the longstanding need to keep *koloa,* at large, circulating as gift in the Tongan ethnoscape.

Conclusion: Why Tongan *Koloa* is not "Like Money"

That textile *koloa* are essential in nation building is evident in more than just their materiality, aesthetics, and exchange value. It is proven by a sense of loss that pervades an event when *koloa* are *not* present and, moreover, when women are not presenting them at ritual events like funerals. As earlier chapters have argued, by keeping *koloa* as the main visual and value-enabling enhancements of a life ritual, women also render ritual events as legitimate sites for their gendered identity production. Besides producing their own identities, women also recreate their societies through the gift (Graeber 2001). The value of *koloa* lies in the textiles' consummate circulation, so the power that exchanging *koloa* gives Tongan women to create and recreate their society anywhere in the world constitutes a form of value. And this is why *koloa* was indispensable to Teuila and why she gifted her textiles at Malia's funeral rather than keeping them.

This idea also explains why, to Tongans, *koloa* is not like Western money: it has a different form of value that money can partially gain beyond its strictly monetary value, but which *koloa* cannot ever lose. Just like *koloa,* in many ways, money is useful in accomplishing duties to family and nation, as well as discharging gender roles. Money more generically bespeaks good Tonganness, but *koloa* materializes appropriate Tongan womanliness. Moreover, as a focal point for interactions that actualize a sense of genealogical connection and abidance through time, *koloa* is endowed with the power to "regenerate people culturally" (Kaeppler 1999b).

The anthropology of Tonga is quite rich in analysis of the material advantages of Tongan gifts and countergifts (Addo 2004; Evans 2001; Gifford 1929; James 1997, 2002; Small 1997; Van der Grijp 1993). Other analysts of this system concur that the form of the gift affects the quality and timing of the countergift. What I have added here is a consideration of the effect of the form of the gift on the politics of the gift's reciprocation. A gift of textiles must be recognized with a countergift that others can read as representing continued sustenance and renewal of the kin group. A most suitable countergift would be *koloa* because these textiles have a long history of embodying Tongan cultural ideals and principles and are "bundles of iconicity and indexicality" (Küchler 2005:175). They underscore Tonga as a homeland with a kin-based system of agrarian production and exchange, and are crucial tools in Tongan nation building abroad.

Modern wealth—as a system encompassing cash, credit money, and even modern consumer goods—cannot replace *koloa* as a system. Based on the fact that cash bills are "generic, cannot accumulate history, and hence cannot add to the holder's identity" (Graeber 2001:213), they cannot symbolize the uniqueness of Tonga or the Tongan people. Ultimately, I contend that members of a Tongan diasporic community consider cash gifts alone to be an inadequate expression of their *'ofa* for a celebrant at a diasporic life crisis ceremony.

The funeral and pawnshop cases that I analyze above are examples of how individuals in the Tongan exchange system actively resist attempts to completely replace *koloa* with cash in ritual exchange, or to afford more opportunities to commodify specific pieces of *koloa* in order to procure cash—even temporarily and for pragmatic reasons. Thus, to some Tongans cloth may be "like money," but cloth and cash are not (yet) symbolic or material equivalents. In fulfilling responses to perform *langa fonua*, commoner Tongans have to meet the (ideological) challenge of performing tradition in contexts that demand sophisticated knowledge of living in modernity, while not appearing to have abandoned the traditions that they say make them uniquely Tongan. They have also brought the Tongan *fonua* to other parts of the world, creating a multiterritorial *fonua, through exchange.* Commoner women's *koloa* plays no small role in this major, modern accomplishment, as evidenced by Teuila's persistence at gifting her *koloa* at the funeral, even after it was refused by the bereaved family, Kakala's exchange of her *koloa* for cash in order to ensure later *koloa* exchanges, and by 'Ofa's resuming the exchange of *koloa* on her and Langi's return to Tonga after the funeral in Auckland.

In concluding, I make no predictions about trends in Tongan exchange, such as whether cash gifts will replace or outweigh cloth gifts in the future or whether *koloa* will becomes increasingly commodified. I do, however, make one suggestion: more nuanced, culturally relevant understandings of both *koloa* and money will contribute to the relevance of theoretical reflections on the sociality and political economy of migrant lives in the contemporary Pacific. The relationship of these two categories of valuables has been historically established in Tongan culture, but, as my discussion here has shown, the relationship is subject to much negotiation, especially as *kavenga* (rituals) and decisions concerning them may be cross-territorially planned and executed. To see cash and cloth as equivalent forms of value such that one form (money) might replace the other (*koloa*) in ritual exchange, would be to ignore just what is at stake for contemporary Tongans in valuing both cash and *koloa*, wherever they may dwell: maintaining social relations that take into account locality and political economy while affirming identity for individuals and re-creating society for the group.

Notes

1. According to Andrew Arno, writing about men's material currency in Fiji, "a ritual *tabua* can only represent itself, and this may be the key to its cultural supremacy as currency" (2005:56).
2. *Liongi* is a state of ritual mourning usually physically characterized by the wearing of large and tattered waist mats over black clothes (Churchward 1959).
3. Similarly, Katherine Rupp reports on *kokorozukai*, a category of Japanese gifts generally given out of gratitude, for example to doctors for healing a sick family member or for delivering a healthy baby: "It is not possible to bring these gifts to the hospital, where there is a sign that reads: 'We humbly ask that you refrain from kokorozukai' [so] patients simply send their gifts directly to the doctors' residences" (2003:163). Here, presumably, the gifts are not refused. In Tonga, just as in Japan, gifts already refused in one context may be accepted in another to save face for both givers and recipients.
4. Several other Tongan loan companies operate in Auckland, but do not accept *koloa faka-Tonga* as collateral (Snow, Druett, and Crawford 2006). All loan businesses have a singular visibility on the Tongan scene in New Zealand, because they announce on Tongan-language radio the names of people who have defaulted on their loans, and publish their names, pictures, villages of origin, and amounts owned in rather sordid full-page displays in the Tongan-language press. As suggested by the names of several of the pawnshops, many of these businesses target their advertising and décor specifically at Pacific Islanders in New Zealand. It is common to see offices decorated with posters of generic tropical beaches and with welcome signs in Tongan, Samoan, Fijian, New Zealand Maori, and Cook Islands Maori. Some, such as one called Pasifika Finance, advertise for other businesses that the owners have going, such as money transfers to the Pacific Islands. One loan business—called Pacific Loans—has a *tapa*-covered suggestion box on a prominently positioned countertop where customers are encouraged to leave comments that managers reputedly review on a weekly basis.

❧ 6
Church, Cash, and Competition
Multicentrism and Modern Religion

One of the contexts that most Tongans consider to symbolize "tradition" is the practice of donations to Christian churches, especially in the various Tongan Methodist denominations. As described earlier, members of these congregations are expected to present cash gifts to their churches at regular donation periods (*misinale*) and material gifts to church ministers, and churches play a key role in facilitating cash and in-kind donations to villages and national projects in Tonga. Since the late nineteenth century in Tonga cash has been a conventional form of church donation, but as we saw in chapter 5, it is not the preferred form in all cases. Another factor in understanding monetary church donations is that communitarian ideals still hold much weight among Tongans. That is, Tongan modernity does not, thus far, entirely follow the model of individual capital accumulation that prevails (at least discursively) in the West. Instead, it encapsulates processes of resource sharing between people using exchange to reinforce their mutual belonging to the same kin group (*kāinga*), congregation (*kāinga lotu*), and nation (*fonua*) and enshrines people's public reputations for sharing and reciprocating as forms of capital. In this chapter, I consider some of the ways in which Tongans perform *langa fonua* through exclusive use of money. I show that, even when *koloa* is excluded from exchange, its status as a category of objects plays a crucial role in shaping participants' ritual exchange behavior and public expression of cultural identity.

As part of my larger project in this book, I am interested in what an ethnography of contemporary Tongan transnationalism can add to the official and popular understandings of how people who are at the margins of modernity use economic capital in support of traditional cultural institutions and as a part of nation-building projects. In this chapter, I show how cash can be dissociated from its foreign origins in impersonal capitalist systems, and I argue that people derive agency from imbuing cash with some of the qualities of traditional gifts. These qualities include the capacity of *koloa* and *ngāue* to index the multiterritorial Tongan nation, Tongan cultural principles, and ideal kinship relations. People use cash to play such a role when they present it at life-crisis *kavenga*, but also when they gift it along with, or in exchange for, performing arts in both secular and religious contexts. I also resume my discussion of multicentrism in relating how multiple generations in Tongan diasporic communities use money in efforts to contribute to, and distinguish themselves within, the various global projects that can be said to constitute Tongan nation building. The example explored here is of Tongans supporting homeland institutions by gifting cash in diaspora.

Like kin-based ritual events, such as the wedding described in chapter 4 and the funeral in chapter 5, church events involve large outlays of cash. Often, this gifting is competitive, with members of different families trying to outdo those of other families in order to gain status from a reputation as the most generous gift givers, or those with the most *'ofa* (love, generosity, empathy; Lātūkefu 1974). Thus, cash is gifted in highly contingent and culturally-deter-mined ways. As Edward LiPuma states: "One of the defects of the ethnography of money is that, influenced by formal economic theory, it has too often as-sumed that there is a dichotomy between primitive and modern monies be-cause the latter has been freed from its social moorings … [when] the reality [is] that, at the existential level, both money and shells have numerous … social [and] socially defined uses and meanings" (LiPuma 2001:192). A particular competitive spirit has been reported as a feature of annual church donations in mainstream Tongan churches, primarily the Free Wesleyan Church (FWC) and the Church of Tonga denominations (Evans 2001; Rutherford 1996; Van der Grijp 1993). In this chapter I explore the relationship of that spirit of com-petition to expressions of love and nationalism.

In addition, I examine the exchange of valuables and sentiments at two other kinds of exchange events—a church youth camp and a fundraising con-cert. Based in Tongan diasporic churches these events expressly provide the context for people to gift cash that will be funneled, through one channel or another, to a community or congregation in other nation-states. Second- and 1.5-generation members were the primary performers. Both events were held in Auckland at branches of the FWC of Tonga. For diasporic communities, these gifts are essentially remittances that play a primary material role in dia-sporans' globalized nation-building projects; and they also exceed a strictly monetary value as expressions of abiding by Tongan cultural principles.

History of Tongan Exchange of Cash Gifts

Like many dimensions of contemporary Tongan life, the use of money as the currency of both faith and nation building among Tongans is intimately tied to the history of Tonga's modernization as a Christian nation (Herda, Reilly and Hilliard 2005; Lātūkefu 1974). When international trade in copra—the oil from the dried flesh of coconuts—burgeoned in the late nineteenth century, Ton-gans had long had their own forms of currency. These included valuables used for reciprocal gift exchange, to compensate for emotional loss or pain, and to recognize people of higher rank. Among these valuables, objects like *koloa* and prestige foods were the most important. Western, state-issued money (cash) entered the world of Tongan exchange alongside Tongan chiefs' experimentation with, and establishment of, a local form of Christianity, although many Tongans initially gave copra as donations to Methodist churches. Metal coin, introduced through the copra trade, soon replaced this currency. Peruvian and Chilean coin ultimately became the main modern money currency for Pacific trade, and were the first state currencies that Tongans used in their kingdom. A trade firm called Goddefroy and Sons was the sole importer of this bullion. A leading Methodist church minister, the Reverend Shirley Baker—who would eventually become Tonga's first premier under Australia's initial administration and then its first prime minister under its first monarch, Taufaʻahau Tupou I—ensured that this remained the case for many decades (Rutherford 1996). The silver coins' shininess rendered them ideal objects for distinguishing one's family and honoring a generous God, from whom all other blessings flowed; as noted previously, shininess remains a feature of great aesthetic value in *koloa* today (Veys 2009; Young Leslie 2004).

Basil Thomson (1894) described a donation practice called *sivi*, which was a sort of competitive game in which devotees walked in single file around a large washbasin set on the floor, tossing in their silver coin contributions, one coin at a time. As a person exhausted his or her coins, he or she would leave the line. The last person left standing was considered to have "won" the *sivi* and was looked highly upon by his or her peers: "it began to appear that the size of [the] contribution was the measure of the man's faith" (ibid.). Missionaries clearly encouraged the spirit of competitiveness with which people performed *sivi*:

> In front of the pulpit stood a table on which lay a common wash-hand basin and an account book. ... After the preliminary religious exercises, the missionary announced the name of [a] patron ... as the name of each patron was called she rose in a stately manner and cast her contribution into the basin as a nest egg. And now those who had promised contributions ... swaggered up the aisle and flung their coins into the basin ... when the basins had drained the congregation of their cash, the contents were quickly counted and the amount whispered to the presiding teacher. In crying aloud the contents of each basin he allowed pauses for the cheering, and artistically kept the largest until the last. (ibid.:187–191)

Sivi became institutionalized by the end of the nineteenth century, closely followed by regular church donation practices that Tongans referred to as "making missionary," or *misinale*. As I have discussed earlier, *misinale* became a financial mainstay of the local Wesleyan mission-run church. It resulted in regular monetary donations to the larger church through the mission's administration in Sydney, Australia.

The need for donations escalated in 1869 when the British Society withdrew its support for the Australian Methodist Missionary Society, at which time the latter turned to its subsidiary missions to raise funds both to support itself and to donate to the larger London Missionary Society's coffers (Rutherford 1996:42). Even in these early days of Pacific Christianity, observers remarked on the propensity among Tongans at the time to gift wealth beyond their apparent immediate material means, which some considered to amounted to "sheer pillage" (ibid.).

In all of the British colonies administered by Australia, the Tongan churches yielded the greatest amount in cash donation, and the amount increased each year. Indeed, Baker was particularly proud of his kingdom-wide campaign to make the Wesleyan church in Tonga the greatest donor of gifts to the church central administration. Money was important to please God and the church, to facilitate trade relations with Australia, and for Taufa'ahau Tupou I to feel that the Tongan nation was developing, under his rule, as a modern one. By the end of the nineteenth century, donations in copra were no longer suitable for the kind of distinction Tupou I wanted his kingdom to have in the eyes of the Church. However, Baker devised a scheme in which he would accept promissory notes from congregants stating an amount of coconut oil equivalent to a sum of money which, Noel Rutherford tellingly states, "they felt impelled to give" (1996:47).

It is worth considering why a people who were new to Christianity and new to Western modernity would embrace the expenditure of extra energy and resources in exchange for a promise. But consider that the promise was one of eternal life—their souls would be saved by a benevolent, but selective God. For commoners who, in original indigenous epistemology, had never been given the privilege of thinking of themselves as people with souls, this was of immeasurable value. Exchanging some worldly wealth for a reward such as this must have seemed a fair proposition. As one of my Tongan women informants in New Zealand stated to me: "death is certain, but what happens after death can only be affected by what we do in life." Thus, as several anthropologists have theorized, continuing to gift—and gifting to excess—offers some measure of assurance that a person will gain a spiritual reward at the end of life (Godelier 1999, Mauss 1990 [1925]; Sykes 2005). Marcel Mauss (1990 [1925]) grappled with this question of the (materially) unanswered gift in discussing gifts made to gods and, thus, with no expectation of reciprocation. He suggested the gifts given with no expectation of material return—such as gifts presented to the gods and gifts given as alms to the poor—are ways of maintaining links, and perhaps agency, between material goods and the world of the sacred.

Today, *misinale* remains the most important church *kavenga*—obligatory gift occasion—among Tongan Methodist adherents. So *misinale* constitutes a public arena in which to demonstrate commitment to Tongan culture and to God, and so another focus around which Tongans create ethnic communities overseas. The structure of *misinale* donations, the way they facilitate the assemblage of cash resources, the public way in which they are gifted, and the ways in which families associate with one another to make composite gifts, continue to epitomize those acts that are recognized as deeply traditional among contemporary, mainstream Methodist Tongans. Individuals contribute to donations made by their immediate families who are further organized into *kalasi 'aho* (groups comprising several distinct families within a given congregation), and donate money as a lump sum to the church. Within a given congregation, *kalasi 'aho* often compete to give the most money at a specific *misinale;* as in the days of Tupou I and Baker, respect and extra blessings assumedly accrue to the group that presents the largest amount.

Tongan nation building continues to be materially and symbolically facilitated through building up church coffers. Tongan diasporans from a range of denominations send "indirect remittances" through formal institutions such as churches (Lee 2009a), thus using the church as a conduit to channel long-distance monetary support (remittances) to groups in the homeland. A commitment to building up the nation is evidenced when a person uses his/her material wealth to "regularly give generously to church," "support schools [they] went to in the past," "host relatives from overseas," and "be[come] known to participate in church" (Evans, Harms, and Reid 2009:118–119).

Cash Gifts, Church, and Nation Building

David Graeber, citing E. E. Evans-Pritchard (1940) suggests that, "[v]alues ... are embodied in words through which they influence behavior." For example, "the notion of home ... [can] serve to determine who one considers a friend, and who an enemy," and in this way "becomes a political value as well[, where] value ... [means] something more like 'importance': one's home is essential to one's sense of self, one's allegiances, what one most cares about" (2001:13). So too notions of value—the complex of things that people in a particular society consider worth striving for—bear a strong relationship to the concepts that people consider essential to their identity and to the practices that they believe make them unique in the world. Among diasporic Tongans these concepts, or cultural values, include love, respect, reciprocity, and mutual help. Certain practices are associated with these concepts, among them the now-institutionalized practices of transnational migration, exchanging gifts within kin groups, and gifting money to church coffers. An additional cultural value—the concept of *lotu* (religion, denomination, church, or prayer)—indexes the cultural expectation that church, the rituals that are performed within it, and the practice of daily prayer are centrally placed in people's lives. For FWC adherents *lotu* also invokes kin-based exchanges as sites of value, along with the Tongan homeland and its Christian identity and history.

Today, there are very strong connections between homeland churches and their branches in the Tongan diaspora. Tongan diasporans' denominational affiliations and kinship identity tend to be closely tied to one another because the majority of commoner Tongans in diaspora are members of Christian congregations with which they and their families had been affiliated before they emigrated from Tonga. Along with loyalty to God, Tongan churches implicitly teach loyalty to the kingdom through their encouragement of congregants to gift cash that the churches then funnel back to the homeland. Like other Pacific Islander churches, Tongan churches are "active local institutions" (Macpherson 2002). They are sites for congregating as a face-to-face community, and provide a physical and spiritual anchor for historical and homeland-established practices and values that are illustrative of *langa fonua*.

The FWC church makes multiple requests for donations from congregants in diaspora. For example, during my fieldwork in Auckland in early 2002, hurricane Waka hit the northern Tongan island group of Vava'u, causing widespread damage in a place that is generally ill prepared with disaster relief supplies. The steward of the Tongan Methodist Church I attended with Kakala, my hostess in Auckland, appealed to congregants for donations of non-perishable food, clothing, and household items to aid the relief efforts in Vava'u. He announced that a shipping container had been placed at a specific site in South Auckland—the location of the largest Pacific Islander immigrant neighborhoods in New Zealand—for the purpose of collecting these items. Appealing to the importance of Tonga and Tongans as a nation, as well as to the Tongan principle of *foaki* (being willing to freely give to others), the steward announced: "so, please, go and give whatever you can before the container leaves next week for Vava'u … you don't have to be from Vava'u to *want* to give a gift." Appealing to a congregant's sense of allegiance to the Tongan nation, rather than to a particular island or region, the pastor reminded congregants that they are crucial parts of what Jon Goss and Bruce Lindquist would call Tongans' "self-sustaining migration networks and institutions" (2000:387). For first-generation Tongans far from the land of their birth, and even for second-generation Tongans in diaspora, such allegiance can continue to provide a framework within which Tongans can feel the benefits of performing *langa fonua* by gifting their cash wealth.

Members travel frequently between Tonga and the diaspora, and diasporans gift cash to churches, youth groups, and charitable causes in Tonga. Homeland churches sometimes send delegations to diasporic churches for purposes of fundraising. When diasporic congregations visit Tonga, there is very little gifting of money by local congregations, because of the assumption that Tongan island churches are much poorer than their diasporic counterparts. This notion is in keeping with many Tongans' belief that Tongans in the diaspora have access to more cash than Tongans based in the homeland. Youth groups from diaspora often perform modern religious songs during church services and traditional Tongan dance and song arts (called *faiva*) during church camps and fundraising concerts that are often held in the halls adjoining diasporic FWC chapels.[1] Members of island-based congregations usually say they feel "enriched" by the chance to host visiting congregations. Such visits often allow for reunions between family members, and youth are encouraged to look for potential mates within the church congregations, as parents assume that the children of fellow congregants would be committed to both Tongan culture and church community. Potentially large cash exchanges facilitate these crucial interactions and people who attend and are witnessed gifting cash in these contexts build up their social and cultural capital.

Yet cash itself lacks the "symbolic density" of traditional valuables. Symbolic density is Annette Weiner's term for a notion that the value of an object that exceeds its material or exchange value (1992). Traditional valuables that are associated with cultivation of the land and that take time to grow or make and prepare for gifting are laden with *mana* (see Douaire-Marsaudon 2008) and with symbolic density. However, the specific ways in which agents use money can affect whether others register a positive or negative association between the money and the person in question. So, for example, gifting money publicly to institutions such as churches and disaster-affected villages that represent Tongan culture, writ large, entangles a person's reputation with the principle of *langa fonua* (nation building) and the public identification with Christian faith. Given that both *langa fonua* and Christianity are lived as kin-based activities, cash can be the currency of professed faith. Moreover, when a person gifts cash in the name of his or her kin group, capital accrues to the kin groups in terms of recognition by others.

Many Tongans still consider cash to be a *pālangi* (Western) valuable and associate money with a different moral universe: one in which capitalist relations, not the reciprocal relations of the gift, rule social interaction. However, Tongans adapt some of the ways they use cash to make it suitable for gift giving in religious contexts. Following principles of *langa fonua* and gifting publicly for the glory of God helps to dissociate money from its origins in the West and relocalize it as valuable suitable for Tongan exchange.

Using cash as a gift is a way of mediating between the materiality of money and the immateriality of the divine (Maurer 2005:141; Miller 2005:31). Many religious communities have developed a modern discourse about the desirability of money for their spiritual enrichment, one that specifically enables their members to dissociate themselves from ungodly characteristics of selfishness or worldliness. For example, in *Money Has No Smell* (2004), Paul Stoller argues that money, while not something that should be coveted, is considered spiritually neutral to many of the rules of Muslim morality for traders from Niger who sell African goods in New York City. In some cases, however, money given as gift can actually combat the negative associations of its being acquired for its own material sake. Contemporary Pacific peoples also engage in a range of discourses about the role of cash in both economic and spiritual development of their communities and have ways of rendering cash appropriate for spiritual purposes. For example, one ideological discourse positions money outside of traditional Fijian constructions of morality that eschew commodity exchange, but gifting cash appropriately in religious situations has the ability to "purify" the cash (Toren 1989). Likewise, Tongans consider cash to become "cleansed" of its negative associations with, and origins in Western cultures and economies when it is gifted with a heart that loves God. Retaining this religious element of the association of cash with modernity renders cash a valuable that is suitable for doing Tongan tradition. Tongans have, thus, a cultural capacity for managing the politics of the assumed disconnect between money and the moral world that it is being used to underwrite.

Moreover, that Tongans gift cash to what some would call excess—and what Karen Sykes (2005), in her discussion of the Kwakiutl potlatch, refers to as "giving beyond reason"—suggests an anxiety with some aspect of life: its inevitable end, perhaps. It explains, in part, why a working-class diaspora family that has little spare cash would give hundreds, sometimes thousands, of dollars to their church when they have bills to pay. The anxiety may well have to do with the fact that, in religious endeavors, one is always focused on the certainty of death and what happens after it (ibid.), but also on the uncertainties of modernity (Besnier 2011).

Fundraising: Culture, Cash Gifts, and Kin-Group Loyalty

The most lucrative forms of fundraising in Tongan communities integrate Tongan performing arts, the ethos of gifting, and kin group or kinlike loyalty. People gift money in support of performances by their relatives, fellow villagers (Evans 2001), fellow ex-students or the members of their *kāinga lotu*, or congregations (Lee 2004). Tongan institutions rarely hold fundraisers that involve outright sale of things—such as in bake sales or raffles that are popular in many other Christian groups' fundraising efforts—as these do not afford everyone who donates a chance to participate as *gifters* and to enjoy beloved forms of cultural entertainment. In the context of gifting for religious purposes, the Tongan body plays a crucial role: the body is a stage upon which the history of Christian devotion continues to be performed, to echo Adrienne Kaeppler (1993 [1987]). The properly comported body is also a sign of the success of the later-eighteenth- and early-twentieth-century Christian project (Besnier 2011; see also Burns 2008 and Douaire-Marsaudon 2008).[2] Those performing—unmarried young girls whose demureness and skill in performing Tongan culture potentially give "face" to their families—are expected to rehearse their routines and perform to the best of their ability. Likewise, female relatives spend many hours making or preparing costumes from barkcloth, fabric, and even fresh leaves sewn onto a fabric base, and they dress and decorate dancers for their performances with much care and precision.

Gifting money in exchange for the joy of watching dance performances is a process that everyone can participate in, and people typically enjoy the social time spent watching them together and the chance to come together as a community. Moreover, interaction with the performers is also a gift-delivery system that involves putting cash bills directly onto the body of the performer, echoing a pre-contact practice of placing *koloa* at the feet of high-ranking performers or wrapping it around their bodies or at their feet. In commoner dances, gifts of money are either pasted (*tā*, literally "slapped") onto the dancers' well-oiled arms, or tucked into their shirt or costume collars and their waistbands (see figure 6.1). The gift giver can present cash in the form of a "*lei*" made of currency bills that have been strung together; and may also throw the cash bills into the air above the head of the dancer(s). Tongan cash gifts are always given in the local state currency of the country where a ritual or event is taking place, regardless of where the giver lives, works, or has traveled from. This is because money needs to be immediately useful to the recipients, who may well need to use it to purchase tickets for further travel or to gift to someone else locally.

Any cash thus gifted is collected by others and put into a box or basket, counted, and eventually presented to the intended recipient, who is either a specific individual or a congregation. Unless the dancer receives a gift as a token after the dance, she does not keep any of the money donated during her performance. By passing the money on to someone else in the group, the dancer evinces generosity and love, and transforms economic capital into social capital—respect for herself and her kin group, whose *'ofa* (love) for fellow congregants, Tongan culture, and God she delivers with her dance (Bourdieu 1986). In the context of the religious institution, the congregation effects a further "transmutation of capital" (ibid.) so that the social and economic capital are transformed into spiritual capital, or people's admiration for, and assumptions that God will bless both the dancer and other believers assembled.

Diasporic groups may also come together under the commitment to the umbrella notion of being Tongan, but people usually show that they are further divided into different kin groups through their competitive gifting to support

Figure 6.1. A young girl performs a *tauʻolunga* dance for a wedding couple. Her relatives present *koloa* and money (tucked into the front of her costume), Nukuʻalofa.

relatives or people from particular villages in Tonga where they have ancestral ties. When attending an event at which a relative is performing a dance or song, Tongans are responsible for doing their part in publicly supporting the *kāinga* by gifting performers with cash. Individuals might represent two different kin groups—their mother's *kāinga* and their father's *kāinga*—and, if so, they are doubly obligated to present cash gifts at fundraising events.

Church camps (*ʻapitanga*) and fundraising "concerts" (or *koniseti*) are two forms of fundraising events that Tongan Methodist churches in diaspora regularly host. They are both contexts for gifting money either to the church or, through the church, to causes in home villages in Tonga and to delegations who visit on church business. Youth groups play a key role in both *ʻapitanga* and *koniseti*: they sing Tongan songs that they have rehearsed numerous times, and perform Tongan dances and skits. Sometimes a family will sponsor the gift of a dance by a young woman or teenage girl in their kin group, donating a lump sum of money. The sum is announced over a loudspeaker as the girl begins to dance and, while she dances, attendees who are members of the sponsoring family approach her and present other smaller sums of money. They each place their money on the dancer's arms, tuck it into her costume, or pin it in her hair. Once they have thus gifted, they often join her and dance behind her for the rest of her time "on stage," showing her further encouragement in representing their *kāinga*. Such gifts demonstrate the presenters' support for the church and for Tongan culture more broadly by rewarding youths' mastery of cultural skills.

Like extended kin-group interactions, the practice of presenting performances and cash in church contexts supports the teaching of cultural roles and responsibilities to Tongan youth. Youth groups are an integral part of Tongan village structure and, being normally associated with the church, they also afford a sense of cultural continuity for diasporic Tongans who are often highly scrutinized by homeland-raised Tongans for signs that they are loyal to and competent in "the Tongan way." Having youth perform endows fundraising events with further cultural value because it provides evidence of a particular Tongan congregation's devotion to and success at raising children to fear God and to honor Tongan culture, family, and nation. In addition, growing up as a member of a church youth group can contribute to Methodist Tongan youth's development of an invaluable sense about how doing Tonganness *feels*. When young people return to Tonga on family visits, they are often expected to perform at family gatherings or with the local church group in their parents' villages. There is much at stake for the performers, their families, and the audience in such performances.

Indeed, public recognition that the youth in the diasporic congregations know, respect, and perform *anga faka-Tonga* (the Tongan way) competently carries a very high value. Since individual's actions are judged as a reflection on their family's attitudes, for the family of the youth in question, a legitimate claim to Tongan identity is at stake. As I discussed in chapter 4, materializing the homeland in diasporic celebrations is integral to authenticating a performance of Tonganness in expatriate contexts, partly because it reifies the links between the homeland *fonua* and its globally dispersed people. Children who grow up socialized through such events, as well as through speaking the Tongan language, learn to perform Tongan identity in ways that reflect positively on their parents and that garner their families' praise from their relatives in the homeland and in other parts of the ethnoscape. The following case studies of ʻ*apitanga* and *koniseti* consider in greater detail how gifting money in the Tongan diaspora, particularly as this involves Tongan youth, articulates with the larger project of creating and maintaining the ties that contribute to—and even more so *constitute*—the multiterritorial Tongan nation.

ʻ*Apitanga:* Gifting Cash at the Church Easter Camp

Church camps often take place during the Lenten season, usually lasting for the week, and culminating on Easter Sunday. Fundraising revolves around monetary gifts presented to dancers and singers during traditional-style Tongan dances, songs, and skits. The participants in 'apitanga are typically members of youth groups from congregations in overseas Tongan communities who have traveled to a specific site where there is a vibrant Tongan community and congregation. During diasporic 'apitanga, and especially at churches that have large building complexes, participants spend all day involved in camp-related activities, eating most of their meals on the premises and often sleeping there as well. One particular Free Wesleyan Church in a South Auckland suburb has kitchen facilities, a large, tiled-floor church hall, and a 300-person capacity chapel. At the 'apitanga at this church, which I observed in 2001, participants slept on mattresses and in sleeping bags on the floor. In keeping with gender avoidance rules within a given generation, makeshift dormitories were arranged so that males and females could sleep separately. Youth especially relish this time to socialize with friends and cousins, stay up late, and spend time outside of their parents' presence. However, elderly people and entire immediate families also look forward to the shared time and space away from household responsibilities and usually consider the 'apitanga a time of relaxation and camaraderie.

In addition to dances and songs that commemorate Tonga's unique performing arts, youth also provide entertainment and help deliver morality lessons in the form of skits (known as "dramas") with religious and moral messages about putting God first and being obedient to parents. They may reenact Bible stories or provide parodic depictions of fictive villagers who turn away from God and are brought back to the truth by members of the church. Youth are rewarded with cash gifts only for traditional performing arts of song (*hiva*) and dance (*tau'olunga*)—but rarely for skits—in which some audience participation is typical. When members rise to dance behind a performer, they usually place some money on the dancer first. 'Apitanga are, first and foremost, religious events and are distinguished from "floor shows," a secular form of fundraising that also plays a role as entertainment at celebrations such as ex-student associations and family reunions.

Among the most anticipated performances are those by members of youth groups from congregations in overseas Tongan communities. Sometimes the performers display symbols, such as national flags of the country where they currently live, consciously honoring their diasporic homes as much as they do Tonga or the FWC. Audience members, who are also congregants, recognize the performers with money that is normally collected by older youth who put them into large buckets or baskets to be counted later.[3] At this particular week-long event, over $50,000 in funds were raised for the church, entirely from donations by congregants attending the 'apitanga.

That weekend's *faiva* (traditional song and dance) were held on a rainy Easter Saturday and were one of highlights of the 'apitanga. Delegations of youth from FWC church in New Zealand, Australia, Hawai'i, and the US mainland performed a series of songs and dances; the youth group from the Auckland church that was hosting performed a skit. It was a highly anticipated event: for several weeks before Easter the 'apitanga was announced at every FWC church service I attended in various parts of Auckland. Congregants were reminded, at preceding church meetings and in Tongan community radio announcements, to "come and support" ("ha'u ke poupou"). The rain that weekend did not deter the hundreds of people who squeezed into a large rented tent that had been erected for the occasion outside of this particular FWC building in South Auckland. They sat as comfortably as they could on layers of cardboard that had been spread on the damp ground under the tent. Virtually everyone in attendance was a Free Wesleyan Church of Tonga member. This was a very special and formal occasion, judging from the fact that people were as finely dressed as they would be for a church service. One local Tongan family, comprising a grandmother and her four grandchildren, wore matching outfits that the grandmother said her daughter had made especially for the event. The daughter was absent from the event that day due to work (see figure 6.2).

Matching attire also distinguished members of youth performance groups. For example, members of the delegation that hailed from a FWC in Sydney, Australia, wore yellow and green, those from Hawai'i wore white shirts with blue and white raffia "grass skirts" around their waists, the group representing the local FWC in Auckland wore white shirts and black wrap "skirts" that were decorated with white curvilinear Maori designs (koru). This latter group performed a song in Maori, incorporating dance movements that had been obviously derived from Maori culture.

During the faiva, individuals from the audience approached the dancers and placed New Zealand currency bills on them, tucking the bills into the collars, necklines, and waistbands of the dancers and (usually male) singers who stood to the rear of the performing group. At the end of each performance, the money that congregants donated during the performance was counted up and the amount announced by the emcee. These announcements fueled people's sense of pride and competitiveness, encouraging those connected to dancers from subsequent groups to gift even more during the group's next dances.

The Hawai'i delegation entered holding aloft both a US flag and a Hawai'i state flag. Many of the young people who performed wore lei (neck garlands) made from strings of polished black candlenuts over the collars of their white button-down shirts; they also wore waist streamers comprising pleated white ribbon suspended from red and white waistbands. Their first act was a group dance performed by several young women dressed in black tops and skirts; the skirts were made of hand-painted barkcloth pieces (ngatu ngatu) that had been decorated with striking examples of traditional barkcloth designs. The national flags and the barkcloth were signs of the different groups' belonging in United States, Tonga, and Hawai'i, as well as of these countries' particular self-constructions as sovereign nations.

After the Hawai'i group performed, the continental American (*Amelika lahi*) group entered holding aloft their US flag, and began their time on the stage with one girl's solo a cappella performance of "The Star-Spangled Banner," during which she held her hand dutifully over her heart. The male flag bearer and some of the other young men, who stood behind the female performers, wore matching t-shirts printed with motifs of the US flag. Taking photographs as best I could from behind viewers who would suddenly rise to recognize performers, I pondered these competitive displays of nationalism: the youth's costumes, their artistic performances, the audience's cheers for particular groups, and their enthusiastic gifting to the youth groups who conspicuously represented the countries where the givers live now.

At one point during this particular performance, Sulieti, an Auckland Tongan woman whom I had met previously, arrive, and tapped me on the shoulder, asking, "Where is the group from America? I want to put some money on them. ... Pingi come with me and we'll go and [put some money on] them. ... I'm so happy I did not arrive any later than this or I would have missed them." With that she pressed a small wad of New Zealand currency bills into my left hand, grabbed me by the right, and pulled me toward the dancers. We walked up to the "stage," bent over at the waist so as not to block the audience's view of the dancers, and tucked bills into collars and waistbands, then we quickly left the stage. Sulieti beamed during the rest of the performance and, having accomplished her duty to recognize her relatives in the group, left soon after the group's last dance. Before she left she informed me that she was planning a trip to visit her relatives in Los Angeles and San Francisco, one of whom had a child who was part of the mainland America delegation. Sulieiti's gift to this youngster was probably as much a gift anticipating the hospitality from which she hoped to benefit during her visit to America as it was a sign of appreciation for the young woman's dancing skills. Sulieti's gift to her cousin's daughter afforded her a form of social value, an accumulation of obligation that others in her social group would feel compelled to reciprocate.

Eventually, the time came for the Tongan delegation to perform. Theirs was the last performance and, as the youth from that delegation entered the tent, bearing aloft the Tongan national flag, there was a noticeable peak in excitement among the audience. As soon as they began to perform, spectators rose with money in their hands and, for the duration of practically their entire *faiva* it was difficult to see many of the performers and their movements at all, so many were the audience members who kept rising to press money upon them. Here, diaspora dwellers were the principle people performing gift-giving acts; this was also their chance to fulfill a duty of being diasporans—to

Figure 6.2. A family in matching outfits of commercially printed cotton; the fabric's patterns resemble traditional barkcloth designs, Auckland.

gift to Tonga, to contribute to *langa fonua,* to do so publicly, and to express all of this in the presence of God.

That people see themselves as interrelating across time and space as they transact cash makes it crucial to consider multicentrism when examining the links between the Tongan exchange, nation building, and diaspora. In this case, the performers are helping to funnel economic capital (money) toward another institution or group: the church or village. Economic capital cannot move without people to send, transfer, and receive it in various stages and various locations, thus gifting cash depends on particular spatial relationships between sending, receiving, and mediating persons or groups. The idiom in which these relationships are ideally developed is kinship, and kinship is also apparent in fundraising concerts, or *koniseti.*

Koniseti: Fundraising Concerts

Koniseti tend to be collective, festive gatherings organized to bring people together in support of particular projects, both religious and secular. The projects *koniseti* help to sponsor include raising money to fix a church building, funding a church youth group's visit to a church in another part of the ethnoscape, and subsidizing village building or infrastructure improvement projects. When secular *koniseti* are held in a village hall in Tonga, they can be highly entertaining events featuring traditional female solo dances and skits that range from the serious and instructive to the hilarious. The performers never keep monetary gifts but donate them to the intended beneficiaries, although sometimes adults will give small token cash gifts to performers who are young children if the audience especially loved their portrayal. *Koniseti* can also double as events to bid farewell to a visiting ex-student group or church youth group from Tonga. The fund raising is a key, if not, the key, aspect of such trips, as it ensures that the group return to Tonga materially enriched.

The particular *koniseti* I analyze here took place right after the week of the *'apitanga* (Easter Camp) at the FWC in Auckland in April 2002, and it was meant for far more than just entertainment. It was a farewell event for the delegation from Tonga whose performance I described earlier and who had "brought the house down" at the Easter Camp the previous weekend. The *koniseti* began with prayers and welcome speeches by the pastor and the steward of the Church. In one evening, sixteen different dances were performed, some by members of the local church and others by members of the visiting delegation from Tonga who had been staying with relatives in various parts of Auckland for the duration of the church camp. The dance performances at the event were meant to raise funds with which the visiting delegation from Tonga would return. Thus, they did not have as strong a religious overtone as the *'apitanga* itself. During some of the women's solo dances, the performers wore costumes made of folded pieces of textile *koloa* that had been wrapped around the body and tied at the waist. Their arms and shoulders were bare, which enabled excited family members to recognize dancers by pasting currency bills directly onto their oiled arms and shoulders. As is traditional in Tongan dance, arms, shoulders and backs are the parts of the body that move the most in the performance of a dance and they also become the material tablet upon which return gifting of money is performed.

Two dances stood out: a solo dance, called a *tau'olunga,* performed by a young woman from the Auckland congregation named Lose, and an impromptu dance by a young man from the Tongan delegation. Lose's dance was fairly typical of dances that a kin group might gift along with some cash at an important ceremonial event, such as a wedding. Kakala, whom I introduced earlier was Lose's great aunt and it was she who sponsored Lose's dance with a $100 gift. The $100 accompanied the gift of the dance and constituted, by extension, a gift from Kakala to the homeland of Tonga. Indeed, I heard onlookers refer to the dance as "Kakala's *tau'olunga.*" Gifts of solo dances are generally not considered to be from the performer herself, but from the member of her family who sponsors her dance. In a competitive arena like this one, where congregations are represented by constituent families, the gifting of money rendered Kakala and her family as generous and full of love to onlookers. The people performing the dance were merely mediums for the transference of this sense of value, their bodies servings as tablets, again, upon which that value—translated into money—was literally placed.

Another solo dance performance by a particular teenaged boy from the visiting Tongan group transformed the audience into a gifting machine. As he approached the front of the church hall, the emcee announced that this boy had no relatives in New Zealand; there were murmurs of "what a pity" (*faka'ofa*) from some in the audience. As the recorded music for his dance began to play, a remarkable frenzy ensued as spectators—mostly women—stood and walked towards him. And as he began to dance there was a flurry of tucking bills in his clothing, pasting them on his skin, and throwing them into the air above his head. It was as if he had suddenly acquired numerous relatives in Auckland. Clearly, feelings of pity and generosity motivated his many supporters, who were from all the different churches represented, and gave the money for the boy to take back to Tonga. Kakala's sister, Talanoa, also rose, changing a $100 bill into ten $10 bills at a table near the side of the stage where a middle-aged man sat giving people change for large bills. She pinned the ten bright blue bills together and then clipped them into the boy's hair so that they bobbed and flowed with his head movements as a decorative comb or feather head ornament would in other dance contexts (Kaeppler 1993). Talanoa's two sisters and some of their children and grandchildren also rose, placed additional cash gifts on him, and then joined Talanoa who was dancing behind the young man, using comical movements that traditionally highlight the grace and beauty of the main dancer's performance (ibid.). One of the elderly sisters suggestively pulled her thirty-something, recently divorced daughter to dance next to the young man. The audience roared with laughter, relishing the humor suggested by the inappropriateness of the match, but also appreciating the older woman's generosity in gifting one of her daughters to this young man, if only jokingly.

Almost regardless of the gift being offered, having a "heart that wants to give" and being inclined to give publicly signals to others that a person has sincere faith in God and has been raised with regard for *anga faka-Tonga*, the Tongan way. Integral to both of these personal qualities is further faith that the Tongan community will recognize one's generosity and will show support when one is faced with ceremonial or monetary needs in the future. Indeed, in a gift society like Tongan culture, the social and spiritual value that accrue to an individual through exchanges like those discussed above inspire still further presentations of gifts. This system provides tacit assurance that the giver will receive gifts and reciprocal relations in the future—an assurance that she will neither starve nor be lonely in lean times. Even though both commodity and gift exchange are perhaps equally deeply embedded in the system of transnational exchange, as both are necessary for daily survival and useful in fulfilling ceremonial obligations, it is the assurance of community support and spiritual protection implied by the gift that motivates Tongans to use money as gift. Rather than simply employing cash as a means to participate in commodity purchase and capitalist exchange—even though both are coveted signs of modernity—Tongans regularly use money in service of "tradition."

Furthermore, in the processes that create such meanings for members of an ethnic community, a mutual interdependence links the generations of diaspora dwellers together (Levitt 2009). When Tongan youth—members of the 1.5 and second generation in the hostland—witness their parents and older relatives gifting money, the cash gift becomes transformed from a "foreign" or *pālangi* valuable with fungibility in modern contexts into a valued expression of their inalienable Tongan cultural identity. Likewise, to constitute the very bodies upon which such gifts are placed gives the younger generation a strong sense of having a stake in, and being instruments for, the maintenance of culture and identity. *'Apitanga* and *koniseti*, like numerous other contexts in which gifts pass between people for the mutual benefit of multiple generations of community members, reference the homeland and the multiterritorial nation in material and affective ways.

Conclusion: Gifting as Multicentrism

This chapter has argued that gifting in the context of events held by or at mainstream Tongan churches in diaspora is a major expression of multicentrism and a key process in global nation building. Just as an idiom of kinship governs

Tongans' exchange of traditional wealth in *kavenga,* or family-based life-crisis ceremonies, it also governs their exchange of cash wealth in both religious and secular contexts. The relatives of performers at fundraising events are culturally bound to show their love and commitment (*'ofa*) for the dancers by bestowing them with cash gifts. The principle of mutual help comes into play at contemporary Tongan fundraising events, but so does the tendency to strategize in order to make the biggest and most impressive gifts. In part motivated by a similar commitment to the notion of God's beneficence toward those who act generously with their material wealth, diasporic Tongan communities contribute cash gifts and thereby compete for spiritual capital on behalf of their families. Besides accruing prestige for such public gifting, these individuals help to materially support their kin from different parts of the ethnoscape and help their own church congregations accumulate social and spiritual capital. First- and second-generation members alike are motivated by this notion of mutual help (*fētokoni'aki*) and the culturally recognizable "face" that they are compelled to give their kin groups and communities.

Cash gifts thus motivated become contributions to Tongans' globalized nation building. Modern diasporic fundraising events are part of the way mainstream Tongan churches funnel money to other locations in the Tongan ethnoscape and, especially, to the homeland. Dances and songs performed simultaneously by a group of performers are considered the ideal acts to reward with money and have become the focal point of modern fundraising in Tongan communities all over the world. That such gifting affords gift givers a chance to reaffirm ties with relatives and friends who may live in another part of the Tongan ethnoscape makes the paired identity projects of nation building and accruing spiritual value through the gift not just possible, but also ultimately desirable and extremely enjoyable. Moreover, the gifting of cash allows people to show approval of, and commitment to, the raising of youth who are devoted to Tongan arts and culture, kinship constructions, and particular contemporary forms of Tongan Christianity.

Events like church camps and concerts gain symbolic value as sites of cash gifting because they are used to demonstrate that diasporic Tongans are generous, interested, and invested on numerous levels in *langa fonua,* or nation building. Rather than simply remitting money to relatives who then gift the money through *misinale* (annual donation) to the church, diasporic Methodist Tongans can also perform their own loyalties to Tonga and to the church by publicly presenting money to other church members who visit their diasporic location from other parts of the ethnoscape. They do so through institutions of kinship and religion and by publicly performing their connections to place and, especially, to Tonga. Churches are thus both the recipients and the conduits of large transfers of wealth between Tongans in diaspora and the homeland. Through the institution of mainstream Methodist churches, Tongans have developed a system of consumption and exchange that intertwines two influential realms of desire: personal distinction and respecting traditions. And, just as they gain spiritual capital by gifting lump sum cash donations to the church, so too Tongans who gift money at more secular fundraising events like *koniseti* also enhance their cultural capital by being recognized as (economically) invested in Tonga, Tongans, and the intertwined globalized projects that constitute Tongan nation building and Tongan modernity.

Notes

1. For a more thorough discussion of the contemporary aspects of *faiva* performances and its constituent elements—song, dance, poetry, oratory—as well as its relationship to other forms of Tongan cultural expression such as barkcloth, see Kaeppler 1993a and Māhina 2004, among others.

2. As I have explored in another publication (Addo 2003), the dressed Tongan body brings together Western and Tongan elements with a syncretism that embodies *anga faka-Tonga,* or "the Tongan way." This most often takes place in the form of a stitched, ankle-length, two-piece outfit for women and a dress shirt and "tailored men's skirt," both with *ta'ovala* (waist mat) or *kie kie* (braided belt with tassels). This mode of dressing was formalized by Queen Sālote in the 1950s, as part of the monarchy's ongoing project of modernizing Tonga through carefully adapting certain expressions of formerly chiefly attire (see Wood-Ellem 1999).

Conclusion ❧

Moving, Dwelling, and Transforming Spaces

For people in diaspora communities, there continues to be a powerful connection between feeling tied to a place and moving between various places. This book has explored this connection through the lens of women's material culture production and exchange, illuminating how the movement of objects maps spaces of significance for social actors and how the roles assigned to certain valuables continue to be shaped by competing ideas about gender roles, cultural and religious identity, history, the present, and the future. Recognizing that movement must be punctuated by culturally significant activity on the ground, the book has also thrown into relief some of the contexts in which a people creatively engage in both movement and dwelling in their ongoing making of a nation. That nation is, today, not bound by territory but is marked by particular social and economic activity whose meanings are encoded in valuables like *koloa faka-Tonga*. As *koloa* are exchanged across time and place, whether over small distances—between family members in a village, for example—or the much greater expanses between sites in the Tongan diaspora, they become tools in how Tongans in various locations establish additional "cores and centers" (Lilomaiava-Doktor 2009) outside of their home villages or the ancestral homeland, Tonga. Living outside of Tonga may help strengthen emigrants' ties to home, as "home" now constitutes a multiterritorial *fonua*—globally dispersed, but intimately connected sites—over which they continue to perpetuate their culture and values.

Since Tongans in diaspora are so deeply and regularly engaged with their relatives in Tonga—people with whom and, in other contexts, in whose name they exchange valuables—a study of diasporic nation building among Tongans today has to take into account the role of spatial relationships articulated through the movements of valuables. Objects move across national boundaries and accrue (or lose) value in people's efforts to (re-)create meaningful cultural spaces and to augment their relationships therein. In this book, these relationships have been understood through an examination of a series of linked themes concerning women, their exchange of material culture as gift, nation building, and globalization. Here I rearticulate these themes and also suggest areas for further research on diasporic communities that follow logically from my analysis of first-generation Tongan women's agency, nation building, and ceremonial exchange. In the latter vein, I explore further areas of development for the study of the second generation in diaspora.

Movement and Dwelling: Constructing a Nation

Movement and dwelling are twin practices in the diasporic construction of place, and the development of spatial relationships is a necessary result of the dialogic interplay between the two. Dwelling, not just movement, is essential in diaspora because it is through dwelling that people can nurture the relationships that develop or are taken for granted reason for people being in specific locations. I have used an indigenous Tongan term for the multiterritorial nation that Tongans construct as they establish diasporic communities and continue to maintain relationships with co-ethnics in the homeland and in other diaspora locations: *fonua*. As a process of place making, *fonua* involves Tongans' cultural construction of their world from the "conjuncture of people and place" (Francis 2007, 2009). Intrinsic to this notion is the experience of people connecting to places as sites for meaningful activity, and not simply to places as locations.

Movement and dwelling encode rupture and reconnection, yet they both have epistemological and ontological value in the Pacific: they are central to how people have come to make and to know their world. For example, Pacific origin stories and mythology feature many accounts of ancestral and divine movement to dwell in new places (see Collocott 1924 and Craig 1989, among others). Ancient and contemporary movement across the Pacific has necessarily been punctuated with dwelling, which has further been marked by ritually recognizing warfare, marriage, birth, and death. Wherever Pacific people dwell, they mark all of these processes with the ceremonial exchange of valuables, which may be tangible, such as *koloa*, or intangible, such as songs and skills of weaving. Spatial relationships are made evident and are celebrated through exchange, in the Tongan diaspora, the multiterritorial Tongan nation is also created through such processes, lending credence to Jana Evans Braziel and Anita Mannur's contention that diaspora is not inimical to nation (2003).

Thus, a nation *can* be forged by movement, but only when actors engage in processes that reify their shared notions of value—conceptions of what they consider most desirable. For Tongans, who actualize value as they engage in exchange, *traveling in order to exchange* is a process whereby the Tongan nation has been constructed, expanded, and regrounded in multiple places. Where Tongans settle, they have continued to meld ancient ideas of *fonua*— land and relationships that sustain and are sustained by people engaging meaningfully with one another—with modern ideas of the respectable citizen who has inalienable rights to a specific place in the world.

Unfortunately, conventional ideas of belonging and nationhood ideas may have marginalized commoner women (Gailey 1987), something that male-led nationalistic movements have also done more generally in the Pacific (Bolton 2003; Jolly 1997 and 2005; Molisa 1983; Trask 1996). Pacific women activists have criticized standard nationalisms as inimical to indigenous women's agency because nation building is often established through processes led by indigenous men, Western people, or both. These agents employ Western models of modernity and the citizen and foreign assumptions about how endowing people with rights can help them as citizens. This book, by contrast, suggests that building a nation that has expanded and modernized through diaspora may afford female agents a chance to strategically redefine their societal roles and even aesthetically augment their material wealth in order to increase their cultural capital in their own communities. For example, some women fulfill traditional roles while pursuing individualistic interests in gaining or saving cash wealth, some work at wage labor while living far away from their families, in order to help theim source and manage the money they must spend on staging ceremonial occasions. Others have reimagined and repurposed Western materials and objects, incorporating them into ritualized and everyday practices to serve specifically Tongan cultural goals. In a process that, elsewhere, Heather Young Leslie and I label "pragmatic creativity" (2007), these women demonstrate that the "Tonganization" of synthetic fabric products can augment the category of women's wealth available for ceremonial exchange.

The most striking example of "Tonganizing" foreign materials that I explore in this book lies in the hybrid form of barkcloth, *ngatu pepa,* which differs from conventional barkcloth in materiality only. It continues to be made by women, in groups, using assembly techniques and aesthetic designs identical to that of older forms. Even though its authenticity remains debated among Tongans and non-Tongans alike, this form of cloth is now a regular feature in the Tongan ceremonial economy, suggesting that, while it has an ambiguous position as *koloa,* pragmatically it confers on women the same kind of prestige and obligation as the more conventional barkcloth made from paper mulberry bark. I argue that this is because, for Tongan women a *ngatu pepa* encodes into modern social contexts women's *mana* (power, efficacy, influence), their place in the history of *koloa* making *and* of the Tongan nation, and their indispensable role in helping those to whom they are bound by *'ofa* realize value through gift exchange.

Movement of Things: Globalization through Gifts

In the Pacific, movement is intrinsic to cultural processes of renewal and reconnection between people—especially kin—*through* interactions in places, and with places. This book also compels us to think about the gift and about Pacific modernity as complex constructions forged at the intersection of new and continuing entanglements between objects, people, and place through *things*. Rather than thinking of the gift as an "add-on" to the formally recognized exchange processes of globalization—large capital transfers, trade between nations, and commodity exchange controlled by multinational corporations, for example, I present the gift as a tool for Pacific modernity. My study shows that the gift is a crucial context for re-examining global economic relations. Valuables such as *koloa* are potential commodities and, indeed, some are commodities in the global art market. However, their primary identity is as gifts intended for circulation through social exchange and Tongan women preferentially and emphatically maintain the status of *koloa* as gift, keeping themselves as indispensable nodes in its global circulation.

Anthropologists have long discussed the potency of exchange in the contexts of rituals. This book has explored exchange as the creation and augmentation of cultural capital both for the gift giver and for recipients. The public context of rituals means that properly executed exchange moments beget opportunities to engage in further gift giving and to do so across global distances spanned by kin and co-ethnics, thus building a globalized nation.

Globalization may be popularly characterized by the numerous modes of moving goods and capital long distances at rapid speeds and could be easily, and mistakenly, attributed solely to the operation of impersonal forces. However, what ethnographies like this one make clear is that globalization is also facilitated by the majority of the world's people who are engaged in "low-level," local, and kin-based transactions in which exchange is accompanied by the expectations of ongoing social relations. In a sense, this is what Arjun Appadurai meant when he theorized globalization as, in part, effected through ethnoscapes, or the interconnected sites of "culture" inhabited by ordinary people (1996). Such sites are also where people experience the everyday politics involved in negotiating how to express allegiance to (the idea of) a nation while managing the demands of making ends meet, caring for kin, fighting for rights that the nation may deny them, or creating culturally-meaningful contexts to realize rights that it does grant them. As Tonga's Queen Sālote recognized when she set up Langa Fonua in the mid-1950s, often these negotiations most deeply affect women in developing nations.

In this book, Tongan women's agency in nation building has also been important to reexamine because women's practices and power permeate the multiple levels on which nationalism is performed—in formal and everyday political arenas, in household and national economics, and especially, in families. At all levels, women are crucial to Tongan people's realization of their highest cultural ideals because women produce the most important objects that people exchange, and thereby reinforce social values through ritual exchange.

Something else that is shared through ritual exchange is the high monetary cost of ritual commemorations for members or branches of an extended family such that the modality of reciprocation of a complex gift of *koloa,* money, and food can actually facilitate a giver's ability to meet other material needs and responsibilities. Because some parts of a complex gift are reciprocated fairly immediately while others incur quite a long time delay, gift givers are able to feel immediately recognized for their bestowal of a complex gift and recipients can hold onto some resources that would otherwise be funneled toward reciprocation in the short term. This is crucial for diasporic families who, for the most part, live in urban locations without access to (much) land for subsistence farming. As people who are usually on the lower end of the socioeconomic scale virtually everywhere they live, *commoner* Tongans are especially vulnerable. Exchanges across further distances with people—and especially exchanges involving modern money, or state currencies—have become increasingly necessary as a way of surviving in a tenuous global economic climate. But even money is subject to cultural assumptions about its foreignness, and it is not universally fungible: it cannot be used in all forms of Tongan exchange. As such, money must first be "Tonganized" in order to fulfill a role as a Tongan ceremonial valuable.

Dwelling, Identity Politics, and the Second Generation

Focusing on numerous things that diasporic Tongan women do with their traditional wealth raises another theme that has been subsumed in my exploration here, but that deserves more in-depth examination in further studies of diaspora and long-distance nationalism. It is the broad-ranging question of how the gift is used as both a tool and a context to socialize members of diaspora-born generations into their Tongan identities. I have touched on this in two main areas. The first concerns the materiality of the gift. Kin-based exchange is probably increasing as the Tongan population in diaspora grows. Thus, Tongan youth continue to be raised in situations where many of their parents regularly gift traditional valuables alongside modern ones such as money. The youth come to understand the relationship between different kinds of valuables, as well as the importance of reciprocating each kind of valuable with a particular material form and a particular kind of timing. However, the gifting of large amounts of cash can be a source of intergenerational strain over how earning resources intertwines with constructions and displays of loyalty to the homeland and to practices that continue to be prevalent there, but that might be attenuated in diaspora.

Various ethnographic moments in the book reveal the dilemmas that some second- and 1.5-generation Tongan-New Zealanders face in deciding how to allocate their relatively low earnings between a seemingly never-ending range of family events, each of which comes with its own demands on their pockets and their time. Even after children have matured into adults, their identities and life choices are strongly influenced by the desires of their parents. So while second generation people may resist conforming to their parents' wishes in everyday contexts, in ritual contexts, and as they age and become parents themselves, young people sometimes adopt their parents' attitudes and behaviors (see Levitt 2009). I noted that younger generations often end up following their parents' desires—usually expressed through material support of and attendance at large, public, family gifting events—because both parents and children hold very high stakes in their family's standing in the community. The experiences of parents as first-generation members in a given society create the contexts in which such second-generation members negotiate notions of homeland, tradition, and choice, and ambitions for engaging with modernity. Thus the lives of both immigrants and their children are shaped by the value, practices, and ideas that originate in the homeland (Somerville 2008; Tupuola 2004) and, indeed, in the "multiple sites and levels of the transnational social fields they inhabit" (ibid.).

The second area in which the identity of Tongan youth in diaspora is reinforced through the gift is when youth are made the front face of their communities in interdiasporic competitive gifting. At public gifting occasions when youth groups compete in dance groups that represent their specific diasporic communities, youth may be more emotionally invested in impressing one another with shows of allegiance to their diasporic communities than to Tonga itself. These messages may be lost on their parents and other senior generation members, adding to the elisions between the generations that are as much a part of the construction of global Tonganness as are realms where all generations agree.

In a reification of movement as an overarching theme in the experience of diaspora, we might examine how youth in diasporic communities move back and forth between their "foreign" identities, their status as native born, and their identification as cultural others by people within their own cities, neighborhoods, or even their own homes. As such, there need to be more studies of second-generation diasporans as they inhabit these ambiguous areas and as others perceive them in their various social contexts. Many studies have agreed that it is difficult to tease out where their Tonganness ends and their New Zealander-ness begins (Koloto 2003; Spoonley 2001; Teaiwa and Mallon 2005). However, my study shows that sophisticated analysis does not rely on separating these apparently independent aspects of identity. We may ask: How do second-generation members switch between realizing their parents' desires and their own? What mechanisms do they use to move between the very different spaces they inhabit in diaspora? What forms and discourses of identity do second-generation members engage with and produce in these crossings? (cf. Tupuola 2004) And—following Maila Stivens (2005:334) who reminds us that anthropological studies have often ignored men as gendered actors—how are these discourses and experiences of crossing *gendered*?

Finally, if there is one thing that my study of competing displays of Tonganness suggests, it is that studying the second generation in diaspora should not be confined to diasporic places but must embrace some consideration of how and with what effect youth in these locations cultivate relationships with Tongans in Tonga. Helen Lee (2009b; 2007; 2006; 2004) and Tupou Hopoate Pau'u (2002), among others, have pioneered such research about diasporic youth and their relationships to their respected Pacific homelands. More such studies are needed, especially those that explore comparatively the lives of the second generation in multiple places, not simply in a single location. Such studies would explore the connections forged by the second generation across these different places, asking, for example, what are the tokens of ethnic identity and valuables exchanged between Tongan youth throughout the diaspora? And what are the effects of these ties being forged, not by government representatives and members of mainstream groups, but by youth and members of immigrant families, people who are marginal in most majority white nations where Tongan diasporans live? What roles do modern technology and communication—online social-networking sites, internet chat rooms, and the instantaneous dissemination of photographs of oneself through electronic means, for example—play in how diasporic youth relate *across* the spaces that seemingly divide their communities globally? And how are they linking these technologies and their connections to co-ethnic youth in other communities to their own embracing and re-creating of traditions outside of the homeland?

Places of "Home"

Pacific Islanders move between such places as they pursue particular projects of personal and cultural value, highlighting movement as a connective and communicative practice. Even as they *dwell* in places scattered across the ocean, within islands, and around the globe or *move* through spaces defined by others as urban or rural, they maintain the right and agency to call some of these places "home." As "rooted cosmopolitans" (Appiah 1998:91), Pacific Islanders often live as if they are currently dwelling in the center of their ancestral homelands, showing that they have found ways to feel meaningfully rooted wherever they dwell at a given time. Throughout this book, I have analyzed aspects of visits that diasporic Tongan individuals make when they return to their home islands, that homeland-based Tongans make to see relatives in diaspora, that diasporans make when they go to other parts of the diaspora to perform temporary stints of wage work, and that other Pacific people make when they journey to Tonga to exchange valuables. Each of these forms of movement conveys a message about the value of kinship and heritage, which are experienced through dwelling together—often temporarily—*and* through engaging in exchange.

In his influential piece "Our Sea of Islands," Epeli Hau'ofa (1993) outlines the movement of a Hawai'i-based Tongan businessman, a seller of Fijian *kava* that he first purchases himself from Fiji. When he leaves Hawai'i for Fiji to secure his purchase, he packs a cooler of t-shirts. While waiting for his *kava* to be bagged in Fiji, he visits Tonga, renewing bonds with kinspeople, in part through these t-shirt gifts. On leaving Tonga, he fills his cooler with frozen fish to take back with him to Hawai'i. This return to Hawai'i takes place via Fiji, where he collects his *kava*. This individual maps out and manages a modern trade triangle that, like the ancient one between Tonga, Fiji, and Samoa, entangles a form of market exchange with modern gift exchange. He also entangles both movement and rootedness—building on routes and roots (Clifford 1994; Gilroy 1993)—within the Tongan ethnoscape in living his modern life.

Likewise, elderly Pacific women like Lina and 'Ofa, whom I introduced here, also engage in travel and exchange relationships. In women's hands, I argue, the project of nation building becomes one of sometimes challenging traditional patriarchal ideas of women's subordination and men's control of family resources in order to pool together enough wealth to finance a gift-giving event. At other times, women find the greatest value—that is, the greatest realization of meaning in their lives—in performing tradition with its concomitant restrictions on their agency and its demands on their labor and time. Women's roles, in particular, in exchange exemplify the negotiation—literally the give and take, if you will—of being embedded in social relations of debt, trust, love, and challenge over time and space. When families interact *through* such reciprocal practices, they establish or augment (*langa*) their places of meaningful dwelling (*fonua*), thus realizing the very meaning of their nation: the conjuncture of people and place in dynamic interaction. This nation has been constructed through acts of movement and, as I have explored here, through the continued exchange of gifts.

Hau'ofa (1993) suggests that movement out of the home islands involves loss, but also obvious gain through expansion of boundaries and possibilities: to those living in the islands, the boundaries of the islands seemingly move outward, across the oceans, and to other lands. Here I have shown that further movement to other places in the diaspora can be equally important in expanding the effective reach of the home islands. The complex process of nation building involves multidirectional flows of people leaving, arriving, visiting, and inhabiting. In this comingling of processes vital to living, movement and dwelling bookend one another continually. Equally vital are the exchanges of valuables that keep people, place, and values connected through time and over space—in a continually renewed sense of being at home.

Glossary of Polynesian Terms ⚜

Note on orthography: In the written Tongan language, elongated vowel sounds are denoted by a macrons or a short line above the letters, known in Tongan as *toloi*. So, for example, a long *o* sound is written as *ō*, and might appear in older written forms of Tongan as *oo*. A glottal stop is indicated by a "backward apostrophe" symbol that Tongans call *fakau'a* and is placed before the vowel that will be sounded with the glottal stop. A few words from other Pacific languages appear in this glossary as well and are included alphabetically among the Tongan words.

'a'āhi	exhibition of newly made Tongan textiles
'anga	behavior
'anga faka-Tonga	ideal modes of Tongan social interaction
anga lelei	well behaved; good behavior
'api	home
'api kolo	a town allotment on which a family house would usually be built
'apitanga	(church) camp
'api 'uta	a bush allotment that is farm land, often located some distance away from villages
apō	all-night vigil; a wake; time before human beings (*kaukakai Tonga*) lived in the world
coco (Fijain)	a single-layer floor mat with yarn fringing
'efinanga	a bundle of traditional cloth, usually comprising a piece of Tongan barkcloth folded within a plaited mat
'eiki	chiefly; person of chiefly rank
fa	pandanus (*Pandanus utilis*); the screw pine plant whose leaves are treated and used for plaiting Tongan (and other Pacific) mats of different varieties: floor mats, waist mats, and also baskets
fa'alealea	pre-wedding celebration between bride and groom's close kin, characterized by clowning and merrymaking

fa'e huki	a ceremonial position for senior generation kin member from the mother's side, typically important at wedding rituals
fahu	highest-ranking person in relation to ego in Tongan kinship terminology
fai tutu	to beat paper mulberry bast for barkcloth making, using a wooden *ike*
faiva	performance (dance, song, music, oratory)
faka'afe	a feast, a treat, or other presentation that is made freely to another
faka'apa'apa	respect shown to one of another rank by remaining distant (both socially and physically)
faka'ofa	sympathy, pity; piteous
faka'ofa'ofa	beautiful
fakalangilangi	to elevate in status; "push toward heaven"
fakatapu	honorific speech made at the opening of events to partially mitigate differences in rank between chiefs, commoners, and God
fakatotolo	to lie down; the wefts of a mat that lie down during the mat's construction
fala	two-layered plaited mat, often with a fringe of colorful yarn used as a floor covering; also used as gift
fale koka'anga	a house or building for doing *koka'anga* (assembling barkcloth)
famili	the smaller groups of kin with whom Tongan individuals maintain close ties; close kin relation
foaki	to give, gift, present
fatongia	duty
fau	hibiscus plant; treated bark of this plant used to plait certain fine (waist) mats
fauniteni	fountain
fea	flea market; fair
fētokoni'aki	mutual support; to give help reciprocally
feta'aki	beaten strips of paper mulberry bark; ready to be assembled into barkcloth
fetongi	to exchange; exchanging one commercial object for another

fefetongi'aki	reciprocity
fie'eiki	wanting to be *'eiki;* uppity
fiefia	joy
fie lahi	putting on airs; being/acting "uppity"
fine mātu'a	elderly woman; respectful term denoting one's "mother"
foaki	present as gifts; giving an outright gift
fohi tutu	to roll fresh strips of paper mulberry tree inner bark into spiral for drying
fo'i hea	black circle design for barkcloth
fola'osi	pieces of barkcloth cut from a large cloth measuring 5-*langanga* pieces
fokotu'u	to stand up; the wefts of a mat that stand up during the mat's construction
fonua	land; country; culture; homeland
fua kavenga	to meet one's cultural obligations; literally, to shoulder the burden
fuatanga	a very high-ranking category to Tongan barkcloth; made pasting beaten paper mulberry bark pieces in a slightly different orientation used when assembling more conventional barkcloth (*ngatu*)
hako fefine	women of the same matriline; unlike the group conventionally denoted as a matriline, this group does not include the women's brothers
hiapo	paper mulberry (*Broussonetia papyrifera*) plant; the inner bark of this plant is used as raw material in barkcloth making throughout the Pacific
ike	carved wooden beater for preparing bark for barkcloth production
'ilokava	collective and ceremonial drinking of *kava* among chiefly people
kafa	sennit fiber; plaited or twisted sennit "rope" used for lashing beams together; can also be used to fasten a waist mat (*ta'ovala*) around one's waist
kāhoa	garland, necklace (similar to a Hawaiian "*lei*")
kāinga toto	church family
kāliko	calico; cotton fabric
kalapu	*kava*-drinking clubs

kalasi 'aho	"class" or a pre-assigned group of congregants whose members pool money for regular church donation
kātoanga	(literally, "celebration") a formally arranged exchange of textiles for other material valuables between two groups of Tongan women
kato teu	decorated plaited basket usually gifted as part of a textile gift at a formal Tongan ceremonial occasion
kaukakai Tonga	Tongan people
kau mōtu'a	term denoting elderly people
kautaha	co-operative group
kautaha nō pa'anga	loan companies
kava	(*Piper methysticum*) plant used to make a drink by the same name that is partaken both informally and ceremonially by men in Tonga; plant is also known for its medicinal properties
kavenga	(literally, "burden") cultural obligation(s)
kelekele	land, soil, mud
kiekie	plaited girdle worn over a Tongan female's clothing to decorate the waist-to-hip area composed of a braided belt and numerous vertical parts that dangle from it
kie tonga	single-layered, "white" pandanus mat often with embroidered wool fringing
koka	large tree (*Bischofia javanica*) whose bark is scraped and soaked in water for making dye for barkcloth; the reddish-brown vegetable dye thus produced and used to decorate Tongan barkcloth
koka'anga	the process whereby a Tongan barkcloth is simultaneously assembled and dyed, usually by several women seated in pairs across a low work table; also a word used to modify related terms (*fale koka'anga*: house/shed for such work)
koloa	"thing of value"; treasure
koloa faka-Tonga	literally, "thing of value to Tongans"; traditional-styled textiles that may be gifted in ceremonies commemorating life stages or national pride
kolo si'i	newer and lesser-valued forms of objects that women exchange as *koloa*
konga fā	a cut piece of barkcloth, four *langanga* in length

koniseti	concert, often for fundraising purposes in Tongan communities
kulasi	colored yarn fringe
kupesi	relief pattern tablets for imprinting designs on barkcloth
kula	exchange system of shell valuables within the Massim region of Papua New Guinea
kuta	Fijian waist mat plaited from reed fibers
lālanga	plaiting; to plait; a plaited item such as a fine mat
langa	to build, to augment, to add to
langa fonua	building up the nation/culture; "nation building"
langanga	a measurement for length of a unit of Tongan barkcloth (approx. 18–21 inches)
lau maʻopoʻopo	a variety of *hiapo* (paper mulberry tree) used for making barkcloth
lau mahaehae	a variety of *hiapo* (paper mulberry tree) used for making barkcloth
launima	a fifty *langanga* (length) *ngatu*
lauteau	a one-hundred *langanga* (length) *ngatu*
lei	(Hawaiian) a garland of flowers worn around the neck and shoulders
liongi	a ritual state of being lower than the deceased during the funeral observances
loi	lie (n.); to lie (v.); fake (adj.)
loto mafana	kind and warm heartedness
lotu	prayer; to pray; church service; to attend church
mālō	thank you
mana	power/spirit imbued in a person or object by qualities that associate that person or object with deities
manulua	ancient and chiefly design for barkcloth that stylizes the image of two birds passing one another in flight; symbolizes the intertwining of genealogies in chiefly marriages
maʻolunga	to be higher than another in rank
masi	(Fijian) barkcloth
mehekitanga	father's eldest sister
meʻaʻofa	a gift; to present a specific thing as a gift

misinale	(regular, lump-sum church) donations by congregants that are a feature of most Tongan Christian churches and for which the Methodist churches are best known
mohenga	bed
mole	to lose or waste
monomono	machine-made quilts often gifted in *kavenga* along with varieties of barkcloth and plaited mats
ngatu	a variety of Tongan barkcloth, customarily made out of beaten, pasted, and painted sheets of *hiapo* inner bark
ngatu hāfekasi	form of barkcloth, made with hybrid materials; one layer of beaten *hiapo* bark and one layer of synthetic fabric (vylene); also generic name for barkcloth with at least one sheet of vylene in its composition; same as *ngatu pepa laulalo*
ngatu pepa	form of barkcloth, made with a base entirely of vylene
ngatu pepa laulalo	textile that has the composite paper mulberry and vylene base; synonym for *ngatu hāfekasi*
ngāue	work; to work or labor; sometimes used for category of men's wealth (from daily agricultural products to prestige foods)
ngaue fakameʻaʻa	handicrafts
ngoue	agricultural products
ʻofa	love, sympathy, kindness
palakū	ugly, unbecoming
papa kokaʻanga	wooden work table for assembling *ngatu*
pālangi	people of European descent; originally, non-Tongan people
pati	plaited pandanus mat with one elaborate embroidered yarn border; said to have originated in the Fijian islands
pōtalanoa	evening (bedtime) stories
poto	skilled
pusiaki	a child raised by someone other than its birth parents; adopted kin-group members
sila paʻaʻanga	envelope containing cash gifts
sivi	test
tabua	(Fijian) a large whale's tooth usu. suspended on a plaited sennit rope

ta'ovala	waist mats
tapa	white border of a Tongan barkcloth; also used to denote barkcloth in general
tauhi	caring; care for; watch over
tauhi vā	to care for one's (social) relationships
tau'olunga	solo dance
teu	ceremonial gift presentation comprising *koloa*
teuteu	to decorate; a decorative element
tivaivai	(Cook Islands Maori) quilted quilts that are women's supreme material valuable Cook Islands culture
tofi'a	estate
tohi	hand painting (on barkcloth); writing; a letter; to write
tongo	mangrove tree; natural dye made from the bark of this tree and used for decorating barkcloth
toulanganga	a group of women doing *koka'anga*, or assembling Tongan barkcloth
toulālanga	group of women working together to process pandanus raw materials and to produce plaited textiles
tu'a	Tongan person of the commoner rank; *kau tu'a* being the plural form
tu'a niu	dried midribs of coconut fronds
tuitui	dye prepared by mixing the soot of burnt candlenuts with water or *koka* dye
tu'i	highest-ranking chief of a particular place; king
tutu	the act of beating the inner bark of the paper mulberry tree for making barkcloth; dried pieces of this material
vā	space between; social relations between specific people
vā lelei	good social relations

References

Addo, Ping-Ann. 2012. "Teaching Culture with a Modern Valuable: Lessons for and from Tongan Youth in New Zealand." *Pacific Studies* 35(1/2):11–43.

———. 2009. "Forms of Tradition, Forms of Transnationalism: Cash and Cloth as Ritual Exchange Valuables in the Tongan Diaspora." In Helen Lee and Stephen Tupai Francis (eds.), *Migration and Transnationalism: Pacific Island Perspectives*, 43–56. Canberra: Australia National University Press.

———. 2007. "Commoner Tongan Women Authenticate Ngatu Pepa in New Zealand." *Pacific Arts* New Series 3–5:63–71.

———. 2004. "Kinship, Cloth, and Community in Auckland New Zealand: Commoner Tongan Women Navigate Transnational Identity using Traditionally-Styled Textiles." Unpublished PhD dissertation. New Haven, CT: Yale University.

———. 2003. "God's Kingdom in Auckland: Tongan Christian Dress and the Expression of Duty." In Chloe Colchester (ed.), *Clothing the Pacific*, 141–163. Oxford: Berg Press.

Addo, Ping-Ann, and Niko Besnier. 2008. "When Gifts Become Commodities: Pawnshops in Tonga and the Tongan Diaspora." *Journal of the Royal Anthropological Institute* 14(1):39–59.

Ahlburg, Dennis. 1991. "Remittances and their impact: a study of Tonga and Western Samoa." Pacific Policy Papers, Australia National University, No. 7. Canberra: National Center for Development Studies.

Ahrens, Prudence, and Charles Zuber. 2004. "Langa Fonua: The Impact of Polynesian Communities on the Landscape of South-East Queensland." *Queensland Review* 11(1): 97–107.

Akin, David, and Joel Robbins. 1999. "An Introduction to Melanesian Currencies: Agencies, Identity and Social Reproduction." In David Akin and Joel Robbins (eds.), *Money and Modernity: State and Local Currencies in Melanesia*, 1–40. Pittsburgh: University of Pittsburgh Press.

Alexeyeff, Kalissa. 2008. "Neoliberalism, Mobility and Cook Islands Men in Transit." *The Australian Journal of Anthropology* 19(2):136–149.

Anae, Melani. 2004. "From kava to coffee: the 'browning of Auckland.'" http://www.anewnz .org.nz/paper_comments.asp?paperid=83 (accessed 30 January 2012).

Anderson, Benedict. 1998. "Long-Distance Nationalism." In *The Spectre of Comparisons: Nationalism, Southeast Asia and the World*, 58–74. London: Verso.

———. 1983. *Imagined Communities: Reflections on the Origin and Spread of Nationalism*. London: Verso.

Appadurai, Arjun. 2000. "Grassroots Globalization and the Research Imagination." *Public Culture* 12(1):1–19.

———. 1996. *Modernity at Large*. Minneapolis: University of Minnesota Press.

Appiah, Kwame Anthony. 1998. "Cosmopolitan Patriots." In Pheng Cheah and Bruce Robbins (eds.), *Cosmopolitics: Thinking and Feeling Beyond the Nation*, 91–144. Minneapolis: University of Minnesota Press.

Arbeit, Wendy. 1994. *Tapa in Tonga.* Honolulu: University of Hawai'i Press.

Arno, Andrew. 2005. "*Cobo* and *Tabua* in Fiji: Two Forms of Cultural Currency in an Economy of Sentiment." *American Anthropologist* 32(1):46–62.

Australia Government. 2009. Department of Foreign Affairs and Trade, Kingdom of Tonga Country Brief. www.dfat.gov.au/geo/tonga/tonga_brief.html (accessed August 2010).

Bailey, Benjamin. 1997. "Communication of Respect in Interethnic Service Encounters." *Language and Society* 26:327–356.

Barker, John. 2007. *Ancestral Lines: The Maisin of Papua New Guinea and the Fate of the Rainforest.* Peterborough, Ontario: Broadview Press.

Barnett, Homer. 1953. *Innovation: The Basis of Cultural Change.* New York: McGraw-Hill.

Bataille-Benguingui, Marie-Claire. 1976. "'Le Salon d'Agriculture' aux Îles de Tonga et sa Relation avec le Passé." *Journal de la Société des Oceanistes* 32(50):67–86.

Bedford, Richard, and Robert Didham. 2001. "Who are the 'Pacific People'? Ethnic Identification and the New Zealand Census." In Cluny Macpherson, Paul Spoonley, and Melani Anae (eds.), *Tangata O Te Moana Nui: The Evolving Identities of Pacific Peoples in Aotearoa/New Zealand*, 21–43. Palmerston North, New Zealand: Dunmore Press.

Berman, Tressa. 2003. *Circle of Goods: Women, Work, and Welfare in a Reservation Community.* Albany: State University of New York Press.

Bertram, Geoffrey, and Ray F. Watters. 1985. "The MIRAB Economy in South Pacific Microstates." *Pacific Viewpoint* 26(3):497–520.

Besnier, Niko. 2011. *On the Edge of the Global: Modern Anxieties in a Pacific Island Nation.* Stanford, CA: Stanford University Press.

———. 2008. "Modernity, Cosmopolitanism, and the Emergence of Middle Class in Tonga." *The Contemporary Pacific* 21(2):215–226.

———. 2007. "Gender and Interaction in a Globalizing World: Negotiating the Gendered Self in Tonga." In Bonnie S. McElhinny (ed.), *Words, Worlds and Material Girls: Language, Gender, Globalization*, 423–446. Berlin and New York: Mouton de Gruyter.

———. 2004. "Consumption and Cosmopolitanism: Practicing Modernity at the Second-Hand Marketplace in Nuku'alofa, Tonga." *Anthropological Quarterly* 77(1):7–45.

Bianco, Barbara, A. 1991. "Women and Things: Pokot Motherhood as Political Destiny." *American Ethnologist* 18(4):770–783.

Bolton, Lissant. 2003. *Upfolding the Moon: Enacting Women's Kastom in Vauatu.* Honolulu: University of Hawai'i Press.

Bott, Elizabeth. 1982. *Tongan Society at the Time of Captain Cook's Visits: Discussion with Her Majesty Queen Sālote Tupou.* Wellington, New Zealand: The Polynesian Society, Inc.

Bourdieu, Pierre. 1990. *The Logic of Practice* (trans. Richard Nice). Palo Alto, CA: Stanford University Press.

———. 1986. "The Forms of Capital." *Handbook of Theory and Research for the Sociology of Education* (John Richardson, ed.), 241–258. Westport, CT: Greenwood Press.

———. 1977. *Outline of a Theory of Practice.* Cambridge: Cambridge University Press.

Braziel, Jana Evans, and Anita Mannur. 2003. *Theorizing Diaspora: A Reader.* Malden, MA, and Oxford: Blackwell Publishing.

Brown, Jo-Marie, and Libby Middlebrook. 2001. "Gay Row Sends Worshippers Down the Road." *New Zealand Herald* (May 7). Accessible online at www.nzherald.co.nz.

Burns, Lucy Mae San Pablo. 2008. "'Splendid Dancing': Filipino 'Exceptionalism' in Taxi Dancehalls." *Dance Research Journal* 40(2):23–40.

Campbell, I. C. 1992. *Island Kingdom: Tonga Ancient and Modern*. Christchurch, New Zealand: University of Canterbury Press.

Chan, Kwok Bun. 1997. "A Family Affair: Migration, Dispersal, and the Emergent Identity of the Chinese Cosmopolitan." *Diaspora* 6(2):195–213.

Chapman, Murray. 1991. "Pacific Island movement and Sociopolitical Change: Metaphors of Misunderstanding." *Population and Development Review* 17(2):263–292.

———. 1978. "On the Cross-Cultural Study of Circulation." *International Migration Review* 12:559–569.

Churchward, C. Maxwell. 1959. *Tongan Dictionary*. London: Oxford University Press.

Clifford, James. 2001. "Indigenous Articulations." *The Contemporary Pacific* 13(2):468–490.

———. 1997. *Routes: Travel and Translation in the Late Twentieth Century*. Cambridge, MA: Harvard University Press.

Cohen, Robin. 2008. *Global Diasporas: An Introduction*. London and New York: Routledge.

Collins, Patricia Hill. 2006. *From Black Power to Hip Hop: Racism, Nationalism, and Feminism*. Philadelphia, PA: Temple University Press.

Collocott, E. E. V. 1924. "Tongan Myths and Legends, III." *Folk-Lore* 35(3):275–283.

Connell, John. 2009a. "Bittersweet Home? The Return Migration of Health Workers in Polynesia." In Dennis Conway and Robert Potter (eds.), *Return Migration of the Next Generations: Twenty-first Century Transnational Mobility*, 139–160. Ashgate: Aldershot.

———. 2009b. "'I Never Wanted to Come Home': Skilled Health Workers in the South Pacific." In Lee and Francis (eds.), *Migration and Transnationalism*, 159–177. Canberra: Australia National University Press.

Connell, John, and Richard P. C. Brown. 2004. "The Remittances of Migrant Tongan and Samoan Nurses from Australia." *Human Resources for Health* 2(2):1–45.

Cornwall, Andrea. 2000. "Missing Men? Reflections on Men, Masculinities and Gender in GAD." *Institute of Development Studies (IDS) Bulletin* 31(2):18–27.

Cowling, Wendy. 1990. "On Being Tongan: Responses to Concepts of Tradition." Unpublished PhD thesis. Sydney, Australia: Macquarie University.

Craig, Robert D. 1989. *Dictionary of Polynesian Mythology*. Westport, CT: Greenwood Press.

DasGupta, Monisha. 1997. "What is Indian about You? A Gendered, Transnational Approach to Ethnicity." *Gender and Society* 11(5):572–596.

Davin, Anna. 1997. "Imperialism and Motherhood." In Frederick Cooper and Ann Laura Stoler (eds.), *Tensions of Empire: Colonial Cultures in a Bourgeois World*, 87–151. Berkeley: University of California Press.

Dektor Korn, Shulamit Rose. 1995. "Household Composition in the Tonga Islands: A Questions of Options and Alternatives." *Journal of Anthropological Research*. 31(3):235–249.

———. 1974. "Tongan Kin Groups: The Noble and the Common View." *Journal of the Polynesian Society* 83(1):5–13.

Denoon, Donald, with Stewart Firth, Jocelyn Linnekin, Malama Maleisea, and Karen Nero. 1997. *The Cambridge History of the Pacific Islanders*. Cambridge: Cambridge University Press.

di Leonardo, Michaela. 1984. *The Varieties of Ethnic Experience: Kinship, Class, and Gender among Italian-Americans*. Ithaca, NY: Cornell University Press.

Douaire-Marsaudon, Françoise. 2008. "Food and Wealth: Ceremonial Objects as Signs of Identity in Tonga and Wallis." In Serge Tcherkezoff and Francoise Douaire-Marsaudon (eds.), *The Changing South Pacific: Identities and Transformations*, 207–229. Canberra: Australia National University Press.

———. 2002. "The *Kava* Ritual and the Reproduction of Male Identity in Polynesia." In *People and Things: Social Mediation in Oceania,* 53–78. Durham, NC: Carolina Academic Press.

———. 1998. *Les premiers fruits. Parenté, identité sexuelle et pouvoirs en Polynésie occidentale (Tonga, Wallis et Futuna).* Paris, CNRS Editions/Editions de la Maison des Sciences de l'Homme (Chemins de l'ethnologie).

Douglas, Bronwyn. 2003. "Christianity, Tradition and Everyday Modernity: Towards an Anatomy of Women's Groupings in Melanesia." In Bronwyn Douglas (ed.), *Women's groups and everyday modernity in Melanesia,* special issue, *Oceania* 74(1–2):6–23.

Dove, Nah. 1998. *Afrikan Mothers: Bearers of Culture, Makers of Social Change.* Albany: State University of New York Press.

Drake, Maile. 2002. "Ngatu Pepa: Making Tongan Tapa in New Zealand." In Sean Mallon and Pandora Fulimalo Pereira (eds.), *Pacific Art Niu Sila: The Pacific Dimension of Contemporary New Zealand Arts,* 53–64. Wellington, New Zealand: Te Papa Press.

Enloe, Cynthia. 1990. *Bananas, Beaches and Bases: Making Sense of International Politics.* Berkeley: University of California Press.

'Esau, Raelyn Lolohea. 2007. "Tongan Immigrants in Japan." *Asian and Pacific Migration Journal* 16(2):289–301.

Evans, Mike. 2001. *Persistence of the Gift: Tongan Tradition in Transnational Context.* Waterloo, Ontario: Wilfred Laurier University Press.

Evans, Mike, Paul Harms, and Colin Reid. 2009. "Attitudinal Divergence and the Tongan Transnational System." Lee and Francis (eds.), *Migration and Transnationalism,* 115–129. Canberra: Australia National University Press.

Evans-Pritchard, E. E. 1940. *The Nuer: The Political System and Mode of Livelihood of a Nilotic People.* Oxford: Oxford University Press.

Eves, Richard. 1996. "Colonialism, Corporeality and Character: Methodist Missions and the Refashioning of Bodies in the Pacific." *History and Anthropology* 10(1):85–138.

Ewins, Rod. 2009. *Staying Fijian: Vatulele Island Barkcloth and Social Identity.* Honolulu: University of Hawai'i Press.

Fairbairn-Dunlop, Peggy. 2003. "Some Markers on the Journey." In Peggy Fairbairn-Dunlop and Gabrielle Sisifo Makisi (eds.), *Making Our Place: Growing up PI in New Zealand,* 19–43. Palmerston North, New Zealand: Dunmore Press.

Fanua, Tupou Posesi. 1986. *Tapa Cloth in Tonga.* Nuku'alofa, Tonga: Tongan Secondary Teacher Education Program.

Ferraiuolo, Augusto. 2009. "Boston's North End: Negotiating Identity in an Italian American Neighborhood." *Western Folklore* 65(3):263–301.

Ferdon, Edwin. 1988. *Early Tonga: As the Explorers Saw It, 1616–1810.* Tucson: University of Arizona Press.

Filihia, Meredith. 2001. "Men are From Maama, Women are from Pulotu: Female Status in Tongan Society." *Journal of the Polynesian Society* 110(4):377–390.

Finau, Makisi. 1992. "The Emergence of the Maamafo'ou Movment from the Free Wesleyan Church of Tonga." In Makisi Finau, Teerur Ieuti, and Jione Langi (eds.), *Island Churches: Challenges and Change,* 141–195. Suva, Fiji: Pacific Theological College and Institute of Pacific Studies.

Fog Olwig, Karen. 2002. "A Wedding in the Family: Home Making in a Global Network." *Global Networks* 2(3):205–218.

Fong, Vanessa. 2004. "Filial Nationalism among Chinese Teenagers with Global Identities." *American Ethnologist* 31(4):631–648.

Foreign Affairs, Defence and Trade Committee, 2005. "Inquiry into New Zealand's relationship with the Kingdom of Tonga." Report presented to the House of Representatives.

Forshee, Jill. 2001. *Between the Folds: Stories of Cloth, Lives, and Travels from Sumba.* Honolulu: University of Hawai'i Press.

Forsyth-Brown, Ivy. N.d. "Maintaining a Transnational Family: A Caribbean Case Study." Draft paper available at http://www.allacademic.com//meta/p_mla_apa_research_citation/1/0/4/8/0/pages104807/p104807-1.php (accessed 30 September 2009).

Forte, Tania. 2001. "Shopping in Jenin: Women, Homes, and Political Persons in the Galilee." *City and Society* 13(2):211–243.

Foster, Robert J. 1997. *Nation Making: Emergent Identities in Postcolonial Melanesia.* Ann Arbor: University of Michigan Press.

Francis, Steven Tupai. 2009. "The View from 'Home': Transnational Movements from Three Tongan Villages." In Lee and Francis (eds.), *Migration and Transnationalism,* 203–213. Canberra: Australia National University Press.

———. 2007 "People and Place in Tonga: The Social Construction of *Fonua* in Oceania." In Thomas Reuter (ed.), *Sharing the Earth, Dividing the Land: Territorial Categories and Institutions in the Austronesian World,* 345–364. Canberra: Australian National University Press. http://epress.anu.edu.au/sharing_citation.html (accessed 28 August 2009).

Fouron, Georges Eugene and Nina Glick Schiller. 2002. "The Generation of Identity: Redefining the Second Generation within a Transnational Social Field." In P. Levitt and M. Waters (eds.), *The Changing Face of Home: The Transnational Lives of the Second Generation,* 168–208. New York: Russell Sage Foundation.

Gailey, Christine Ward. 1992. "A Good Man is Hard to Find: Overseas Migration and the Decentered Family in the Tongan Islands." *Critique of Anthropology* 12(1):47–74.

———. 1987. *Kinship to Kingship: Gender Hierarchy and State Formation in the Tongan Islands.* Austin, TX: University of Texas Press.

Geertz, Clifford. 1977. *The Interpretation of Cultures.* New York: Basic Books.

Gell, Alfred. 1993. *Wrapping in Images: Tattooing in Polynesia.* Oxford: Clarendon Press.

Gellner, Ernst. 1983. *Nations and Nationalism.* Ithaca, NY: Cornell University Press.

Gershon, Ilana. 2012. *No Family is an Island: Cultural Expertise among Samoans in Diaspora.* Ithaca, NY: Cornell University Press.

———. 2007. "Viewing Diasporas from the Pacific: What Pacific Ethnographies Offer Pacific Diaspora Studies." *The Contemporary Pacific* 19(2):474–502.

———. 2001. "How to Know When Not to Know: Strategic Ignorance When Eliciting for Samoan Migrant Exchanges." *Social Analysis* 44(2):84–105.

Gibson, John, and Karen Nero. 2008. "Why Don't Pacific Island Countries' Economies Grow Faster?" In Alistair Bisley (ed.), *Pacific Interactions: Pasifika in New Zealand; New Zealand in Pasifika,* 191–244. Wellington, New Zealand: Institute of Policy Studies, Victoria University of Wellington.

Gilroy, Paul. 1993. *The Black Atlantic: Modernity and Double Consciousness.* Cambridge, MA: Harvard University Press.

Giddens, Anthony.1992. "Modernity and Self-Identity: Self and Society in the late Modern Age." In Francis Frascina and Jonathan Harris (eds.), *Art in Modern Cultures: An Anthology of Critical Texts,* 17–22. London: Phaidon Press.

―――. 1990. *The Consequences of Modernity.* Cambridge: Polity Press.

Gifford, Edward Winslow. 1929. *Tongan Society.* Bernice P. Bishop Museum Bulletin, no. 16. Honolulu, HI: Bishop Museum.

Glick Schiller, Nina, Linda Basch, and Christina Blanc Szanton. 1992. *Towards a Transnational Perspective on Migration: Race, Class, Ethnicity, and Nationalism reconsidered.* New York: New York Academy of Sciences.

Godelier, Maurice. 1999. *The Enigma of the Gift* (trans. Nora Scott). Chicago, IL: University of Chicago Press.

Goldsmith, Michael. 2003. "Culture, For and Against: Patterns of 'Culturespeak' in New Zealand." *Journal of the Polynesian Society* 112(3):280–294.

Gopinath, Gayatri. 1995. "'Bombay, U.K., Yuba City': Bhangra Music and the Engendering of Diaspora." *Diaspora* 4(3):303–322.

Gordon, Tamar. 1990. "Inventing the Mormon Tongan Family." In John Barker (ed.), *Christianity in Oceania: Ethnographic Perspectives,* 197–219. Lanham, MD: University Press of America.

Goss, Jon, and Bruce Lindquist. 2000. "Placing Movers: An Overview of the Asian-Pacific Migration System." *The Contemporary Pacific* 12(2):385–414.

Government of Tonga. 2009a. "First group of Tongan seasonal workers under the Pacific Seasonal Workers Pilot Scheme (PSWPS) departs to Tonga," 14 September 2009. https://www.pmo.gov.to/first-group-of-tongan-seasonal-workers-under-the-pacific-seasonal-workers-pilot-scheme-pswps-departs-to-tonga.html (accessed 2 November 2009).

―――. 2009b. Prime Minister's office. https://www.pmo.gov.to/index.php/Weathering-the-Global-Storm-The-Case-of-Tonga.html (accessed 5 November 2009).

Graeber, David. 2001. *Towards an Anthropological Theory of Value: the False Coin of Our Own Dreams.* New York: Palgrave.

Grainger, Gareth. 1998. "Tonga and Australia since World War II." In Deryck Scarr, Niel Gunson, and Jennifer Terrell (eds.), *Echoes of Pacific War,* Papers from the 7th Tongan History Conference, Canberra, 64–75.

Gregory, Christopher A. 1982. *Gifts and Commodities.* London: Academic Press.

Grieco, Elizabeth. 2004. "Will Migrant Remittances Continue Through Time? A New Answer to an Old Question." *International Journal on Multicultural Societies* 6(2):243–252.

Gupta, Akhil. 1997. "Song of the Nonaligned World: Transnational Identities and the Reinscription of Space in Late Capitalism." In Akhil Gupta and James Ferguson (eds.), *Culture, Power, Place: Explorations in Critical Anthropology,* 179–199. Durham, NC: Duke University Press.

Hall, Stuart. 1990. "Cultural Identity and Diaspora." In Jonathan Rutherford (ed.), *Identity: Community, Culture, Difference,* 222–237. London: Lawrence and Wishart.

Harvey, David. 2001. "Globalization and the Spatial Fix." *Geographische Revue* 2:23–20.

―――. 2004 [1989]. *The Condition of Postmodernity: An Enquiry into the Origins of Cultural Change.* Malden, MA: Wiley-Blackwell.

Hau'ofa, Epeli. 1993. "Our Sea of Islands." In Eric Waddell, Vijay Naidu, and Epeli Hau'ofa (eds.), *A New Oceania: Rediscovering Our Sea of Islands,* 16. Suva, Fiji: School of Social and Economic Development, University of the South Pacific.

Helu, 'I Futa. 1991. *Critical Essays: Cultural Perspectives from the South Seas.* Canberra: Journal of Pacific History, Research School of Asian and Pacific Studies, Australia National University.

Henare, Amiria. 2005. "Nga Aho Tipuna (Ancestral Threads) Maori Cloaks from New Zealand." In Susanne Küchler and Daniel Miller (eds.), *Clothing as Material Culture*, 121–138. London: Berg.

Herda, Phyllis. 1999 "The Changing Texture of Textiles in Tonga." *Journal of the Polynesian Society* 108(2):149–167.

Herda, Phyllis, Michael Reilly, and David Hilliard. 2005. *Vision and Reality in Pacific Religion (Essays in Honor of Neil Gunson)*. Christchurch and Canberra: Macmillan Brown Centre for Pacific Studies, University of Canterbury and Pandanus Books, Australia National University.

Hereniko, Vilsoni. 1995. *Woven Gods: Female Clowns and Power in Rotuma*. Honolulu: University of Hawai'i Press and Center for Pacific Island Studies, University of Hawai'i.

Hermkens, Anna-Karina. 2005. *Engendering Objects: Barkcloth and the Dynamics of Identity in New Guinea*. PhD thesis. Nijmegen, Netherlands: Radboud University Nijmegen.

Hill, Richard S. 2010. "Fitting Multiculturalism into Biculturalism: Maori-Pasifika Relations in New Zealand." *Ethnohistory* 57(2):291–318.

Ho, Christine. 1993. "The Internationalization of Kinship and the Feminization of Caribbean Migration: The Case of Afro-Trinidadian Immigration in Los Angeles." *Human Organization* 52(1):32–40.

Hobsbawm, Eric J. 1992 [1983]. "Introduction: Inventing Traditions." Eric J. Hobsbawm and Terence Ranger (eds.), *The Invention of Tradition*, 1–14. Cambridge: Cambridge University Press.

Hong, Joann, and Pyong Gap Min. 1999. "Ethnic Attachment among Second Generation Korean Adolescents." *Amerasia Journal* 25:165–180.

Horan Jane Catherine. 2012. "*Tivaivai* in the Cook Islands Ceremonial Economy: An Analysis of Value." Unpublished PhD thesis. Auckland, New Zealand: University of Auckland.

———. 2002. "Indigenous Wealth and Development: Micro-Credit Schemes in Tonga." *Asia-Pacific Viewpoint* 43(2):205–221.

Hoskins, Janet. 1998. *Biographical Objects: How Things tell the Stories of People's Lives*. London: Routledge.

Jackson, Cecile. 2001. *Men at Work: Labour, Masculinities, Development*. London: Routledge.

James, Kerry. 2002. "The Cost of Custom: A Recent Funeral in Tonga." *Journal of the Polynesian Society* 111(3):223–238.

———. 1997. "Reading the Leaves: The Role of Tongan Women's Traditional Wealth and Other 'Contraflows' in the Processes of Modern Migration and Remittance." *Pacific Studies* 20(1):1–27.

———. 1988. "'O, lead us not into commoditisation': Christine Ward Gailey's changing gender values in the Tongan islands." *Journal of the Polynesian Society* 97:31–48.

———. 1983. "Gender Relations in Tonga 1780–1984." *Journal of the Polynesian Society* 92: 233–243.

Jolly, Margaret. 2008. "Of the Same Cloth? Oceanic Anthropologies of Gender, Textiles and Christianities." Distinguished Lecture. Association for Social Anthropology in Oceania Conference, Australian National University, 14 February.

———. 2005. "Beyond the Horizon? Nationalisms, Feminisms, and Globalization in the Pacific." *Ethnohistory* 52(1):137–166.

———. 2003. "Epilogue." In Bronwyn Douglas (ed.), *Women's Groups*, special issue, *Oceania* 74(1–2):134–147.

———. 1997. "Woman-Nation-State in Vanuatu: Women as Signs and Subjects in the Discourses of Kastom, Modernity, and Christianity." In Ton Otto and Nicholas Thomas (eds), *Narratives of Nation in the South Pacific*, 133–162. Amsterdam, Netherlands: Harwood Academic.

Jolly, Margaret, and Nicholas Thomas. 1992. "The Politics of Tradition in the Pacific." Special issue, *Oceania* 62(4).

Jowitt, Glen, with Graeme Lay. 2002. *Feasts and Festivals: A Celebration of Pacific Island Culture in New Zealand*. Auckland, New Zealand: New Holland Publishers.

Kamehiro, Stacy L. 2007. "Hawaiian Quilts: Chiefly Self-Representations in Nineteenth-Century Hawai'i." *Pacific Arts* New Series 3–5:23-36.

Kaeppler, Adrienne L. 2007. "*Me'a lālanga* and the category *Koloa*: intertwining value and history in Tonga." In Atholl Anderson, Kaye Green, and Foss Leach (eds.), *Vastly Ingenious: The Archaeology of Pacific Material Culture, in Honor of Janet Davidson*, 145–154. Dunedin, New Zealand: Otago University Press.

———. 2005. "Animal Designs on Samoan Siapo, and Other Thoughts on Polynesian Barkcloth Design." *Journal of the Polynesian Society* 114(3):197–225.

———. 1999a. *From the Stone Age to the Space Age: Tongan Art and Society on the Eve of the Millennium*. Tofoa, Kingdom of Tonga: Tongan National Museum.

———. 1999b. "*Kie Hingoa*: Mats of Power, Rank, Prestige and History." *Journal of the Polynesian Society* 108(2):168–231.

———. 1995. "Poetics and Politics of Tongan Barkcloth." In Dirk A. M. Smidt, Pieter ter Keurs, and Albert Trouwborst (eds.), *Pacific Material Culture: Essays in honor of Dr. Simon Kooijman on the occasion of his 80th birthday*, 101–121. Leiden: Rijksmusem voor Volkenkunde.

———. 1993a [1987]. "Melody, Drone and Decoration: Underlying Structures and Surface Manifestations in Tongan Art and Society." In *Poetry in Motion: Studies in Tongan Dance*, 98–108. Nuku'alofa, Tonga: Vava'u Press.

———. 1993b. "Poetics and Politics of Tongans Laments and Eulogies." *American Ethnologist* 20(3):474–501.

———. 1978a. "Exchange Patterns in Goods and Spouses: Fiji, Tonga, and Samoa." *Mankind* 11(3):246–252.

———. 1978b. "*Me'a faka'eiki*: Tongan Funerals in a Changing Society." In N. Gunson (ed.), *The Changing Pacific: Essays in Honour of Henry Maude*, 174–202. Melbourne: Oxford University Press.

———. 1971. "Rank in Tonga." *Ethnology* 10(2):174–193.

Ka'ili, Tēvita O. 2008. "Tauhi Vā: Creating Beauty Through the Art of Sociospatial Relationships." Unpublished PhD dissertation. Seattle: University of Washington.

———. 2005. "Tauhi vā: Nurturing Tongan Sociospatial ties in Maui and Beyond." *The Contemporary Pacific* 17(1):83–114.

Kingma, Mireille. 2006. *Nurses on the Move: Migration and the Global Health Care Economy*. Ithaca, NY: Cornell University Press.

Kluckhohn, Clyde. 1951. "Value and Value Orientations in the Theory of Action: An Exploration in Definition and Classifications." In Talcott Parsons and Edward Shils (eds.), *Towards a General Theory of Action*, 388–433. Cambridge, MA: Harvard University Press.

Kooijman, Simon. 1972. "Tonga." In *Tapa in Polynesia*, 297–341. Honolulu, HI: B. P. Bishop Museum Press.

Kavaliku, Langi S. 1977. "'Ofa! The Treasure of Tonga." *Pacific Perspective* 6:247–267.

Keesing, Roger M. 1989. "Creating the Past: Custom and Identity in the Contemporary Pacific." *Contemporary Pacific* 1(1):19–42.

Koloto, ʻAna Hauʻalofaʻia. 2003. "Growing up as a Tongan in Aotearoa." In Fairbairn-Dunlop and Sisifo Makisi (eds.), *Making Our Place*, 171–188. Palmerston North, New Zealand: Dunmore Press.

Koloto, ʻAna Hauʻalofa, and Sashi Sharma. 2005. "Pasifika Women's Economic Well-Being Study." Final Report. Prepared for Ministry of Women's Affairs, Wellington, New Zealand.

Kondo, Dorinne. 1990. *Crafting Selves: Power, Gender, and Discourses of Identity in a Japanese Workplace.* Chicago: University of Chicago Press.

Küchler, Suzanne. 2005. "Why are Quilts Big in Polynesia?" In Küchler and Miller (eds.), *Clothing as Material Culture,* 175–192. London: Berg Publishers.

Kuehling, Susanne. 2005. *Dobu: Ethics of Exchange on a Massim Island, Papua New Guinea.* Honolulu: University of Hawaiʻi Press.

Lātūkefu, Sione. 1974. *Church and State in Tonga: The Wesleyan Methodist Missionaries and Political Development, 1822–1875.* Canberra: Australia National University Press.

Laguerre, Michel S. 2006. *Diaspora, Politics, and Globalization.* New York: Palgrave Macmillan.

Leckie, Jacqueline. 1993. "Pacific Islands Women's Organisations." In A. Else (ed.), *Women Together: A History of Women's Organisations in New Zealand. Nga Ropu Wahine o te Motu,* 521–530. Wellington, New Zealand: Daphne Brasell and Associates / Historical Branch, Department of Internal Affairs.

Lee, Helen. 2009a. "Pacific Migration and Transnationalism: Historical Perspectives." In Lee and Francis (eds.) *Migration and Transnationalism,* 7–41. Canberra: Australia National University E-Press.

———. 2009b. "The Ambivalence of Return: Second-generation Tongan Returnees." In Conway and Potter (eds.) *Return Migration of the Next Generations,* 41–58. Aldershot: Ashgate.

———. 2007. "Generational change: The children of Tongan migrants and their ties to the homeland." In E. Wood-Ellem (ed.), *Tonga and the Tongans: Heritage and identity,* 203–217. Melbourne, Australia: Tonga Research Association.

———. 2006. "'Tonga Only Wants Our Money': The Children of Tongan Migrants." In Stewart Firth (ed.), *Globalization and Governance in the Pacific Islands,* 121–135. Canberra: Australia National University E-Press.

———. 2004. "'Second generation' Tongan transnationalism: Hope for the future?" *Asia Pacific Viewpoint* 45(2):235–254.

Lee, Helen Morton. 2003. *Tongans Overseas: Between Two Shores.* Honolulu: University of Hawaiʻi Press.

Levin, Michael J., and Dennis A. Ahlburg. 1993. "Pacific Islanders in the United States Census Data." In Grant McCall and John Connell (eds.), *A World Perspective on Pacific Islander Migration: Australia, New Zealand and the USA,* 95–145. Australia: University of New South Wales Press.

Levitt, Peggy. 2009. "Routes and Roots: Understanding the Lives of the Second Generation Transnationally." *Journal of Ethnic and Migration Studies* 35(7):1225–1242.

———. 2001. *The Transnational Villagers.* Berkeley: University of California Press.

Levitt, P., and B. N. Jaworsky. 2007. "Transnational Migration Studies: Past Developments and Future Trends." *Annual Review of Sociology* 33:129–156.

Liava'a, Viliami Tupou Futuna. 2007. "Transnational Tongans: The Profile of Re-integration of Return Migrants." Unpublished MA thesis. Hamilton, New Zealand: University of Waikato.

Lilomaiava-Doktor, Sai'iliemanu. 2009. "Samoan Transnationalism: Cultivating 'Home' and 'Reach.'" In Lee and Francis (eds.), *Migration and Transnationalism*, 57–71. Canberra: Australia National University E-Press.

Lindley, Ana. 2009. "The Early-Morning Phonecall: Remittances from A Refugee Diaspora Perspective." *Journal of Ethnic and Migration Studies* 35(8):1315–1334.

Linnekin, Jocelyn. 1990a. *Sacred Queens and Women of Consequence: Rank, Gender, and Colonialism in the Hawaiian Islands*. Ann Arbor: University of Michigan Press.

———. 1990b. "The Politics of Culture in the Pacific." In Jocelyn Linnekin and Lin Poyer (eds.), *Cultural Identity and Ethnicity in the Pacific*, 149–174. Honolulu: University of Hawai'i Press.

LiPuma, Edward. 2001. *Encompassing Others: The Magic of Modernity in Melanesia*. Ann Arbor: University of Michigan Press.

Loto, Robert, et al. 2006. "Pasifika in the news: The portrayal of Pacific peoples in the New Zealand press." *Journal of Community and Applied Social Psychology* 16(2):100–118.

Lukere, Nancy, and Margaret Jolly 2002. *Birthing in the Pacific: Beyond Tradition and Modernity*. Honolulu: University of Hawai'i Press.

Lythberg, Billie Jane. 2010. "*Mama'o 'a Folau* (Far Away, but Only Travelling): Context and Performativity in the Making and Display of Contemporary *Ngatu*." Unpublished PhD thesis. Auckland, New Zealand: University of Auckland.

MacKenzie, Maureen Anne. 1991. *Androgynous Objects: String Bags and Gender in Central New Guinea*. Switzerland: Harwood Academic Publishers.

Macpherson, Cluny. 2002. "From Moral Community to Moral Communities: The Foundations of Migrant Solidarity Among Samoans in Urban Aotearoa/New Zealand." *Pacific Studies* (Judith Modell, ed.) 25(1/2):71–93.

Macpherson, Cluny, and La'avasa Macpherson. 2010. *Warm Winds of Change: Globalization in Contemporary Samoa*. Auckland, New Zealand: Auckland University Press.

Māhina, 'Okusitino. 2010. *16/11: Tonga he Fepaki—Tonga in Crisis*. Auckland, New Zealand: Lo'au Research Society Publishing.

———. 2004. "Art as *tā-vā*, 'time-space' transformation." In Tupeni Baba et al. (eds.), *Researching the Pacific and Indigenous Peoples: Issues and Perspectives*, 86–93. Auckland, New Zealand: Centre for Pacific Studies, University of Auckland.

———. 1999. *The Tongan Traditional History Tala-ē-Fonua: A Vernacular Ecology-Centered Historico-Cultural Concept*. Canberra: Australian National University.

Mahmood, Saba. 2005. *Politics of Piety: The Islamic Revival and the Feminist Subject*. Princeton, NJ: Princeton University Press.

Malinowski, Bronislaw. 1922. *Argonauts of the Western Pacific: An Account of Native Enterprise and Adventure in the Archipelagoes of Melanesian New Guinea*. London: Routledge and Keegan Paul.

Malkki, Lisa. 1997. "National Geographic." In Gupta and Ferguson (eds.), *Culture, Power, Place*. Durham, NC: Duke University Press.

Marcus, George. 1998. "Ethnography in the World System: Emergence of Multi-Sited Ethnography." In *Ethnography Through Thick and Thin*, 79–104. Princeton, NJ: Princeton University Press.

————. 1993. "Tonga's Contemporary Globalizing Strategies: Trading on Sovereignty Amidst International Migration." In Victoria Lockwood, Thomas G Harding, and Ben J. Wallace (eds.), *Contemporary Pacific Societies: Studies in Development and Change,* 21–33. Englewood Cliffs, NJ: Prentice Hall.

Maron, Nicole, and John Connell. "Back to Nukunuku: Employment, Identity and Return Migration to Tonga." *Asia Pacific Viewpoint* 49(2001):168–184.

Martin, John. 1991 [1817]. *Tonga Islands: William Mariner's Account.* Nuku'alofa, Tonga: Vava'u Press.

Marx, Karl. 1990 [1867]. *Capital Volume 1* (trans. Ben Fowkes). London: Penguin.

Maurer, Bill. 2005. "Does Money Matter? Abstraction and Substitution in Alternative Financial Forms." In Daniel Miller (ed.), *Materiality,* 140–164. Durham, NC: Duke University Press.

Mauss, Marcel. 1990 [1925]. *The Gift: Forms and Functions of Exchange in Archaic Societies* (trans. I. Cunnison). New York: W.W. Norton.

McClintock, Anne. 1997 "'No Longer in a Future Heaven': Gender, Race and Nationalism." In Anne McClintock, Aamir Mufti, and Ella Shohat (eds.), *Dangerous liaisons: Gender, nation, and postcolonial perspectives,* 89–112. Minneapolis: University of Minnesota Press.

Meintjes, Helen. 2001. "Washing Machines Make Women Lazy: Domestic Appliances and the Negotiation of Woman's Propriety in Soweto." *Journal of Material Culture* 6(3): 345–363.

Miller, Daniel. 2005. "Materiality: An Introduction." In *Materiality,* 1–50. Durham, NC: Duke University Press.

Molisa, Grace 1983. *Black Stone: Poems.* Suva, Fiji: Mana Publications.

Morton, Helen. 1996. *Becoming Tongan: An Ethnography of Childhood.* Honolulu: University of Hawai'i Press.

Munn, Nancy. 1992. *The Fame of Gawa: A Symbolic Study of Value Transformation in a Massim Society.* Durham, NC: Duke University Press.

Ongley, Patrick, 1991. "Pacific Islands' Migration and the New Zealand Labour Market." In Paul Spoonley, David Pearson, and Cluny Macpherson (eds.), *Nga Take: Ethnic Relations and Racism in Aotearoa/New Zealand,* 17–36. Palmerston North, New Zealand: Dunmore Press.

Ostraff, Joseph, and Melinda Ostraff. 2001. *Kuo Hina 'e Hiapo: The Mulberry is White and Ready for Harvest.* 27-min. Document Educational Resources, Watertown, MA.

Parmentier, Richard J. 1987. *The Sacred Remains: Myth, History, and Polity in Belau.* Chicago and London: University of Chicago Press.

Pau'u, Tupou Hopoate. 2002. "My Life in Four Cultures." In Paul Spickard, Joanne Rondilla, and Debbie Hippolite Wright (eds.), *Pacific Diaspora: Island Peoples in the United States and Across the Pacific,* 31–39. Honolulu: University of Hawai'i Press.

Pearson, David G. 1990. *A Dream Deferred: The Origins of Ethnic Conflict in New Zealand.* Wellington, New Zealand: Allen & Unwin and Port Nicholson Press.

Philips, Susan U. 2007. "Symbolically Central and Materially Marginal: Women's Talk in a Tongan Work Group." In McElhinny (ed.), *Words, Worlds and Material Girls,* 41–76. Berlin and New York: Mouton de Gruyter.

Poirine, Bernard. 1998. "Should we Hate or Love MIRAB?" *The Contemporary Pacific* 10(1):65–106.

Potauaine, Semisi Fetokai, and ʻOkusitino Māhina. 2011. "Kula mo e ʻUli: Red and Black in Tongan Thinking and Practice." In T. Moimoi and N. Drescher (eds.), *Tonga: Land, Sea and People* (papers from the 2011 Tonga Research Association Conference, Nukuʻalofa, Tonga). Kingdom of Tonga: Vavaʻu Press.

Rasmussen, Susan. 2000. "From Child-bearers to culture-bearers: Transition to post-child-bearing among Tuareg women." *Medical Anthropology* 19(1):91–116.

Renne, Alisha. 1995. *Cloth That Does Not Die.* Seattle: University of Washington Press.

Rethmann, Petra. 1999. "Skins of Desire: Poetry and Identity in Koriak Women's Gift Exchange." *American Ethnologist* 27(1):52–71.

Rogers, Garth. 1977. "The Father's Sister is Black: A Consideration of Female Rank and Powers in Tonga." *Journal of the Polynesian Society* 86:157–183.

Rovine, Victoria L. 1984. *Bogolan: Shaping Culture through Cloth in Contemporary Mali.* Washington, DC: Smithsonian Press.

Rupp, Katherine. 2003. *Gift-Giving in Japan: Cash, Connections, Cosmologies.* Stanford, CA: Stanford University Press.

Rutherford, Noel. 1996. *Shirley Baker and the King of Tonga.* Honolulu: University of Hawaiʻi Press.

Safran, William. 1991. "Diaspora in Modern Societies: Myths of Homeland and Return." *Diaspora* 1(1):83–89.

Sahlins, Marshall D. 1999. "What is Anthropological Enlightenment? Some Lessons of the Twentieth-Century." *Annual Reviews of Anthropology* 28:x–xxiii.

———. 1988. "Cosmologies of Capitalism: The Trans-Pacific Sector of 'the World System.'" *Proceedings of the British Academy* LXXIV:1–51.

Scaife, Annabel. 2009. "Sharing Skills and Good Laugh." *Central Leader.* Friday November 9:6.

Schoeffel, Penelope. 1999. "Samoan Exchange and 'Fine Mats': An Historical Reconsideration." *Journal of the Polynesian Society* 108(2):117–147.

Schoone, Adrian. 2010. "Re-scripting life: New Zealand-born Tongan 'youth-at-risk' narratives of return migration." *Mai Review* 1:1–11. Accessible online at www.review.mai .ac.nz (accessed 25 May 2010).

Shankman, Paul. 1993. "The Samoan Exodus." In Lockwood, Harding, and Wallace (eds.), *Contemporary Pacific Societies,* 156–170. Englewood Cliffs, NJ: Prentice-Hall.

Shipton, Parker. 1995. "How Gambians Save: Culture and Economic Strategy." In Jane I. Guyer (ed.), *Money Matters: Instability, Values, and Social Payments in the Modern History of West African Communities,* 245–276. Portsmouth, NH: Heineman.

Sinclair, K. P. 1990. "*Tangi:* Funeral rituals and the construction of Maori identity." In Linnekin and Poyer (eds.), *Cultural Identity and Ethnicity in the South Pacific,* 218–236. Honolulu: University of Hawaiʻi Press.

Sissons, Jeffrey. 1999. *Nation and Destination: The Making of Cook Islands Identity.* Suva, Fiji and Rarotonga, Cook Islands: Institute of Pacific Studies, University of the South Pacific and University of the South Pacific Centre in the Cook Islands.

Small, Cathy. 1997. *Voyages: From Tongan Villages to American Suburbs.* Ithaca, NY: Cornell University Press.

———. 1995. "The Birth and Growth of a Polynesian Women's Exchange Network." *Oceania* 65(3):234–256.

———. 1987. "Women's Associations and their pursuit of Wealth in Tonga: A Study in Social Change." PhD thesis. Philadelphia, PA: Temple University.

Small, Cathy, and David Dixon. 2004. "Tonga: Migration and the Homeland." Accessible online at www.migrationinformation.org/Feature/display.cfm?ID=198 (accessed 27 April 2009).

Smith, Anthony D. 2001. *Nationalism: Theory, Ideology, History.* Cambridge: Polity Press.

———. 1995. *Nations and Nationalism in a Global Era.* Malden, MA: Wiley-Blackwell.

Smith, M. P., and L. E. Guarnizo. 1999. *Transnationalism from Below: Comparative Urbana and Community Research,* vol. 6. New Brunswick, NJ: Transaction Publishers.

Snow, Amanda, Kate Druett, and Vicky Crawford. 2006. "The High Cost of Easy Cash: Are poorer Auckland communities being exploited by loan sharks?" *Te Waha Nui,* 6 June, 1. Accessible at www.tewahanui.info/pdfs/12/twn12pg20.pdf.

Somerville, Kara. 2008. "Transnational Belonging among Second Generation Youth: Identity in a Globalized World." In Anand Singh (ed.), Special Issue on Youth and Migration, *Journal of Social Sciences* 10:23–33.

Spoonley, Paul. 2001. "Transnational Pacific communities: Transforming the politics of place and identity." In Macpherson, Spoonley, and Anae (eds.), *Tangata O Te Moana Nui: The Evolving Identities of Pacific Peoples in Aotearoa/New Zealand,* 81–96. Palmerston North, New Zealand: Dunmore Press.

Stahl, Charles W., and Reginald T. Appleyard. 2007. "Migration and Development in the Pacific Islands: Lessons from the New Zealand Experience." Canberra: Australian Agency for International Development.

St. Cartmail, Keith. 1997. *The Art of Tonga: Ko e Ngaahi 'Aati o Tonga.* Honolulu: University of Hawai'i Press.

Stivens, Maila. 2005. "Gender." In James G. Carrier (ed.), *A Handbook of Economic Anthropology,* 323–338. Cheltenham, UK: Edward Elgar Publishing, Ltd.

Stoler, Ann Laura, and Frederick Cooper. 1997. "Between Metropole and Colony: Rethinking a Research Agenda." In *Tensions of Empire: Colonial Cultures in a Bourgeois World,* 1–56. Berkeley: University of California Press.

Stoller, Paul. 2002. *Money Has No Smell: The Africanization of New York.* Chicago, IL: University of Chicago Press.

Strathern, Marilyn. 1990. *The Gender of the Gift: Problems with Women and Problems with Society in Melanesia.* Berkeley: University of California Press.

Sykes, Karen Margaret. 2005. *Arguing with Anthropology: An Introduction to Critical Theories of the Gift.* London: Routledge.

Tamahori, Maxine. 1963. "Cultural Change in Tongan Bark-Cloth." MA thesis. Auckland, New Zealand: University of Auckland.

Taumoefolau, Melenaite. N.d. "'Tongans—Migrations', Te Ara—the Encyclopedia of New Zealand." Accessible at www.teara.govt.nz/en/tongans/1, updated 4 March 2009. (accessed 20 December 2009).

Teaiwa, Teresia. 2005. "Solidarity and Fluidarity: Feminism as product and productive force for regionalism in the Pacific." Paper presented. "Gender, Globalization, and Militarism," Conference. University of Hawai'i at Manoa, Honolulu. February 4.

Teaiwa, Teresia, and Sean Mallon. 2005. "Ambivalent Kinships? Pacific People in New Zealand." In James Liu, et al. (eds), *New Zealand Identities: Departures and Destinations,* 207–229. Wellington, New Zealand: Victoria University Press.

Teilhet-Fisk, Jehanne. 1991. "To Beat or Not to Beat, That is the Question: A Study on Acculturation and Change in an Art-making Process and its Relation to Gender Structures." *Pacific Studies* 14(3):41–67.

Thomas, Nicholas. 1991. *Entangled Objects: Exchange, Material Culture, and Colonialism in the Pacific.* Cambridge, MA: Harvard University Press.

Thomson, Basil. 1894. *Diversions of a Prime Minister.* Edinburgh and London: Blackwood.

Tilley, Christopher. 2006. "Objectification." In Christopher Tilley, et al. (eds.), *Handbook of Material Culture,* 60–73. London: Sage.

Tonga Department of Statistics. 2006. "Tonga 2006 Census of Population and Housing." Accessible at www.spc.int/PRISM/country/to/stats/Census06/cen-ind.htm (accessed 10 December 2009).

Toren, Christina. 1989. "Drinking Cash: The Purification of Money through Ceremonial Exchange in Fiji." In Jonathan Parry and Maurice Bloch (eds.), *Money and the Morality of Exchange,* 143–164. Cambridge: Cambridge University Press.

Troxler, Gale Scott. 1972. *Fijian Masi: A Traditional Art Form,* 2nd edition. Greensboro, NC: Piedmont Press.

Trager, Lilian. 2005. "Women Migrants and Hometown Linkages in Nigeria: Status, Economic Roles, and Contributions to Community Development." In *Migration and Economy: Global and Local Dynamics,* 225–255. Walnut Creek, CA: Altamira Press.

Trask, Haunani-Kay. 1996. "Feminism and Indigenous Hawaiian Nationalism." *Signs: Journal of Women in Culture and Society* 21:906–916.

Tsing, Anna. 2005. *Friction: An Ethnography of Global Connection.* Princeton, NJ: Princeton University Press.

Tuʻitahi, Sione. 2007. *Langa Fonua: In Search of Success. How a Tongan Kāinga Strived to be Socially and Economically Successful in New Zealand.* MA thesis. Auckland, New Zealand: Massey University.

Tupuola, Anne-Marie. 2004. "Pasifika Edgewalkers: Complicating the Achieved Identity Status of Youth in Research." *Journal of Intercultural Studies* 25(1):87–100.

United States Census Bureau. 2007. "The American Community: Pacific Islanders, 2004." Washington, DC: United States Department of Commerce, Economics and Statistics Administration, May 2007. Accessible at www.census.gov/prod/2007pubs/acs-06.pdf.

Van der Grijp, Paul. 2003. "Between Gifts and Commodities: Commercial Enterprise and the Trader's Dilemma on Wallis ('Uvea)." *The Contemporary Pacific* 15(2):277–307.

———. 2002. "Selling is Poverty, Buying a Shame: Representations of Work, Effective Leadership and Market Failures on Wallis." *Oceania* 73:17–34.

———. 1993. *Islanders of the South: Production, Kinship and Ideology in the Polynesian Kingdom of Tonga* (trans. Peter Mason). Verhandelingen Series, no. 154. Leiden, Netherlands: KITLV Press.

Vete, Mele Fuka. 1995. "The Determinants of Remittances among Tongans in Auckland." *Asian and Pacific Migration Journal* 4(1):55–67.

Veys, Fanny Wonu. 2009. "Materialising the king: The royal funeral of King Tāufaʻāhau Tupou IV of Tonga." *The Australian Journal of Anthropology* 20:131–149.

Wagner, Roy. 1981. *The Invention of Culture.* Chicago and London: University of Chicago Press.

Wallis, Joanne. 2008. "Transnationalism and the Development of the Deterritorialized Tongan Nation-State." *Studies in Ethnicity and Nationalism* 8(3):408–432.

Watson, James 1988. "The Structure of Chinese Funerary Practices: Elementary Forms, Ritual Sequence and the Primacy of Performance." In James L. Watson and Evelyn S. Rawski (eds.), *Death Ritual in Late Imperial and Modern China.* Berkeley: University of California Press.

Weiner, Annette. 1994. "Cultural Difference and the Density of Objects." *American Ethnologist* 21(2):391–403.

———. 1992. *Inalienable Possessions: The Paradox of Keeping While Giving.* Berkeley: University of California Press.

———. 1989. "Why Cloth? Wealth, Gender, and Power in Oceania." In Annette Weiner and Jane Schneider (eds.), *Cloth and Human Experience,* 33–72. Washington, DC: Smithsonian Institution Press.

———. 1980. "Stability in Banana Leaves: Colonialism, Economics and Trobriand Women." In Eleanor Leacock and Mona Etienne (eds.), *Women and Colonization: Anthropological Perspectives.* New York: J. F. Bergin.

Werbner, Pnina. 1990. *The Migration Process: Capital, Gifts and Offerings among British Pakistanis.* New York: Berg Press.

White, Geoffrey. 2008. "Foreword." In Epeli Hau'ofa (ed.), *We are the Ocean: Selected Works.* Honolulu: University of Hawai'i Press.

Wimmer, Andreas, and Nina Glick Schiller. 2002. "Methodological Nationalism and Beyond: Nation-State Building, Migration, and the Social Sciences." *Global Networks* 2(4):301–334.

Wood-Ellem, Elizabeth. 1999. *Queen Sālote of Tonga: The Story of an Era 1900–1965.* Honolulu: University of Hawai'i Press.

World Bank. 2006. "Pacific Islands At Home and Away: Expanding Job Opportunities for Pacific Islanders Through Labor Mobility." Report of the Poverty and Economic Management Sector Unit, East Asia and Pacific Region.

Yan, Yunxiang. 2005. "The Gift and Gift Economy." In James G. Carrier (ed.), *A Handbook of Economic Anthropology,* 246–261. Cheltenham, UK: Edward Elgar Publishing, Ltd.

———. 1996. *The Flow of Gifts: Reciprocity and Social Networks in a Chinese Village.* Stanford, CA: Stanford University Press.

Yuval-Davis, Nira. 1997. *Gender & Nation.* London and Thousand Oaks, CA: Sage Publications.

Young Leslie, Heather E. 2007. "Tonga" [Political Reviews]. *The Contemporary Pacific* 19(1): 262–276.

———. 2004. "Pushing Children Up: Maternal Obligation, Modernity, and Medicine in the Tongan Ethnoscape." In Victoria Lockwood (ed.), *Globalization and Culture Change in the Pacific Island,* 390–413. Upper Saddle River, NJ: Prentice Hall.

———. 1999. "Tradition, Textiles and Maternal Obligation in the Kingdom of Tonga." Unpublished PhD thesis. Toronto: York University.

Young Leslie, Heather E., and Ping-Ann Addo. 2007. "Introduction: Pragmatic Creativity and Authentic Innovations in Pacific Cloth." *Pacific Arts* New Series 3–5:12–21.

Index